Praise for
Through the Brick Wall

"On behalf of eight million New Yorkers, I commend and thank
The Five O'Clock Club. Keep the faith and
keep America working!"
—David N. Dinkins, Mayor, The City of New York

"In eighteen years of career counseling and coaching, I have seen
nothing as good as this book. It combines sound, practical advice
about the hiring process with profound wisdom and humor
regarding the inner issues stirred up by transition. Kate has struck:
shrewdness about the hiring process and the courage
to face inner issues. Great work!"
—William Pilder, Chairman, TransKey

"Kate Wendleton offers a wealth of pragmatic, uplifting advice for
the job seeker. A person who follows Kate's formula would
certainly get my attention, even if I'd already
rejected his or her resume."
—Carole F. St. Mark
President, Pitney Bowes Logistics Systems & Business Services

"*Through the Brick Wall* is a great book for a success-oriented
transitional executive. It breaks the process into do-able
steps that are easy to understand."
—Albert Prendergast
Senior Vice President, Human Resources,
Mastercard International

"I am living proof that you can change your career for the better
with the techniques described in *Through the Brick Wall*.
Take a look at Chapter 2."
—Bart ("Ted" in Chapter 2) Pestrichello
Director of Casino Administration,
Tropicana Resort, Las Vegas

"*Through the Brick Wall* provides specific and innovative
suggestions and has a seasoning of inspiration and motivation. For
anyone who is in, or may be in, the job market, this book
would be a good place to start."
—Theodore F. Brophy,
former Chairman of the Board, GTE

"Harlem adults want to work. We have a high rate of unemployment, and our people often feel hopeless and can see no way out. They feel they are often the last hired and the first fired in times of recession. The Five O'Clock Club is part of the healing process and is helping our people be competitive when they need this kind of help the most."
—Rev. James Russell, III
Executive Director, Harlem YMCA

"Kate is one of the most singularly creative and energetic persons I have ever met. She is completely dedicated to the 'proposition of possibilities' in peoples' lives, and that dedication comes shining through in this book. For those of you not lucky enough to have in person the benefit of Kate's experience, talent, energy and wisdom, *Through the Brick Wall* is the next best thing to being there."
—Dan Ciporin
Vice President, Director, Worldwide Brand Management, major credit card company

"During the time I was looking for a job I kept Kate's book by my bed. I read a little every night, a little every morning. Her common-sense advice, methodical approach, and hints for keeping the spirits up were extremely useful."
—Harold Levine
Coordinator, Yale Alumni Career Resource Network

"*Through the Brick Wall* is 'what works now.' This indispensible, no-excuses guide to job-hunting and career building provides a step-by-step approach to organizing your search . . . targeting the job you want . . . getting in for the meetings . . . beating out the competition . . . and turning the interview into an offer."
—Jack Schlegel
New York Advertising & Communications Network

"Thank you, Kate, for all our help. I ended up with four offers and at least fifteen compliments in two months—all attributed to your work on my resume. Thanks!"
—President and CEO, large banking organization

"I'm an artistic person, and I don't think about business. Kate provided the disciplined business approach so I could practice my art. After adopting her system, I landed a role on Broadway in *Hamlet*."
—Bruce Faulk
Actor, Manhattan

THROUGH THE BRICK WALL

HOW TO JOB-HUNT IN A TIGHT MARKET

KATE WENDLETON

VILLARD BOOKS / NEW YORK / 1992

For my parents

who had the strength to impose their own terms upon life
—with generosity and caring

Most of the contents of this work appeared previously in somewhat different form in
Changing Jobs and *The Job Changing Workbook* published by The Five O'Clock Club.

Villard Books is a registered trademark of Random House, Inc.

The Five O'Clock Club and Workforce America are registered trademarks.

Library of Congress Cataloging-in-Publication Data

Wendleton, Kate.
  Through the brick wall: how to job-hunt in a tight market/Kate Wendleton.
    p. cm.
  Includes index.
  ISBN 0-679-74498-3
    1. Executives—United States.   2. Executives—United States—Supply and demand.
3. Management—Vocational guidance—United States.   4. Job hunting—United
States.   5. Career changes—United States.   I. Title.
HD38.25.U6W46   1992
650.14'0951—dc20   92-13904

Manufactured in the United States of America on acid-free paper
Design by Robert Bull Design

If you haven't the strength
to impose your own terms upon life,
then you must accept the terms
if offers you.
      T. S. ELIOT,
      The Confidential Clerk

PREFACE

Dear Reader:

I am very happy to bring you this book.

When I started The Five O'Clock Club in Philadelphia in 1978, professionals and managers who were job hunting came to my apartment every Thursday evening. Career consultants from corporations and consulting firms taught us their job hunting techniques. I will be forever grateful to those experts who helped us get started. We were able to compare their approaches. We experimented. We tried various job hunting techniques and reported our results back to the group.

In The Five O'Clock Club, it was not enough for us to learn about job hunting—we wanted to learn about the job *hiring* process. What happens when your résumé crosses the desk of a hiring manager? How effective are direct-mail campaigns? Why does one person find a job quickly, while someone else takes longer—even though they both work hard and are equally well qualified?

This book answers those questions. We found that there is no one job hunting technique that works. Job hunting formulas hold true in the aggregate, but may not for a specific situation. The techniques that work depend, to a large extent, on the industry you are interested in, the kind of job you want to have within that industry, and on your own style and personality.

This book gives you guidelines, but also gives you flexibility in deciding which job hunting approach is right for you. When you understand what is happening and why, you can be in a better position to plan your own job hunting campaign, and not rely so much on chance or on what a specific expert tells you.

Job hunting can be thought of as a project—much like any project you might handle in your regular job. Most of the approaches in this book are businesslike rather than intensely psychological. Thinking of job hunting in a business-type way allows you to use the problem-solving skills you might use at work.

This book is organized to be used by busy people like you. Skip to the part you need. If you already know what you want in your next job, go directly to Part III to learn the most powerful, up-to-date techniques available today for getting interviews. If you have an interview coming up, go to Part IV to find the latest ideas for getting what you want, including how to assess the interview and turn it into a job offer.

I felt duty-bound to write about career planning. Most people are interested only in job hunting techniques and don't want to give much thought to what they should do with their *lives*. But I included the section on career planning just in case you decide to spend the time it takes to give your life some direction and a sense of real satisfaction.

Finally, you will find a lot of inspirational material in this book. I needed it myself often enough. I have worked with many unemployed and unhappy working people. I believe that techniques by themselves are worthless without the right frame of mind. I hope the quotes and the inspirational writing will inspire you as they have inspired me and my fellow job hunters. I can guarantee that these quotes have been "tested" on job hunters for years.

Good luck!

Kate Wendleton
New York City
January 1992

ACKNOWLEDGMENTS

With appreciation to the entire Dobbs Family, of which I am the eldest, for being dependable cheerleaders. To Nancy O'Shea Mercante, my friend and partner at The Five O'Clock Club. To Robert Dobbs, my brother, and Dan Wendleton, my former husband, for their help in editing the first book in 1987. To Kay Shadley, my friend and attorney, who has helped me start Five O'Clock Clubs in other cities. And to my friends Barbara Goldenberg and Deirdre Cavanagh for lots of fun.

I appreciate all Five O'Clock members, old and new, some of whose stories are contained herein: Members provide feedback on our job hunting techniques, which allows our approach to continually evolve with the changing job market.

I thank the excellent and devoted staff of The Five O'Clock Clubs. I am especially grateful to the staff of the mid-Manhattan Club, which serves as a model for other Clubs. The counselors include: Ellis Chase, Roy Cohen, Barbara Earley, Shelli Kanet, John Leonard, Wendy Rothman, and Gloria Waslyn. The administrative staff includes Nancy Mercante and Lucille Paterniani.

We are all especially proud of Workforce America: The Five O'Clock Club of Harlem. It was started with the help of the Reverend James Russell, executive director of the Harlem YMCA, Kathy Fanning and Louise Stuetley, our first counselors there, and Sandy Bowers, vice president of career services at Citibank, who gave me consulting assignments that enabled me to pay for the start-up of The Five O'Clock Club of Harlem. My deepest appreciation also to Spike Lee, our honorary chairman, who gave us a tremendous lift; the churches and mosques of Harlem, who welcomed us; my pastor, Reverend Herbert Anderson at The Brick Church, for inspiring me to do more in Harlem; and the following folks who have contributed to the success of this effort: Debbie Brown, Deirdre Cavanagh, Deborah Dahl, Stacy Feldman, Bob Follek, Dr. Barbara Jackson, Shawn LaBorde, Terry McGuinness, Luther Mook, Yvonne Wallace, and Beulah Walton. My apologies to those who joined us too late to be recognized here.

Since I came to New York in 1985, I have gotten a number of big breaks from people who believed in me. Edith Wurtzel at The New School for Social Research, encouraged me to speak there. Three hundred and fifty people attended, and I later became director of their career center. Abe Fiss at Barnes & Noble agreed to carry my first self-published book, then my second, and kept reordering them for five years. Jonathan Dolger, my agent, rescued me from years of self-publishing: He quickly sold this book to Diane Reverend at Villard whose influence is on every page. I thank them all. I also appreciate the help of Maureen McMahon, Carsten Fries, and Jackie Duval.

Finally, my deepest appreciation and fondest gratitude go to the faculty and staff of Chestnut Hill College, Philadelphia. Attending Chestnut Hill was the most important experience of my life because there I saw women leaders who were nurturing, intelligent, and professional. May I follow in their footsteps.

TABLE OF CONTENTS

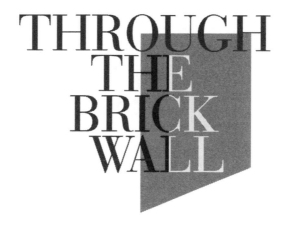

THROUGH THE BRICK WALL

INTRODUCTION

We've all heard too many painful stories: out of work for over a year . . . networking, mailings, search firms, ads—but can't get a job . . . lots and lots of interviews but . . .

At The Five O'Clock Club, we get impressive results. The average professional, manager or executive who attends on a regular basis gets a job within ten to fifteen weeks. (Many had been looking for a year or more.) That's because they used the principles taught in this book. As you will see, these techniques work at *all* levels—and for all types of people. They have even successfully been used by actors and actresses, and at least one orchestra conductor. Whatever your field, this book will give you the inside track.

When a job hunter finds a job, he reports to the group. Last week, a man reported that he had been unemployed for three years. His wife had a good job, he spent time with his kids, and he found a few temporary assignments, but he was essentially unemployed, and was trying very hard to get a job. After only four Five O'Clock Club sessions, he found a great one.

The week before, a woman spoke who had been unemployed for a year and a half; she had come to six sessions. Her first session had been a full year earlier, and she had decided to search on her own. After a year, she came back, attended five more sessions, and got a great job.

The week before that, a man who had been unemployed for six months before joining The Five O'Clock Club was able to find a great job. In his four months with the club, the group had helped him see how he was coming across in interviews (very stiff and preachy) and how to expand his job targets. Some people take longer because they are at the beginning of their search or because they have not searched in many years and need to learn this new skill.

Many job hunters think they have to lower their salary expectations because they are unemployed or have been job searching for a long time. You may have to lower your salary expectations for other reasons, but none of these three people did. Their unemployment did not affect their salary negotiations. In this book you will learn how to negotiate properly and increase your chances of getting what you deserve—whether you are employed or unemployed.

The Five O'Clock Club techniques in this book work whether a job hunter is employed or unemployed. Most job hunters try to get interviews and then try to do well in them. They are skipping two important parts of the process, and are therefore probably not doing the two remaining parts very well. At The Five O'Clock Club, we consider all four parts to be important. They are:

- **Assessment:** Deciding what you want results in better job targets. (Part II of this book)
- **Campaign Preparation:** Planning your campaign results in lots and lots of interviews in each job target. (Part III)
- **Interviewing:** Interviews result in an assessment of the *company's* needs. (Part IV)
- **Interview Follow-Up:** Follow-up after the interview results in job offers. (Part IV)

As you can see, job hunters who think that interviews lead to offers have skipped a step. Interviews lead to a better understanding of what the company wants. What you do *after* the interview leads to an offer.

Here are a few quick stories to get you started.

CASE STUDY: PHIL
Expanded his job hunting targets—and went through the brick wall to get the job.

Phil had been earning hundreds of thousands of dollars a year as a senior executive in a large publishing company. When I met him, he had been job searching for a year, focusing on twenty-four publishing and health care companies in his geographic area. Given his level, his search was obviously not going to work: his target was too small. He needed to look into other industries and other geographic areas.

In addition, Phil needed a new attitude. He expected people to recognize his credentials and simply hire him—something that had always happened in the past. Now he needed to go through the brick wall to get a job.

Phil found a job within three weeks after our meeting. He answered an ad in the paper for a job—not in publishing or health care—in another state. (It doesn't matter how you get the interview: through a search firm, an ad, networking, or direct contact.) He was called in for two interviews and then received a rejection letter: the company had decided against him.

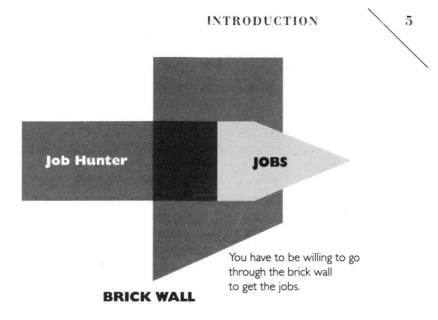

Job Hunter   JOBS

BRICK WALL

You have to be willing to go
through the brick wall
to get the jobs.

But this time Phil wanted to fight for the job. He wrote to the president of the company and said there had obviously been a big mistake. The company reconsidered and hired him.

CASE STUDY: STEELWORKERS
Who gets hired?

A colleague of mine, Aaron Nierenberg, tells of a counselor who did a workshop for steelworkers a few years back when many of them were losing jobs. They were not of a mind to do résumés (many of them didn't even speak English), so the counselor concentrated on the most important part of the search process—follow-up.

The counselor asked, "How many of you have already contacted companies about getting a job?" Sixteen hands went up. "Your homework for tomorrow," he said, "is to *recontact* those companies and report back here." The next day, four workers had gotten jobs.

The explanation for this is simple. Look at it from the hiring manager's point of view. The steel industry was laying off thousands of workers, who went to other steel mills looking for work. Hundreds of workers went to the hiring managers and said, "Have you got any work?" How could a manager easily decide which workers he should hire? But when a worker said, "I was here last week looking for work. Do you have anything now?" the manager then knew whom to select.

Much of the selection process is a *self*-selection process: the *job hunter* decides which companies he or she wants to work for, and behaves very differently toward those companies than toward others he or she is not interested in.

Job hunters put most of their effort into getting interviews and doing brilliantly well in those interviews. Then they stop. Five O'Clock Club job hunters keep going and turn more interviews into offers. Don't follow up with a silly thank-you note. Instead, *influence* the person. This book will give you a process for analyzing the interview so you can decide what to do next.

SEE PEOPLE TWO LEVELS HIGHER THAN YOU ARE

Norman had been searching for a job for over a year. He did what he had been told: he networked. By now he had met with almost 250 people! Yet he could not find a job. The problem: he was meeting with people at his own level. When he started meeting with higher-level people (through direct contact), he started seeing results. Within two months, he found a great job.

Most job hunters network incorrectly. In this book, we will tell you exactly how to network so you can get the most out of it. We'll also cover the other techniques for getting interviews: through search firms, answering ads, and directly contacting companies.

TAKE THE LONG VIEW

The next job you take will not be your last. Where will you go after that one? When deciding between two or more possibilities, select the one that positions you best for the long term.

Christine is a good example. She had three job offers—which is what we like people to have. Two offers paid $10,000 more than the third one. Which job should she take?

Christine selected the one that positioned her best for the long term —which happened to be the lower-paying job. She is now as happy as a person can be, getting tremendous experience and meeting lots of important people. After a few years, she could easily leave (if she wants) and get much more money than she ever would have gotten had she taken one of the other two positions.

Julio is a portfolio manager with strong connections to South America. He had five job offers and wondered which one he should take. I couldn't help him until I knew his long-term plans. Otherwise, his decision would be based strictly on the money or the kind of people at each company. We spent ten minutes working on his Forty-Year Plan, which you will read about later. It turned out that he imagined himself working out of his house five to ten years down the road. Then, the decision-making process became easy. Only two of the companies would eventually allow him to work from home. He selected one of them. Had he selected one of the others, he would have had a problem in a few years.

This book will help you think about *your* long-term plan. Your next job is simply a step, and we'll help you plan that step and the ones after that. Job hunters are not powerless. They can do a lot to influence the hiring process and their own long-term careers.

THE FIVE O'CLOCK CLUB COACHING APPROACH

Our approach is methodical. Our counselors are the best. Five O'Clock Club counselors are full-time career coaches. Each one has met with hundreds of job hunters. Often we can pinpoint what is wrong with a person's search and turn it around. In this book, you will get that same information. Like our Five O'Clock Club job hunters, you will learn the techniques and hear the stories of other people so you can job hunt more effectively.

> It is other people's experience that makes the older man wiser than the younger man.
> —YORUBA PROVERB

Sometimes we call our techniques the *Parachute* for the nineties. The original *Parachute* book (*What Color is Your Parachute?* by Richard Nelson Bolles, Ten Speed Press) was first published more than twenty years ago. It teaches first-time job hunters or career changers how to get jobs. Now we have a nation of skilled workers, managers, executives, and professionals who are out of work or unhappy in their jobs—people who used to be routinely wooed and solicited for their talents. Now these people have to do the selling. They need a very different and specific approach to finding jobs and changing careers.

HOW THE FIVE O'CLOCK CLUB WORKS

The groups vary from place to place. Some groups, such as the main one in mid-Manhattan, is for professionals, managers, and executives. Others may focus on recent college graduates, for example, or blue-collar workers. Generally, half the people who attend are employed (and perhaps unhappy); half are unemployed. Members are from various industries and professions—usually difficult situations, or they wouldn't need us. The basic format is the same: the group meets every week for two hours. During the first hour, members hear a presentation on an important job hunting technique. These techniques are presented in this book. In between the first and second hours, those who have found jobs report on their searches, and we learn from what they did.

During the second hour, a career counselor leads the group of job hunters in a strategy-planning session for each job hunter: how can this person move his or her search along? How can he get more interviews in his target market or turn those interviews into offers? Job hunters learn from the counselor and from the strategies other job hunters are pursuing. They get feedback on their own searches and critique the searches of others. They aim to get six to ten contacts in the works, and have three job offers. Those who stick with the process find that it works. That process is presented in this book.

PART ONE

FINDING GOOD JOBS

THE CHANGING JOB HUNT PROCESS

(START HERE IF YOU ARE JUST BEGINNING YOUR JOB HUNT.)

People can be divided into three groups:
those who make things happen,
those who watch things happen—
and those who wonder, What happened?

— ANONYMOUS

CHAPTER 1

HOW TO JOB-HUNT IN A TIGHT MARKET

I'm going to fight hard.
I'm going to give them hell.
    —HARRY S TRUMAN
        Remark on the presidential campaign, August 1948

YOUR EMPLOYER HAS GOT TO BE SHARPER AND SO DO YOU

IN A GROWING economy, the market favors the job hunter. There are more jobs than there are job applicants. Sloppy job hunting techniques work "well enough." Companies can hire more people than they need and hope someone will do the job right.

In today's economy, job hunters face greater competition for the jobs that are available. Everyone has to be sharper. Just as your employer cannot be sloppy when competing in world markets, you cannot be sloppy when competing in job markets. Your prospective employers have to be more serious about every position they fill. You, too, must take your job hunt more seriously.

DON'T BE SCARED BY THE HEADLINES

Labor is the superior of capital, and deserves much the higher consideration.
    —ABRAHAM LINCOLN

Job hunters are starting to realize that a large number of people may be laid off in one part of a company, while different kinds of people are hired in other parts of the same company. In the news, you will hear about the layoffs, but you will not hear about the hiring—the company would be deluged with résumés.

Get used to the headlines. Companies must react quickly to changing world circumstances, and they no longer have time to figure out where the laid-off people could fit into other parts of the same company. Some companies now allow laid-off employees to job hunt both inside and outside the company. It can be an efficient way for the company to change direction, and save perhaps 10 percent of the laid-off employees who can fit into the new direction.

The laid-off employee is usually able to find a position outside more quickly because, by definition, there are more positions outside. No matter how big the old company is, it is small compared to the outside world. A smart employee would devote 10 percent of his efforts to an inside search, and 90 percent outside.

A CHANGING ECONOMY

> Security is mostly a superstition. It does not exist in nature, nor do the children of men as a whole experience it. Avoiding danger is no safer in the long run than outright exposure. Life is either a daring adventure or nothing.
> —HELEN KELLER

Today, we know that doing a good job is not enough. Our career prospects can now change for reasons that have nothing to do with our personal job performance, but with the performance of our employers. It's a new economy—a world economy—and the changes are not going to slow down. Not only will things *not* return to the way they were, the amount of change will increase.

Government statistics show the impact of change on job hunters:

- The average American has been in his or her job only four years.
- The average American getting out of college today can expect to have five careers during his or her lifetime—that's not five jobs, but five separate careers!
- We will probably have twelve to fifteen jobs in the course of those five careers.

Ten years from now, half the working population will be in jobs that have not yet been invented. Let's make that more personal: ten years from now, half the people reading this book will be in jobs that do not exist today.

The economy is changing too fast for you to use the same old job hunting techniques. And you can't have the same old attitudes about job hunting.

TECHNOLOGICAL CHANGE IS THE MOST PERVASIVE

Probably no change will affect our careers more than technological change. It's not like a stock market crash, or tearing down the Berlin Wall. It doesn't make the headlines, because it's happening everywhere —every day. When you want money from a bank, you can go to a machine. The human—the middleman doing the drudgery—is no longer required in that job. People are required in *new* jobs—to design and make the machines, service them, sell them, and so on—jobs that did not exist a few years ago.

Computers are part of the reason companies have been able to cut the ranks of middle management. Companies no longer need layers of management to pass information up and down. The reports and studies and controls that were the domain of these managers are now that of computers.

As a result of technology, new industries are possible, such as direct marketing and the express-mail industry. Desktop publishing has affected the publishing, typesetting, and printing industries.

Professions are changing. Many artists now work at a computer keyboard instead of a drawing board. Their jobs did not exist ten years ago. Accountants are no longer needed to do compounded-growth rates and other complex calculations. Their jobs are changing. Salespeople are being replaced by computers and the UPC codes you see on packages. Musicians are being replaced by electronic synthesizers, which can replicate virtually every instrument.

Whether you are talking about manufacturing or hospital technology, artists or accountants, salespeople or teachers—virtually every industry and profession has or will be affected. There are no secure jobs because the jobs themselves are changing. If you think your industry or profession is not being affected, think again.

THE GOOD OLD DAYS—PEOPLE WERE STUCK

I remember the "good old days"—the days of one employer and one career. It used to be that when you found a job, you had found a home. You expected to get in there, do what the company wanted, learn to play the game, rise through the ranks, and eventually retire. People had secure jobs with large, stable employers.

People may have had job security, but the downside is that they were often stuck. Changing jobs was frowned upon. For every satisfied person, there was someone stifled, who knew he or she had made a dreadful mistake.

Today, many of us might fear losing our jobs—even from week to week—but no one—*absolutely* no one—needs to feel stifled, deadened, or stuck in a career they no longer find satisfying. *Everyone has an opportunity to do something that is better.*

What we see now is that many of the people pushed out of companies after twenty years are actually relieved to get out of jobs they'd found deadening. Some decide to think about what they really want to do and make the second phase of their lives much more fulfilling than the first.

In this book you will learn how to take more control of your life, how to plan for your own future and not be at the mercy of others. Many people who are laid off say, "This will never happen to me again. I will never again be caught off guard and unprepared."

A NEW DEFINITION OF JOB HUNTING

> People are always blaming their circumstances for what they are. I don't believe in circumstances. The people who get on in this world are the people who get up and look for the circumstances they want, and if they can't find them, make them.
> —GEORGE BERNARD SHAW

Job hunting in our changing economy is a *continuous* process and requires a new definition. Job hunting now means continually becoming aware of market conditions both inside and outside of our present companies, and learning what we have to offer—to both markets. This new definition means we must develop new attitudes about our work lives, and new skills for doing well in a changing economy.

Today's economy requires job hunters to be more proactive, more sophisticated, and more willing to go through brick walls to get what they want. Employers no longer plan your career for you. You must look after yourself, and know what you want and how to get it.

UNDERSTANDING HOW THE JOB HUNT MARKET WORKS

Knowing why things work the way they do will give you flexibility and control over your job hunt. Knowing how the hiring system works will help you understand why things go right and why they go wrong—why certain things work and others don't. Then you can modify the system to fit your own needs, temperament, and the workings of the job market you are interested in.

It is overly simplistic to say that only one job hunting system works. The job selection process is more complicated than that. Employers can do what they want. You need to understand the process from their point of view. Then you can plan your own job hunt, in your own industry. You will learn how to compete in this market.

Always remember, the best jobs don't necessarily go to the most qualified people, but to the people who are the best job hunters. You'll increase your chances of finding the job you want by using a methodical job hunting approach.

Even if you have worked for the same employer for many years, learn how to job hunt in a changing economy. At first it will seem strange. It's a new skill, but one you can use for the rest of your life. For a while you may feel as though things will never be the same. And they won't. No job is secure. At the same time, we now know that no one has to be locked into one job, one boss, one employer. Skilled job hunters have a real ability to plan their careers.

CHANGES MEAN NEW OPPORTUNITIES

The world is changing. What's hot today is not tomorrow. You can use these changes to your advantage. You can choose to head your career in the direction that's right for you.

You can impose your own terms upon life. You don't have to accept the terms it offers you. Read on, and see what others have done.

> Alice said nothing: she had sat down with her face in her hands, wondering if anything would ever happen in a natural way again.
> —LEWIS CARROLL
> *Alice in Wonderland*

CHAPTER 2

HOW TO CHANGE CAREERS

If an idea, I realized, were really a valuable one, there must be
some way of realizing it.
—ELIZABETH BLACKWELL
        (the first woman to earn a medical degree)

TED HAD SPENT ten years in marketing and finance with a
large cosmetics company. His dream was to work in the casino industry.
He selected two job targets: one aimed at the cosmetics industry, and one
aimed at his dream.

All things being equal, finding a job similar to your old one is quicker.
A career change will probably take more time. What's more, the job
hunting techniques are different for both.

Let's take Ted's case. The casino industry was small, focused in
Atlantic City and Las Vegas. Everyone knew everyone else. The industry
had its special jargon and personality. What chance did Ted have of break-
ing in?

Ted had another obstacle. His marketing and finance background
made him difficult to categorize. His hard-won business skills became a
problem.

IT'S NOT EASY TO CATEGORIZE JOB CHANGERS

The easier it is to categorize you, the easier it is for others to see where
you fit in their organizations, and for you to find a job. Search firms, for
example, generally will not handle career changers. They can more easily
market those who want to stay in the same function in the same industry.
Search firms that handled the casino industry would not handle Ted.

YOU MUST OFFER PROOF OF YOUR INTEREST
AND COMPETENCE

> . . . civility is not a sign of weakness, and sincerity is always
> subject to proof.
> —JOHN F. KENNEDY
> Inaugural Address, January 20, 1961

Many job changers essentially say to a prospective employer, "Give me a
chance. You won't be sorry." They expect the employer to hire them on
faith, and that's unrealistic. The employer has a lot to lose. First, you may
lose interest in the new area after you are hired. Second, you may know
so little about the new area that it turns out not to be what you had
imagined. Third, you may not bring enough knowledge and skill to the job
and fail—even though your desire may be sincere.

The hiring manager should not have to take those risks. It is the job
hunter's obligation to prove that he or she is truly interested and capable.

HOW YOU AS A CAREER CHANGER
CAN PROVE YOUR INTEREST AND CAPABILITY

- Read the industry's trade journals.
- Get to know the people in that industry or field.
- Join its organizations; attend the meetings.
- Be persistent.
- Show how your skills can be transferred.
- Write proposals.
- Be persistent.
- Take relevant courses, part-time jobs, or do volunteer work related
  to the new industry or skill area.
- Be persistent.

Ted, as a career changer, had to offer proof to make up for his lack
of experience. One proof was that he had read the industry's trade newspapers for more than ten years. When he met people in his search, he
could truthfully tell them that he had followed their careers. He could also
say he had hope for himself because he knew that so many of them had
come from outside the industry.

Another proof of his interest was that he had sought out so many
casino management people in Atlantic City and Las Vegas. After a while,
he ran into people he had met on previous occasions. Employers want
people who are sincerely interested in their industry, their company, and

the function the new hire will fill. Sincerity and persistence count, but they are usually not enough.

Another proof Ted offered was that he figured out how to apply his experience to the casino industry and its problems. Writing proposals to show how you would handle the job is one way to prove you are knowledgeable and interested in an area new to you. Some people prove their interest by taking courses, finding part-time jobs, or doing volunteer work to learn the new area and build marketable skills.

Ted initially decided to "wing it," and took trips to Atlantic City and Las Vegas hoping someone would hire him on the spot. That didn't work and took two months and some money. Then he began a serious job hunt —following the system which will be explained in the pages that follow. He felt he was doing fine, but the hunt was taking many months and he was not sure it would result in an offer.

After searching in the casino industry for six months, Ted began a campaign in his old field—the cosmetics industry. Predictably, he landed a job there quickly. Ted took this as a sign that he didn't have a chance in the new field. He lost sight of the fact that a career change is more difficult and takes longer.

Ted accepted the cosmetics position, but his friends encouraged him to continue his pursuit of a career in the casino industry—a small industry with relatively few openings compared with the larger cosmetics industry.

Shortly after he accepted the new position, someone from Las Vegas called him for an interview, and he got the job of his dreams. His efforts paid off because he had done a thorough campaign in the casino industry. It just took time.

Ted was not unusual in giving up on a career change. It can take a long time, and sometimes the pressure to get a paycheck will force people to take inappropriate jobs. That's life. Sometimes we have to do things we don't want. There's nothing wrong with that.

What *is* wrong is forgetting that you had a dream. What *is* wrong is expecting people to hire you on faith and hope, when what they deserve is proof that you're sincere and that hiring you has a good chance of working. *What is wrong is underestimating the effort it takes to make a career change.*

In the future, most people will have to change careers. Your future may hold an involuntary career change, as new technologies make old skills obsolete. Those same new technologies open up new career fields for those who are prepared—and ready to change. Know what you're up against. Don't take shortcuts. And don't give up too early. Major career changes are normal today and may prove desirable or essential tomorrow.

Ruth made a great mistake when he gave up pitching. Working once a week, he might have lasted a long time and become a great star.
> —TRIS SPEAKER, manager of the Cleveland Indians, commenting on Babe Ruth's plans to change from a pitcher to an outfielder, spring 1921

To establish oneself in the world, one does all one can to seem established there already.
> —LA ROCHEFOUCAULD

The secret of success is constancy of purpose.
> —BENJAMIN DISRAELI

CHAPTER 3

A SYSTEMATIC JOB HUNT

You only live once, but if you play your cards right, once is enough.
—Joe E. Brown

SUCCESSFUL JOB HUNTING IS A SYSTEM

WORKING THE SYSTEM increases your chances of getting the job you want—faster. Working the system also helps relieve your natural anxiety about what you should be doing next.

The system is the same whether you are employed or unemployed, and even if you are not interested in changing jobs now. That's because job hunting in a changing economy means: *continuously becoming aware of market conditions inside as well as outside your present company. And learning what you have to offer—both inside and outside your company.*

The time to become aware of your opportunities is *not* when the pressure is on to find a new job, but *now.*

THE JOB HUNTING PROCESS

You select or target a job market by selecting a geographic area you'd be willing to work in, an industry or company size, and a job or function within that industry. For example, you may want to be a pressman in the publishing industry in New Hampshire. That's your target market.

Then conduct a campaign for the sole purpose of getting interviews in your target area. A number of those interviews might eventually lead to acceptable job offers.

Job hunting seems to have dozens of equally important steps. There are résumés and cover letters to write, personal contacts to make, search firms to contact, ads to answer, notes to write, and so on. You can lose sight of what is most important.

There are only four main parts in a job hunt campaign: targeting, getting interviews in each target, interviewing, and following up. Do your best and put your effort into those areas. Everything you do in a job hunt grows out of your targets, which lead to interviews and then to offers. If you have targeted well, can get interviews, are well prepared for them, and know how to turn interviews into offers, you will be focused and less affected by mistakes in other areas of your search.

HOW LONG A JOB HUNT WILL TAKE

The length of each step in your search can vary considerably. For example, selecting the area in which you want to work (Part II of this book) can be as simple as saying, "I want to be a controller in a small firm." Or it can be as complex as saying, "I want a position of leadership in a growing computer services business in any major U.S. city, where I can run my part of the operation—working with fast-paced but ethical people who are imaginative and leaders in their field. The job should lead to the position of partner."

The entire campaign can be very short. Let's say, for example, that:

- you have focused on a specific, realizable target
- there are openings in the area that interests you
- you know of someone in a position to hire you
- you and the hiring manager "strike sparks" during the interview and it progresses naturally.

Start to finish could take a month or two.

The average job hunt does take longer. Statistics show that for professionals and middle managers, it takes an average of six months or more to find the job they want. As the previous chapter establishes, *career changers take longer*. And people currently employed usually take longer to find a new job because they often don't work as hard at the hunt.

It can take you longer than a month or two because, among other things:

- You may not be that clear about what you want.
- What you want may not be realistic.
- Maybe it *is* realistic, but there are no immediate openings.
- There may be openings, but you may not know where they are.

- You may hear of some openings, but may not know someone in a position to hire you.
- You may meet someone in a position to hire you, but the two of you don't hit it off.

Devote a large amount of time and energy to your search if you seriously intend to find a suitable job. A thorough search is so much work that the job you finally land will seem easy by comparison.

On the other hand, job hunting is like any other skill: you'll get better at it with practice. You'll learn the techniques, and you'll learn more about what's right for you. You'll become aware of what's happening in your chosen field, so that when you start a formal search it won't take so long.

THE NEW APPROACH TO JOB HUNTING

Keep up with changes in your company and your target area. To compete in today's competitive market, you must know:

- yourself
- the market—both inside and outside your company
- how to compete against "trained" job hunters.

JOB HUNTING—AN EVERYDAY AFFAIR

Job hunting is no longer something that happens only when you want to change jobs. Do it informally *all the time* to stay sharp in your present position.

You should always be aware of what may adversely affect your present security. Don't expect your employer to tell you that the company or your department is heading in a different direction. Be ready when the time for change comes. Take advantage of changes so you can move your career in the direction *you* want it to go. Take control and "impose your own terms upon life."

In today's world, many people job hunt virtually all the time. Twelve years ago, at a time when U.S. corporations were more stable, I met an executive at a major pharmaceuticals company. He had been with that company thirty years, and planned to stay there until retirement.

Yet, while I was talking to him, he reached into his bottom drawer and pulled out an up-to-date résumé. He was not starting a new job hunt; he believed he should always have an up-to-date résumé and keep on looking—even though he had been working at the same company for thirty

WHAT A JOB HUNT LOOKS LIKE

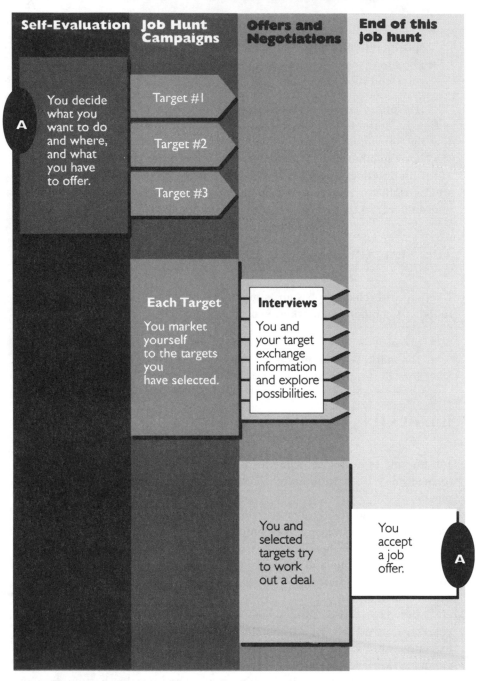

Self-Evaluation

A

You decide what you want to do and where, and what you have to offer.

Job Hunt Campaigns

Target #1

Target #2

Target #3

Each Target

You market yourself to the targets you have selected.

Offers and Negotiations

Interviews

You and your target exchange information and explore possibilities.

You and selected targets try to work out a deal.

End of this job hunt

You accept a job offer.

A

NOTE: After you are in your new job for a while (such as six months, one year, two years), you will want to reevaluate your situation and make sure you are still on track. That's why this chart points back to the beginning after you've landed your job.

years! A good number of his job hunts were "successful" in that his outside exploration got him to his high position in the same company.

Job hunting does not necessarily mean you want to change jobs now. Maybe you'll make your next actual job change a few years down the road. Or maybe someone will change your job for you—without asking. When are you going to start thinking about your next move?

PLAN YOUR NEXT MOVE

Plan your career transitions—your moves from one job to the next—don't have them thrust upon you. First, know which job is right for you: a job in which you will excel and feel satisfied doing. Then see how well your present job fits those desires. Don't leave your job for another one that is equally unsatisfying. On the other hand, don't remain in your current job out of inertia.

Career transitions are prompted by changes in a company—such as when it cuts back or introduces major technological or strategic changes —or by a change in you and your goals for your life. Be alert for a coming transition.

IF YOU'RE THINKING ABOUT CHANGING JOBS

If you don't like your present job, don't leave yet . . . a good job hunt starts at home. Try to enrich your present job or move elsewhere in the company. Leave only after you are convinced that there is nothing there for you.

Whether you want to stay or leave, find out what your options are and what marketable skills you possess. Figure out what would make a good growth move for you.

One way to find out is to talk, on an informal basis, to people in other companies who are at least two levels higher than you are. They have an overview of the broad spectrum of job possibilities and are also in a position to hire you, or know others who might.

Another way to find out what is marketable is to look at the ads in the paper. You could get ideas for growing in your present position.

Let me give you an example. As soon as I accepted the job of vice president of operations for an advertising agency, I started clipping ads for v.p. of personnel, company controller, v.p. of finance, general manager —anything that would apply, even remotely, to my new position. The ads gave me ideas that neither my new employer nor I would have thought of.

I expanded the job and organized the categories of work I should be concentrating on.

These ads also told me the likelihood of being able to get one of those jobs. Even though I clipped lots of ads for v.p. of finance, I would never qualify because they required skills I did not have and was not interested in acquiring.

Ads also let you see who is hiring and what is in demand. Ads teach you the buzzwords of certain professions, and indicate how to tailor your résumé—just in case.

The fact that you're constantly job hunting can only be *good* for your present employer. It motivates you to do better, keeping your company more competitive than if you were not aware of what was happening outside.

WHAT TO DO IF YOU ARE ABOUT TO BE FIRED

> I don't deserve this, but I have arthritis and I don't deserve that either.
> —JACK BENNY

When people are being fired, many say to themselves, "I'm good at what I do. I won't have trouble finding a job." Unfortunately, job hunting calls for special skills. If you are being fired, ask for outplacement help as part of your separation agreement. In full outplacement, counselors guide you in your search until you find a job, and you are given office space and administrative help. It makes all the difference in finding new employment quickly and confidently. Partial outplacement may consist of a one- or two-day workshop on résumé writing, interviewing, and general job hunting techniques, and may also include a few hours with a counselor. You are then left to fend for yourself.

You cannot purchase the services of an outplacement firm yourself. Your old company pays the fee, which usually amounts to 10 to 20 percent of your previous compensation. Full outplacement help will be worth more to you than an extra month's pay. You can get the *Directory of Outplacement Firms* from Kennedy Publications, Templeton Road, Fitzwilliam, NH 03447; 603-585-6544.

If you are currently employed, or outplacement is not available to you, consider your options. A seminar is fine but will not see you through the job hunt process. Job counseling firms often charge from four to six thousand dollars up front, and some have been known to lose interest once the fee is paid.

You need job hunting advice and support. Job hunting is stressful and lonely. You may feel that you are the only one going through what you are going through. You may even feel as though you will never work again.

Join a group such as The Five O'Clock Club or Forty Plus. They complement each other. The Five O'Clock Club offers job search training and coaching from professional career counselors. You can also meet with a counselor privately to help you figure out your job targets, prepare your résumé, or get individualized help on a specific part of your campaign. Forty Plus offers office space, typing equipment, phones, and lectures. You will be with others who feel exactly as you do. See *The Wall Street Journal*'s "National Business and Employment Weekly" for listings of these and other programs in your area.

Unemployed people sometimes become embarrassed by their situation and pretend they are not looking—which is the worst thing they can do. *When you are unemployed and looking for a job, the more people who know what you are looking for, the better.* Spend time regularly with other job hunters, and also with a professional counselor who can give you solid advice.

THE PRACTICE OF JOB HUNTING TECHNIQUES

Job hunting is a specialized skill just as is public speaking or cooking a gourmet meal. You probably wouldn't, for example, get up to speak before an important audience without preparation and practice.

Job hunting takes planning to decide what your message is; some research; some thinking about your audience and how your message will sound to them; writing and rewriting résumés, letters, and interview presentations; and then some practice to hear how it all sounds.

Successful job hunting is a formal process. But once you know the basics, you can and should put your own personality into your presentations, just as you would in public speaking.

Follow the "rules" for job hunting the same way you would follow the "rules" for public speaking or cooking. As a wise beginner, do everything by the book. After you become skilled, you can deviate a bit—for the better—because you have mastered the basics. You will do what is right for you and the situation you are in. You can exercise sound judgment.

You will then be at the point where it flows. You will find that you are operating from an inner strength, and you'll feel what is important and what is not. It is *your* job hunt, and you are the one calling the shots. You will feel sure enough to do what is appropriate regardless of what some expert says. You will know when it is to your advantage to break the rules.

You cannot stop change, so don't develop a siege mentality. Practice job hunting now—even if you happen to enjoy what you're doing, and even if you want to continue in your present job. In fact, you will be more effective in your job if you become sharper about what is happening in the world.

The rules of the game keep changing and that's part of the game. Only those who change along with them will be allowed to continue to play.

Our rate of progress is such that an individual human being, of ordinary length of life, will be called on to face novel situations which find no parallel in his past. The fixed person, for the fixed duties, who, in older societies was such a godsend, in the future will be a public danger.
—ALFRED NORTH WHITEHEAD

CHAPTER   4

HOW LONG WILL IT TAKE TO FIND A JOB?

Nothing in the world can take the place of persistence. Talent will not; nothing is more common than unsuccessful men with talent. Genius will not; the world is full of educated derelicts. Persistence and determination alone are omnipotent. The slogan "press on" has solved and always will solve the problems of the human race.
—CALVIN COOLIDGE

MOST OF THE factors that influence the length of a job hunt are under your control. Scan the following topics and read the ones that interest you now. Read the others later.

Factor #1: Career continuation vs. career change

All things being equal, changing careers takes two to three months longer than looking for a job in the field you are in now. If you want to head your career in a new direction, do it—but realize that it will take longer. (See Chapter 2: How to Change Careers.)

Factor #2: A clear target

You dramatically reduce your chances of finding the job you want if you don't have clearly defined targets, or if you have more than three or four targets.

A job target is a clearly selected geographic area, industry or company size, and function within that industry. For example, a job hunter may target the advertising industry in New York or Chicago, and aim at positions in the account management area. That's one target. That same job hunter may target media sales positions in the publishing industry, also in New York or Chicago. That's a second target. They are related, but require quite different campaigns.

You may feel you are willing to take any job that comes along, but attaining results with that approach takes longer than with a targeted approach. When you target, your campaign is focused and more convincing to hiring managers. Your pitch is more polished, and you'll find it is easier to network. Serendipitous leads can certainly be worthwhile, but the core of your campaign should be targeted.

Factor #3: A clear positioning statement or pitch within that target

You are selling an expensive product—yourself—and you cost many thousands of dollars. To sell this product, know what the customer (your prospective employer) wants, what you have to offer, and why the customer would want to buy this product. As you position yourself, figure out what to say about yourself in light of what your "customer" needs. Know how you fit in.

Factor #4: Favorable conditions within your target market

If your target area is growing or desperately needs what you are offering, or if there are plenty of jobs for which you would qualify, your job hunt will not take as long.

On the other hand, if you decide to go for a tough target, expect to work hard to overcome the difficulties. Find out how to get in, and then do it.

Factor #5: True desire to find a job

The people most likely to succeed are the ones who sincerely want to find a job, and work hard at getting it.

Job hunting is a job in itself. If you are unemployed, work at it full-time (with time off for a little fun). If you are employed, treat job hunting as a serious part-time job and work at it.

Many job hunters do not treat finding a job as their top priority. Some may spend time suing their former employer. Others work hard at a job hunt doing the wrong things: when choosing between doing two things, they seem to choose the one less likely to result in job hunt progress. A person may spend months in the library getting ready, for example, when they know they should be out meeting people. They may consciously or unconsciously sabotage their own efforts because they were recently fired and are afraid of getting fired again. If you find everything is going wrong all the time, ask yourself if you may be afraid of the future. Honestly ask yourself how sincere you are about finding a job now.

Factor #6: Attitude. Attitude. Attitude.

You may have the right target, the perfect market, and be the perfect match for a company, but if your attitude is wrong, you'll have a hard time. The worst attitude is to expect someone else to find a job for you. Successful job hunters are those who take responsibility for their own success or failure rather than blaming the counselor or the system when things go wrong.

"Attitude" includes:

- taking responsibility for your own job hunt
- the self-confidence you portray
- being able to think and act like a winner even if you don't feel like it (who wants to hire a loser?)
- your drive, your energy level.

Your attitude is as important as the actual job hunt techniques you use. Flawless technique is worthless with a bad attitude.

Factor #7: Working the system

In addition to being willing to work hard, you must be willing to work the system. Those most likely to find a job quickly are those who go through every step—even if they go through certain steps quickly or find other steps distasteful.

A job hunt is going to take time. The time you think you're saving by skipping a phase will haunt you later. Do not bypass the system. *There are no shortcuts.*

Factor #8: Good interviewing and follow-up skills

Some people get lots of interviews but no job offers.

You cannot get a job without an interview, in which you'll have to do well. Interviewing is a skill that requires preparation, practice, and an ability to notice what is important to the interviewer so you can take whatever next steps are required.

Factor #9: Support and encouragement from friends and family/absence of personal disruptions

Recently divorced people, for example, tend to do less well in their jobs and less well in their job hunting efforts. If you have other things on your mind, they may adversely affect your job hunt. Try to be effective despite these problems.

Job hunters usually need emotional support because this can be a trying experience. Our egos are at stake. Job hunting is not an easy thing to do.

Sometimes the support of family and friends is not enough because they are not going through what you are going through. That's why people join job hunt groups or get outplacement counseling. You need realistic, honest support from people who know what you are going through. Studies have proved that *those who get ongoing counseling during their searches get jobs faster and at higher rates of pay* than those who simply take a course or decide to search on their own.

Factor #10: Previous job hunt experience

If you haven't job hunted in a while, you're probably rusty. People will ask questions you're not used to answering and you may not sound polished. The process requires skills we don't use in our everyday work lives. Inexperienced job hunters usually take longer than those who are used to marketing themselves. You need to develop the skills you'll need to land the job that is right for you.

> It is only by risking our persons from one hour to another that we live at all. And often enough our faith beforehand in an uncertified result is the only thing that makes the result come true.
> —WILLIAM JAMES
> *The Will to Believe*

> Life shrinks or expands in proportion to one's courage.
> —ANAÏS NIN

> Everyone has a mass of bad work in him which he will have to work off and get rid of before he can do better; and, indeed, the more lasting a man's ultimate work, the more sure he is to pass through a time, and perhaps a very long one, in which there seems to be very little hope for him.
> —SAMUEL BUTLER

CHAPTER 5

WHEN YOU'VE LOST THE SPIRIT TO JOB HUNT

"I can't explain myself, I'm afraid, Sir," said Alice, "because I'm not myself, you see." "I don't see," said the Caterpillar.
—LEWIS CARROLL
Alice in Wonderland

THEY'RE ALL DOING terrific! You're not. You're barely hanging on. You used to be a winner, but now you're not so sure. How can you pull yourself out of this?

I've felt like that. Everyone in New York had a job except me. I would never work again. I was ruining interviews although I knew better —I had run The Five O'Clock Club for years in Philadelphia. Yet I was unable to job hunt properly. I was relatively new to New York and divorced. Even going to my house in the country depressed me: a woman wanted me to sell it, join her cult, and have a seventy-one-year-old as my roommate. It seemed to be my fate.

Then I got a call from my father—a hurricane was about to hit New York. When I told him my situation, he directed me to get rid of the cult lady and take the next train out. I got out just as the hurricane blew in, and he and I spent three beautiful days alone at my parents' ocean place. He nurtured me, including playing ten motivational tapes on "being a winner"!

The winners in life think constantly in terms of I can, I will and I am. Losers, on the other hand, concentrate their waking thoughts on what they should have or would have done, or what they can't do.
—DENIS WAITLEY
The Psychology of Winning

He wined and dined and took care of me. We watched a six-hour tape of my family history—the births and birthdays, Christmases past, marriages and parties. We talked about life and the big picture. I had no strength. He nurtured me and gave me strength.

What can you do if you can't get this kind of nurturing? Perhaps I've learned a few lessons that may help you.

PUT THINGS IN PERSPECTIVE

> A depressing and difficult passage has prefaced every new page I have turned in life.
> —CHARLOTTE BRONTË

You've worked ten or twenty years, and you'll work ten or twenty more. In the grand scheme of things, this moment will be a blip: an aberration in the past.

Focusing on the present will make you depressed, and will also make you a poor interviewee. You will find it difficult to brag about your past or see the future. You will provide too much information about what put you in this situation.

Interviewers don't care. They want to hear what you can do for them. When they ask why you are looking, give a brief, light, logical explanation, and then drop it.

Focus on what you have done in the past, and what you can do in the future. You do have a future, you know—although you may feel locked in your present situation. Even some young people say it is too late for them. But a lot can happen in ten years—and *most* of what happens is up to you.

GET SUPPORT

> Woe to him that is alone when he falleth, for he hath not another to help him up.
> —THE WISDOM OF SOLOMON: APOCRYPHA

Gone are the old support systems: Extended families, and even nuclear families, are gone. We no longer look to our community for support. Today, we are more alone than at any other time; yet we are supposed to be tougher and take care of ourselves. But relying solely on yourself is not the answer. How can you fill yourself up when you are emotionally and spiritually empty?

Job hunters often need some kind of emotional and spiritual support because this is a trying time. Our egos are at stake. We feel vulnerable and uncared for. We need realistic support from people who know what we are going through.

> There is no such thing as a self-made man. I've had much help and have found that if you are willing to work, many people are willing to help you.
> —O. WAYNE ROLLINS

• *Join a job hunt counseling group* to be with others who know what you are going through. A job hunt group gives emotional support, concrete advice, and feedback.

> The more lasting a man's ultimate work, the more sure he is to pass through a time, and perhaps a very long one, in which there seems to be very little hope for him.
> —SAMUEL BUTLER

• If possible, *rely on your friends and family*. I could count on a call from my former husband most mornings after I returned from breakfast—just so we both could make sure I was really job hunting. I scheduled lunches with friends and gave them an honest report or practiced my job hunting lines with them.

Don't abuse your relationships by relying on one or two people. Find lots of sources of support. Consider joining a church or synagogue (they're supposed to be nice to you there).

REMEMBER THAT THIS IS PART OF A BIGGER PICTURE

> We, ignorant of ourselves, beg often our own harms, which the Wise Power denies us for our own good; so we find profit by losing of our prayers.
> —SHAKESPEARE
> *Antony and Cleopatra*

> . . . so are my ways higher than your ways, and My thoughts than your thoughts.
> ISAIAH 55:9

Why me? Why now? Shakespeare thought there might be someone bigger than ourselves watching over everything—a Wise Power. My mother (and probably yours, too) always said that "everything happens for the best."

> And we know that all things work together for good of them that love God.
> —ROMANS 8:28

If you believe that things happen for a purpose, *think about the good in your own situation*. What was the "purpose" of my unemployment? Because of it I experienced a closeness with my father that still affects me, I became a better counselor, and I stopped working twelve-hour days.

Though shattered when they lose their jobs, many people say in retrospect it was the best thing that could have happened to them. Some say the time of transition was *the most rewarding experience of their lives*.

> Every adversity has the seed of an equivalent or greater benefit.
> —W. CLEMENT STONE

Perhaps you, too, can learn from this experience and also make some sense of it. This is a time when people often:

- decide what they really should be doing with their careers (I had resisted becoming a full-time career consultant because I liked the prestige of the jobs I had held).
- better their situations, taking off on another upward drive in their careers.
- develop their personalities; learn skills that will last their entire lives.
- reexamine their values and decide what is now important to them.

> For what shall it profit a man, if he shall gain the whole world, and lose his own soul?
> —MARK 8:36

> The trouble with the rat race is that if you win, you're still a rat.
> —LILY TOMLIN

CONTINUE TO DO YOUR JOB

When you were in your old job, there were days when you didn't feel like doing it, but you did it anyway because it was your responsibility. *Job hunting is your job right now*. Some days you don't feel like doing it, but you must. Make a phone call. Write a proposal. Research a company. Do your best every day. No matter how you feel. And somehow it will get done, just as any job gets done. Some practical suggestions:

- Job hunting is your job. Make it professional. Organize it. Get a job hunt calendar to track what you are doing. Use The Five O'Clock Club's Interview Record to more professionally track your efforts and results.

- Set goals. Don't think of whether you want to make calls and write letters. Of course you don't. *Just do them anyway.* Spend most of your time interviewing—that's how you get a job. Remember that depression leads to inactivity, which leads to more depression.
- If you're at the three-month mark or beyond, you may be at a low point. It's hard to push on. Get a fresh start. Pretend you're starting all over again.
- Finding a job is your responsibility. Don't depend on anyone else (search firms, friends) to find it for you.
- Watch your drinking, eating, smoking. They can get out of hand. Take care of yourself physically. Get dressed. Look good. Get some exercise. Eat healthy foods. *You may need a few days off to recharge.*
- Don't postpone having fun until you get a job. If you are unemployed, schedule at least three hours of fun a week. Do something you normally are unable to do when you are working. I went out to breakfast every morning, indulged in reading the *Times*, and then went back to my apartment to job hunt. I also went to auction houses, and bought a beautiful desk at Sotheby's when I sold my country house.
- Assess your financial situation. What is your backup plan if your unemployment goes on for a certain number of months? If need be, I had planned to take in a roommate, sell furniture, and take out a loan. It turned out not to be necessary, but by planning ahead I knew I would not wind up on the street.
- *Remember: you are distracted.* Job hunters get mugged, walk into walls, lose things. This is not an ordinary situation, and extraordinary things happen. Be on your guard.
- Observe the results of what you do in a job hunt. Results are indicators of the correctness of your actions and can help refine your techniques.
- Become a good job hunter so you can compete in this market. It takes practice, but the better you are, the less anxious you will be.

In nature there are neither rewards nor punishments—there are consequences.
  —ROBERT GREEN INGERSOLL

Finally, two sayings especially helped me when I was unemployed: *You don't get what you want. You get what you need.* And, *When God closes a door, He opens a window.* Good luck, and remember: *All's well that ends well.* (Shakespeare).

Now, let's get on with your search.

PART TWO

DECIDING WHAT YOU WANT

HOW TO SELECT YOUR JOB TARGET

(IF YOU ALREADY HAVE A TARGET, GO TO PART THREE)

ALICE: *"Will you tell me please, which way I ought to go from here?"*
CAT: *"That depends a good deal on where you want to get to."*
ALICE: *"I don't care much where—so long as I get somewhere."*
CAT: *"Oh, you're sure to do that if only you walk long enough."*
　　　　　　　　　　—LEWIS CARROLL
　　　　　　　　　Alice in Wonderland

CHAPTER 6

HOW TO FIND YOUR PLACE IN THE WORLD

You are a child of the universe no less than the trees and the stars; you have a right to be here. And whether or not it is clear to you, no doubt the universe is unfolding as it should.
—DESIDERATA

CHANGE AS OPPORTUNITY

When written in Chinese, the word "crisis" is composed of two characters—one represents danger and the other represents opportunity.
—JOHN F. KENNEDY, Address, United Negro College Fund Convocation April 12, 1959

DON'T EXPECT TO hold on to the way things have worked for you in the past. Get on with the new way the world is operating. You cannot stop the changes, but you *can* choose the way you will respond. You can see change as a threat to resist—or an opportunity to move forward.

Change represents danger to you when you choose to resist it. While your energy goes into trying to keep your situation the same, you will become more dissatisfied as you see others taking advantage of changes.

You can use change to your advantage if you decide to see it as a source of opportunity. Then, it won't be so threatening. You will reduce your chances of being run over. You will be running your own life.

To look at change as a source of opportunity, become more aware of the changes taking place around you—the events that can affect you and your job. Decide which are best for you and how to take advantage of those that interest you. The pace of change in today's economy can be overwhelming—unless you can assess changes more objectively. In doing so, you will have more control *over the way you respond.*

AN INTERNAL REFERENCE POINT

> God grant me the serenity to accept the things I cannot change, the courage to change the things I can, and the wisdom to know the difference.
> —"SERENITY PRAYER"

How can you make the most of changes? How can you decide which ones bode well for you and which ones bode ill? You need a stable, internal point of reference—a clear picture of what you need to feel satisfied with your job and with your life. You can measure a changing situation against your list of the *elements* you require, to decide if a change is in your favor or not. You can perhaps alter the situation to suit you, or to get out of there at the earliest point.

To feel in control and actually to *be* in control of your life, make choices based on your inner direction. With so many changes swirling around, the only stabilizing point must be inside of you. Nothing outside can be your anchor. The next chapter has exercises to help you determine your inner direction.

A CAREER COUNSELOR CANNOT DECIDE FOR YOU

> We can help one another find out the meaning of life. . . . But in the last analysis, each is responsible for "finding himself."
> —THOMAS MERTON
> *No Man Is an Island*

Let's be practical about it: a career counselor cannot possibly know all the options out there for you. There are so many choices and the world is changing so fast, how *could* one person know the answer that is right for you? And when things change again, as they will, will you expect a career counselor to tell you what to do then?

What you do with your life is *your* decision. A counselor cannot decide for you, but can only *help* you decide.

Blaming someone else for your lack of progress can be a reflection of your attitude about life. Do you basically feel you control what happens to you? Or do you feel what happens is essentially in the hands of others? When you blame others, you give up your power. You are saying that someone else is deciding what will happen to you. When you do not blame others, you have more power: you are taking control over your own life.

Those who take responsibility for their own lives do better than those who expect others to solve their problems.

Accepting responsibility means, generally, not blaming others for your situation. You accept that your choices have gotten you where you are. You are in control. You can make new choices to head your life where you want.

WHY USE A CAREER COACH?

> Nobody owns a job, nobody owns a market, nobody owns a product. Somebody out there can always take it away from you.
> —RONALD E. COMPTON, president-chairman, Aetna,
> as quoted in *The New York Times*, March 1, 1992

In this changing marketplace, increasingly we all have to be out there selling ourselves. This is causing people a great deal of understandable stress. Most of us would rather just do our jobs and trust that we will be treated fairly. Since we cannot depend on this, some people have made a career coach a normal part of their lives—as normal as having a regular tune-up on your car or an annual physical. They go to their coach not only when they are conducting a job search or when they have problems, but perhaps once or twice a year for a checkup.

> An important component of the career assessment process is to help clients accept themselves: their strengths as well as what does not come naturally to them.
> —BARRY LUSTIG
> Director of The Professional Development Institute, Federation Employment and Guidance Services of New York

Clients working with a career coach learn what works for them personally and what does not, come to better understand the kinds of environments they should be working in (bosses, corporate cultures, pace, and so on), learn how to be more effective in their work relationships (bosses, peers, subordinates, clients), learn how to balance their lives more effectively, and also lay the groundwork for the next career move they may have to make. They talk about their long-term career goals and the steps they need to take to reach them—or perhaps simply to stay even. They make sure they are doing what they must to develop their careers as the economy changes, such as getting specific experience, taking courses, or joining organizations.

Over time, your coach gets to know you, just as your family doctor gets to know you, and can warn you against things that may cause you problems, or advise you about things you could be doing next. Just as a family doctor would want to give you a complete physical if you are to become his patient, so, too, your coach would want to give you an assessment to find out as much as possible about you. I tell clients that if I don't know enough about them, it is as if they were someone on the street coming up to me to ask advice. I need to know something about them so I can be a real coach.

If you decide to use a private coach, use someone who charges by the hour. Do not pay a huge up-front fee. After you have worked with the counselor a number of times, assess your relationship with that person. There should be a good personality fit between you and your counselor. For example, some counselors are very intense, while others have a softer approach. If the relationship is not good, or if the meetings damage your self-worth, go to someone else.

For your part, make sure you are willing to make the necessary commitment. If you go only for one hour to have the counselor handle an emergency you are facing, do not expect that counselor to come to know very much about you. If you decide to use a counselor, you are likely to learn more about the wonderful person you are, so you can figure out how you fit into this changing world. You will have increased self-esteem and increased effectiveness.

> One of the most important aptitudes we all have to offer is our personality.
> —BARRY LUSTIG

DEVELOP A VISION; MAKE A COMMITMENT

> The field cannot well be seen from within the field.
> —RALPH WALDO EMERSON

Take a stand. Decide where you want to head, and go for it. You'll be happier because you'll have a goal and you'll work toward it. Work will no longer be "work," but an activity that brings pleasure, pride, and a sense of accomplishment, and carries out your vision.

When you know yourself and make a commitment, things become clearer. You act more decisively, have less stress, and cope better with the progress of your career and the changes around you. Negative things will not bother you as much. The direction will not be coming from someone else, but from inside you.

Without commitment, we are wanderers without roots in a rapidly changing world. We feel a lack of meaningful goals in our lives. "Commitment" means accepting that you are responsible for your own career direction. It means *choosing* what you want to do in this changing society without losing your inner bearings.

LOOKING FOR WHERE YOU FIT IN

> For I know the plans I have for you, declares the Lord, plans to prosper you and not to harm you, plans to give you a hope and a future.
> —JEREMIAH 29:11

We each fit in. What you're looking for is *where* you fit in. As you learn more about what is inside you, as well as what is outside, you will progressively change your situation to suit yourself better, and so you will also fit better into the world.

To grow with the world, know what you want and what you want to offer. Knowing yourself, in the context of career development, means knowing how you prefer to operate, what you like to do, and what you can do well. Knowing what you want to offer means stepping outside yourself to see what the world values. Take what you want to offer and market it.

Don't be *too* specific about what you want. If you are open to new opportunities, surprising things can happen. A large number of jobs are created with a certain person in mind. A job created with you in mind would probably be more satisfying than one in which you would have to mold yourself to fit a rigid job description. You would enjoy your job more and do better because you would be doing what you want.

What are the chances of having a job created to suit you? If you don't know what would suit you, chances are slim. Having definite ideas increases your chances of finding such a job, or even of changing your present job to better suit your goals. Opportunities come along all the time. You won't recognize them unless you know what you are looking for.

We change the world and the world changes us. As we grow, we are developing ourselves—in relation to the world. We are each trying to know what we want and how to get it, while we are also trying to understand and fit into a changing world. It is a lifelong process, but a happy one. It is a process of seeing change as an opportunity while accepting the limitations of the world.

> The earth is a medium-sized planet orbiting around an average star in the outer suburbs of an ordinary spiral galaxy, which is itself only one of about a million million galaxies in the observable universe.
> —STEPHEN M. HAWKING, *A Brief History of Time*

CASE STUDY: HENRY
Aiming too low

> You can never enslave somebody who knows who he is.
> —ALEX HALEY

Henry, an executive of about forty-five, had just been fired, and I was asked to be his counselor. Henry said he already had a clear idea of what he wanted to do next—something that was quite in demand—loan work-outs (when loans go bad, he would try to salvage them). Henry could certainly get a job like that, and quickly, but I felt as though I didn't know him at all, so I asked if we could do a few exercises. If I understood him better, I would be in a better position to coach him.

In his Seven Stories (an exercise you will do in the next chapter), Henry stated that he was proud that he had grown up in a tiny Midwestern town (there were only sixty people in his entire high school), had gotten into Harvard, and graduated very high in his class.

Where was that little boy now? What had caused him to settle for a loan workout position that would have been right for lots of *other* people? I told Henry that I thought he could do better than that. I asked him to aim to find a job that would make him so proud it would wind up on his *future* Seven Stories list. Within two and a half months, Henry had landed a job that was better than anything he had ever dreamed possible. At an excellent salary, he became a very senior executive in a major corporation. Henry was so proud, he beamed. He's still there now and doing very well.

YOU NEED INFORMATION—OUT IN THE WORLD

> It is the first of all problems for a man to find out what kind of work he is to do in this universe.
> —THOMAS CARLYLE
> *Sartor Resartus*

You need information about yourself and about the changing world of work. Find an optimal fit by matching what you learn about yourself against what you learn about the world.

If you're like most people, at least part of your career plans was decided by someone else. If that decision was not best for you, something has to change. You must either change to fit the job, or you must change the job to fit you. If you have often changed yourself to suit the job you were in, you may not know what you want. The next chapter helps you figure out what you would enjoy doing in a job.

You cannot find out about yourself in a vacuum. Go out and test your ideas about yourself against what others think of you. That's the only healthy way. With more knowledge about the world, and with a clearer sense of our place in it, options will appear that we never noticed before.

THE STEPS TO FINDING YOUR PLACE

The basic steps to finding your place are covered in greater detail in the other chapters in this section. Spend as much or as little time as you want on each. The process can go on forever. Do what you want now, and do more later.

Step 1: Determine what you want (Chapter 7) Develop a long-term view of yourself—a guiding light that can see you through a number of jobs. In fact, you could develop a view that will see you through your entire life.

Step 2: Decide what you want to offer (Chapter 8) Notice that I say what you *want* to offer—not what you *have* to offer. You may be tempted to offer what you have been offering all along. Although a pragmatic choice may see you through a job transition, it is more important to decide what you *want* to offer. If you offer things you do not want to do, you increase your chances of *doing* things you do not want to do.

I looked at a secretary's résumé. It mentioned heavy phone work as one of her duties. When I asked her if she liked phone work, she responded, "I hate phone work." I advised her to remove it from her résumé, or someone would say, "That's just what we need: someone who can do heavy phone work."

Of course, every job has parts you don't like. In fact, you may decide to offer such an aspect as one of your strong skills until you develop yourself in the areas you want to focus on. That's often a good approach.

I'll use my own life as an example. I started out in computers as a way of working my way through school. After learning so much about them, I have always used computers to my advantage even though working with them was not central on my list of life goals. Sometimes the fact that I knew computers gave me an edge over other job hunters. While I didn't want working with computers to be a central part of my job, the skill has been a handy one to offer.

In this step you will develop a menu of everything you have to offer, and then you can decide to offer what you want.

Step 3: A combination of the results of Steps 1 and 2 (Chapter 9) You'll do best in a job that relies on some of your strengths and experiences, but also provides you with some growth toward your goals. Bring something to the job. Chapter 9 will help you select a job target that considers both.

CAST STUDY: AARON
Knowing where he wants to end up

> Having gifts that differ according to the grace given to us, let us use
> them.
> —ROMANS 12:6

Aaron has been in corporate marketing for eight years. Through the Seven
Stories exercise and his Forty-Year Plan (which you will see in the next
chapter), he developed a long-term view of himself: the head of a five-
hundred-person public-sector-related agency or organization, such as the
World Wildlife Fund.

Now that he knows where he wants to end up, he can work backward
to figure out how he could get there. To head up such a large organization,
he has two choices: he can start such an organization from scratch, or he
can take over an existing organization. Aaron decided that five years from
now, he would prefer to become the head of an existing fifty-person organization and expand it to a five-hundred-person organization.

But how can he go from where he is now to becoming the head of a
fifty-person organization? What he has to offer is his corporate marketing
background. Therefore, his next logical step is to try to get a marketing
job in a not-for-profit organization that is similar to the one he would
eventually like to head up. That way, his next job will be one that positions
him well for the moves after that, and increases his chance of getting
where he wants to go.

THE BENEFITS OF KNOWING WHAT YOU WANT

As I have stressed so far, you are responsible for your own career development. Decide what you want, rather than hoping someone will think
about it for you. The next chapter will get you started.

> Now, I can look at you, Mr. Loomis, and see you a man who done
> forgot his song. Forgot how to sing it. A fellow forget that and he
> forget who he is. Forget how he's supposed to mark down life.
> —AUGUST WILSON
> *Joe Turner's Come and Gone*

CHAPTER 7

HOW TO DECIDE WHAT YOU WANT

Let me listen to me and not to them.
—GERTRUDE STEIN

LOOKING AHEAD—A CAREER INSTEAD OF A JOB

What seems different in yourself; that's the rare thing you possess.
The one thing that gives each of us his worth, and that's just what
we try to suppress. And we claim to love life.
—ANDRÉ GIDE

IF YOU DON'T decide where you want to go, you may wind up
drifting from one company to another each time you're dissatisfied, with
pretty much the same job in each case. Even if you decide that you want
to continue doing what you're doing right now, that's a goal in itself and
may be difficult to achieve.

The first step in career management is goal setting. There are a lot
of processes involved in the goal-setting area. But the one considered most
central is that by which a person examines his or her past accomplishments, looking at the strongest and most enjoyable skills.

This process is not only the one favored by counselors, it is also the
one most often used by successful people. In reading the biographies of
such people, I see again and again how they established their goals by
identifying those things they enjoy doing and also do well. This process of
identifying your "enjoyable accomplishments" is the most important one
you can go through.

WHAT SUCCESSFUL PEOPLE DO

When Steven Jobs, the founder of Apple Computers, was fired by John Sculley, the man he had brought in to run the company, he felt as though he had lost everything. Apple had been his life. Now he had lost not only his job, but his company. People no longer felt the need to return his phone calls. He did what a lot of us would do. He got depressed. But then:

> Confused about what to do next . . . he [Jobs] put himself through an exercise that management psychologists employ with clients unsure about their life goals. It was a little thing, really. It was just a list. A list of all the things that mattered most to Jobs during his ten years at Apple. "Three things jumped off that piece of paper, three things that were really important to me," says Jobs.
> —MICHAEL MEYER, *The Alexander Complex*

The exercise Steven Jobs went through is essentially what you will do in the Seven Stories exercise. The threads that ran through his stories formed the impetus for his next great drive: the formation of NeXT computers. If the Seven Stories exercise is good enough for Steven Jobs, maybe it's good enough for you.

"Successful managers," says Charles Garfield, head of Performance Services, Inc., in Berkeley, California, "go with their preferences." They search for work that is important to them, and when they find it they pursue it with a passion.

Lester Korn, Chairman of Korn, Ferry, notes in his book *The Success Profile*: "Few executives know, or can know, exactly what they aspire to until they have been in the work force for a couple of years. It takes that long to learn enough about yourself to know what you can do well and what will make you happy. The trick is to merge the two into a goal, then set off in pursuit of it."

This chapter will help you decide what you want to do in your next job as well as in the long run. You will become more clear about the experiences you have enjoyed most and may like to repeat. You will also examine your interests and values, and look at past positions to analyze what satisfied you and what did not. In addition, you will look farther ahead (through your Forty-Year Plan) to see if some driving dream may influence what you will want to do in the short term. I did my Forty-Year Plan about fifteen years ago, and the vision I had of my future still drives me today. Knowing where you would like to wind up broadens the kinds of jobs you would be interested in today. Look at it this way:

A B   C

The line represents your life. Right now, you are at A. Your next job is B. If you look only at your past to decide what to do next, your next job is limited by what you have already done. For example, if you have been in finance and accounting for the past fifteen years, and you base your next move on your past, your next job is likely to be in finance or accounting.

If you know that at C you would like to wind up as vice president of finance and administration, new possibilities open up. Think of all the areas you would manage:

- Finance
- Administration
- Accounting
- Operations
- Personnel
- Computers

Experience in any one of these would advance your career in the right direction. For example, you may decide to get some computer experience. Without the benefit of a Forty-Year Plan, a move to computers might look like the start of a career in computers, but *you* know it's just one more assignment that leads to your long-term goal. You'll keep your plan in mind and take jobs and assignments that will continually position you for the long run. For example, in the computer area, you may focus on personnel or administrative systems, two areas that fit your goal. Then your computer job will be more than a job. You will work hard for your employer, but you will also know why you are there—you are using your job as a stepping stone to something bigger and better.

HAPPY IN YOUR WORK

> Make no little plans; they have no magic to stir men's blood and probably themselves will not be realized. Make big plans; aim high in hope and work.
> —DANIEL BURNHAM

People are happy when they are working toward their goals. When they get diverted—or don't know what their goals are—they are unhappy. Many people are unhappy in their jobs because they don't know where they are going.

People without goals are more irked by daily petty problems than are those with goals who are less bothered because they have bigger plans. To control your life, know where you are going, and be ready for your next move—in case the ax falls on you. When you take that next job, continue to manage your career. Companies rarely build career paths for their employees any more. Make your own way. There are plenty of jobs for those who are willing to learn and change with the times.

SEVEN STORIES EXERCISE

The direction of change to seek is not in our four dimensions: it is getting deeper into what you are, where you are, like turning up the volume on the amplifier.
—THADDEUS GOLAS, *Lazy Man's Guide to Enlightenment*

In this exercise, you will examine your accomplishments, looking at your strongest and most enjoyable skills. The core of most counseling exercises is some version of the Seven Stories exercise. A counselor may give you lots of tests and exercises, but this one requires *work* on your part and will yield the most important results. An interest or personality test is not enough. There is no easy way. Remember, busy executives take the time to complete this exercise—if it's good enough for them, it's good enough for you.

Do not skip the Seven Stories exercise. It will provide you with information for your career direction, your résumé, and your interviews. After you do the exercise, brainstorm about a number of possible job targets. Then research each target to find out what the job possibilities are for someone like you.

If you're like most people, you have never taken the time to sort out the things you're good at and also are motivated to accomplish. As a result, you probably don't use these talents as completely or as effectively as you could. Too often, we do things to please someone else or to survive in a job. Then we get stuck in a rut—that is, we're *always* trying to please someone else or are *always* trying to survive in a job. We lost sight of what could satisfy us, and work becomes drudgery rather than fun. When we become so enmeshed in survival or in trying to please others, it may be difficult to figure out what we would rather be doing.

When you uncover your motivated skills, you'll be better able to identify jobs that allow you to use them, and recognize other jobs that don't quite fit the bill. "Motivated skills" are patterns that run through our lives. Since they are skills we get satisfaction from, we'll find ways to do them even if we don't get to do them at work. We still might not know what these skills are—for us, they're just something we do, and we take them for granted.

Tracking down these patterns takes some thought. The payoff is that our motivated skills do not change. They run throughout our lives and indicate what will keep us motivated for the rest of our lives.

THE SEVEN STORIES APPROACH—BACKGROUND

This technique for identifying what people do well and enjoy doing has its roots in the work of Bernard Haldane, who, in his job with the U.S. government forty-five years ago, helped to determine assignments for executives entering the armed forces. The Seven Stories (or enjoyable accomplishments) approach, now quite common, was taught to me by George Hafner, who used to work for Haldane.

The exercise is this: make a list of all the enjoyable accomplishments of your life, those things you enjoyed doing *and also* did well. List at least twenty-five enjoyable accomplishments from all parts of your life: work, from your early career up to the present, volunteering, hobbies; your school years. It doesn't matter how old you were or what other people thought about these accomplishments, and it doesn't matter whether you got paid for doing them.

Examine those episodes that gave you a sense of accomplishment. Episodes from your childhood are important, too, because they took place when you were less influenced by trying to please others.

You are asked to name twenty-five accomplishments so you will not be too judgmental—just list anything that occurs to you. Expect this exercise to take you four or five days. Most people carry around a piece of paper so they can jot down things as they occur to them. When you have twenty-five, select the seven that are most important to you by however you define important. Then rank them: list the most important first, and so on.

Starting with your first story, write a paragraph about each accomplishment. Then find out what your accomplishments have in common. If you are having trouble doing the exercises, ask a friend to help you talk them through. Friends tend to be more objective and will probably point out strengths you never realized.

You will probably be surprised. For example, you may be especially good interacting with people, but it's something you've always done and therefore take for granted. This may be a thread that runs through your life and may be one of your motivated skills. It *may* be that you'll be unhappy in a job that doesn't allow you to deal with people.

When I did the Seven Stories exercise, one of the first stories I listed was from when I was ten years old, when I wrote a play to be put on by the kids in the neighborhood. I rehearsed everyone, sold tickets to the adults for two cents apiece, and served cookies and milk with the proceeds. You might say that my direction as a "general manager"—running the whole show, thinking things up, getting everybody working together— was set in the fourth grade. I saw these traits over and over again in each of my stories.

After I saw those threads running through my life, it became easy for me to see what elements a job must have to satisfy me. When I interview for a job, I can find out in short order whether it addresses my motivated skills. If it doesn't, I won't be as happy as I could be, even though *I may decide to take the job as an interim step toward a long-term goal*. The fact is, people won't do as well in the long run in jobs that don't satisfy their motivated skills.

Sometimes I don't pay attention to my own motivated skills, and I wind up doing things I regret. For example, in high school I scored the highest in the state in math. I was as surprised as everyone else, but I felt I finally had some direction in my life. I felt I had to use it to do something constructive. When I went to college, I majored in math. I almost flunked because I was bored with it. The fact is that I didn't enjoy math, I was simply good at it.

There are lots of things we're good at, but they may not be the same things we really enjoy. The trick is to find those things we are good at, enjoy doing, and feel a sense of accomplishment from doing.

To sum up: Discovering your motivated skills is the first step in career planning. I was a general manager when I was ten, but I didn't realize it. I'm a general manager now, and I love it. In between, I've done some things that have helped me toward my long-range goals, and other things that have not helped at all.

It is important to realize that the Seven Stories exercise will *not* tell you exactly which job you should have, but the *elements* to look for in a job that you will find satisfying. You'll have a range of jobs to consider, and you'll know the elements the jobs must have to keep you happy. Once you've selected a few job categories that might satisfy you, talk to people in those fields to find out if a particular job is really what you want, and the job possibilities for someone with your experience. That's one way to test if your aspirations are realistic.

After you have narrowed your choices down to a few fields with some job possibilities that will satisfy your motivated skills, the next step is to figure out how to get there. That topic will be covered in Part III: How to Get Interviews in Your Target Area.

A DEMONSTRATION OF THE SEVEN STORIES EXERCISE

> . . . be patient toward all that is unsolved in your heart and try to love the questions themselves like locked rooms and like books that are written in a foreign tongue.
> —RAINER MARIA RILKE
> *Letters to a Young Poet*

To get clients started, I sometimes walk them through two or three of their achievement stories, and tell them the patterns I see. They can then go off and think of the seven or eight accomplishments they enjoyed the most and also performed well. This final list is ranked and analyzed in depth to get a more accurate picture of the person's motivated skills. I spend the most time analyzing those accomplishments a client sees as most important. Some accomplishments are more obvious than others. But all stories can be analyzed.

Here is Suzanne, as an example: "When I was nine years old, I was living with my three sisters. There was a fire in our house and our cat had hidden under the bed. We were all outside, but I decided to run back in and save the cat. And I did it."

No matter what the story is, I probe a little by asking these two questions: What gave you the sense of accomplishment? and What about that made you proud? These questions give me a quick fix on the person.

The full exercise is a little more involved than this. Suzanne said at first: "I was proud because I did what I thought was right." I probed a little, and she added: "I had a sense of accomplishment because I was able to make an instant decision under pressure. I was proud because I overcame my fear."

I asked Suzanne for a second story; I wanted to see what patterns might emerge when we put the two together:

> "Ten years ago, I was laid off from a large company where I had worked for nine years. I soon got a job as a secretary in a Wall Street company. I loved the excitement and loved that job. Six weeks later, a position opened up on the trading floor, but I didn't get it at first. I eventually was one of three finalists, and they tried to discourage me from taking the job. I wanted to be given a chance. So I sold myself because I was determined to get that job. I went back for three interviews, said all the right things, and eventually got it."

What was the accomplishment? What made her proud?

- "I fought to win."
- "I was able to sell myself. I was able to overcome their objections."

- "I was interviewed by three people at once. I amazed myself by saying, 'I know I can do this job.' "
- "I determined who the real decision-maker was, and said things that would make him want to hire me."
- "I loved that job—loved the energy, the upness, the fun."

Here it was, ten years later, and that job still stood out as a highlight in her life. Since then she'd been miserable and bored, and that's why she came to me.

Normally after a client tells two stories, we can quickly name the patterns we see in both stories. What were Suzanne's patterns?

Suzanne showed that she was good at making decisions in tense situations—both when saving the cat and when interviewing for that job. She showed a good intuitive sense (such as when she determined who the decision-maker was and how to win him over). She's decisive and likes fast-paced, energetic situations. She likes it when she overcomes her own fears as well as the objections of others.

We needed more than two stories to see if these patterns ran throughout Suzanne's life and to see what other patterns might emerge. After the full exercise, Suzanne felt for sure that she wanted excitement in her jobs, a sense of urgency—that she wanted to be in a position where she had a chance to be decisive and operate intuitively. Those are the conditions she enjoys and under which she operates the best. Armed with this information, Suzanne can confidently say in an interview that she thrives on excitement, high pressure, and quick decision-making. And, she'll probably make more money than she would in "safe" jobs. She can move her life in a different direction—whenever she is ready.

Pay attention to those stories that were most important to you. The elements in these stories may be worth repeating. If none of your enjoyable accomplishments were work-related, it may take great courage to eventually move into a field where you will be happier. Or you may decide to continue to have your enjoyment outside of work.

People have to be ready to change. Fifteen years ago, when I first examined my own motivated skills, I saw possibilities I was not ready to handle. Although I suffered from extreme shyness, my stories—especially those that occurred when I was young—gave me hope. As I emerged from my shyness, I was eventually able to act on what my stories said was true about me.

People sometimes take immediate steps after learning what their motivated skills are. Or sometimes this new knowledge can work inside them until they are ready to take action—maybe ten years later. All the while internal changes can be happening, and people can eventually blossom.

One's prime is elusive. . . . You must be on the alert to recognize your prime at whatever time of life it may occur.
    —MURIEL SPARK
    The Prime of Miss Jean Brodie

MOTIVATED SKILLS—YOUR ANCHOR IN A CHANGING WORLD

If one advances confidently in the direction of his dreams, and endeavors to live the life which he has imagined, he will meet with success unexpected in common hours.
    —HENRY DAVID THOREAU

Your motivated skills are your anchor in a world of uncertainty. The world will change, but your motivated skills remain constant.

Write them down. Save the list. Over the years, refer to them to make sure you are still on target—doing things that you do well and are motivated to do. As you refer to them, they will influence your life. Five years from now, an opportunity may present itself. In reviewing your list, you will have every confidence that this opportunity is right for you. After all, you have been doing these things since you were a child, you know that you enjoy them, and you do them well!

Knowing our patterns gives us a sense of stability and helps us understand what we have done so far. It also gives us the freedom to try new things regardless of risk or of what others may say, because we can be absolutely sure that this is the way we are. Knowing your patterns gives you both security and flexibility—and you need both to cope in this changing world.

Now we'll take a look at other information about you: your work-related values and your special interests. These, too, might provide some hints about your future career path.

EXAMINING YOUR WORK-RELATED VALUES

For deep in our hearts
We do believe
That we shall overcome
someday.
        —"We Shall Overcome"
        African-American freedom song
        (An example of someone's values)

What is important to you? Your values change as you grow and change, so they need to be reassessed continually. At various stages in your career, you may value money, or leisure time, or independence on the job, or working for something you believe in. See what is important to you *now*. Then you won't be upset if a job provides you with the freedom you wanted, but not the kind of money your friends are making.

Look at the list of values below. Think of each in terms of your overall career objectives. Rate the degree of importance that you would assign to each for yourself, using this scale:

1. Not important at all
2. Not very but somewhat important
3. Reasonably important
4. Very important in my choice of job

Add other of your values that don't appear on the list or substitute words you feel more comfortable with.

__ the chance to advance	__ artistic or other creativity
__ work on frontiers of knowledge	__ learning from the job
__ having authority	__ location of the workplace
(responsibility)	__ job tranquility
__ helping society	__ money earned
__ meeting challenges	__ change and variety
__ helping others	__ having time for personal life
__ working for something I	__ fast pace
believe in	__ power
__ public contact	__ adventure/risk-taking
__ enjoyable colleagues	__ prestige
__ competition	__ moral fulfillment
__ ease (freedom from worry)	__ recognition from superiors,
__ influencing people	society, peers
__ enjoyable work tasks	__ security (stability) of
__ working alone	employment
__ being an expert	__ physical work environment
__ personal growth and	__ chance to make an impact
development	__ clear expectations and
__ independence on the job	procedures

Of those you marked "4," circle the five *most* important to you today:

- If forced to compromise on any of these, which would you give up?
- Which would you be most reluctant to give up?

Describe in your own words what you want most in your life/career.

CASE STUDY: LAURA
Using Her Special Interests

For many people, interests should stay as interests—things they do on the side. For others, their interests may be a clue to the kinds of jobs they should do next or in the long run. Laura had food as her special interest. She had spent her life as a marketing manager in cosmetics, but she assured me that food was *very* important to her.

We redid her résumé to downplay the cosmetics background. Next, Laura visited a well-known specialty food store. She spoke to the store manager, a junior person, asked about the way the company was organized, and found that there were three partners, one of whom was the president, Laura said to the store manager, "Please give my résumé to the president, and I will call him in a few days." We prepared for her meeting with the president, in which she would find out the company's long-term plans, and so on. At the meeting, he said he wanted to increase revenues from $4 million to $40 million. Laura and I met again to decide how she could help the business grow through her marketing efforts, and to decide what kind of compensation she would want, including equity in the company. She met with the president again, and got the job!

It was the Interests exercise that prompted her to get into that field. Remember, all you need to do is make a list of your interests. Laura simply wrote "food." Other people list twenty things. Here is the exercise:

INTERESTS EXERCISE

List all the things you really like to do. List anything that makes you feel good and gives you satisfaction. List those areas where you have developed a relatively in-depth knowledge or expertise. For ideas, think back over your day, your week, the seasons of the year, places, people, work, courses, roles, leisure time, family, etc. These areas need not be work-related. Think of how you spend your discretionary time.

If you cannot think of what your interests may be, think about the books you read, the magazines you subscribe to, the section of the newspaper you turn to first. Think about the knowledge you've built up simply because you're interested in a particular subject. Think about the volunteer work you do—what are the recurring assignments you tend to get and enjoy? Think about your hobbies—are there one or two you have become so involved in that you have built up a lot of expertise/information in those areas? What are the things you find yourself doing—and enjoying—all the time, things you don't *have* to do.

Your interests may be a clue to what you would like in a job. Rob was a partner in a law firm, but loved everything about wine. He left the law firm to become general counsel in a wine company. Most people's interests should stay as interests, but you never know until you think about it.

SATISFIERS AND DISSATISFIERS EXERCISE

Simply list every job you have ever had. List what was satisfying and dissatisfying about each job. Some people are surprised to find that they were sometimes most satisfied by the vacation, pay, title, and other perqs, but were not satisfied with the job itself.

BOSSES EXERCISE

Simply examine those bosses you have had a good relationship with and those you have not, and determine what you need in your future relationship with bosses. If you have had a lot of problems with bosses, discuss this with your counselor.

LOOKING INTO YOUR FUTURE

> There are more things in heaven and earth, Horatio, than are
> dreamt of in your philosophy.
> —SHAKESPEARE
> *Hamlet*

Your motivated skills tell you the *elements* you need to make you happy, your Values exercise tells you the values that are important to you right now, and the Interests exercise may give you a clue to other fields or industries to explore. But none of them give you a feel for the *scope* of what may lie ahead.

Dreams and goals can be great driving forces in our lives. We feel satisfied when we are working toward them—even if we never reach them. People who have dreams or goals do better than people who don't.

A study was made of alumni ten years out of Harvard to find out how many were achieving their goals. An astounding 83 percent had no goals at all. Fourteen percent had specific goals, but they were not written down. Their average earnings were three times what those in the 83 percent group were earning. However, the 3 percent who had written goals were earning ten times that of the 83 percent group.

—FORREST H. PATTON, *Force of Persuasion*, as quoted by Ronald W. Miller, *Planning for Success*

Setting goals will make a difference in your life, and this makes sense. Every day we make dozens of choices. People with dreams make choices that advance them in the right direction. People without dreams also make choices—but their choices are strictly present-oriented, with little thought of the future. When you are aware of your current situation, and you also know where you want to go, a natural tension leads you forward faster.

When you find a believable dream that excites you, don't forget it. In the heat of our day-to-day living, our dreams slip out of our minds. In some respects this is good, because it means we're absorbed by the daily events of our lives. If we focused *only* on the future, we'd all be very upset and worried people. We each should be appropriately challenged and involved in what we're doing in the present, with a reminder every once in a while of where we want to go. Happy people keep an eye on the future as well as the present.

"FREEING-UP" EXERCISES

In my practice as a psychiatrist, I have found that helping people to develop personal goals has proved to be the most effective way to help them cope with problems.

—ARI KIEV, M.D.
A Strategy for Daily Living

This next group of exercises may help you imagine broader dreams for yourself—dreams to inspire you and move you forward, add meaning to your everyday life, and give it some long-term purpose.

Its OK if you never reach your dreams. In fact, it can be better to have some dreams that you will probably never reach, so long as you enjoy the *process* of trying to reach them. For example, a real estate developer may dream of owning all the real estate in Phoenix. He may wind up owning much more than if he did not have that dream. If he enjoys the *process* of acquiring real estate, that's all that matters.

EXERCISE #1—WRITE YOUR OBITUARY

Every now and then I think about my own death, and I think about my own funeral. . . . I ask myself, "What is it that I would want said?" . . . Say I was a drum major for justice; say that I was a

drum major for peace; say that I was a drum major for
righteousness. And all of the other shallow things will not matter. I
won't have any money to leave behind. I won't have the fine and
luxurious things of life to leave behind. But I just want to leave a
committed life behind.
　　—MARTIN LUTHER KING, JR.

Martin Luther King, Jr., knew how he wanted to be remembered. He had
a dream, and it drove his life. Write out what you would want the newspapers to say about you when you die. Alfred Nobel had a chance to
rewrite his obituary. The story goes that his cousin, who was also named
Alfred, died. The newspapers, hearing of the death of Alfred Nobel,
printed the prepared obituary, which Alfred read the day after his cousin's
death. Alfred was upset by what the obituary said because it starkly
showed him how he would be remembered: as the well-known inventor of
a cheap explosive called dynamite.

　　Alfred resolved to change his life. Today, he's remembered as a
Swedish chemist and inventor who provided for the Nobel Prizes.

　　Write your obituary as you want to be remembered after your death.
It should also include parts that are *not* related to your job. If you don't
like the way your life seems to be headed, change it—just as Alfred Nobel
did. Some people do this exercise every five or ten years. It keeps them
on track and moving forward. Write your own obituary, and *then make a
list of the things you need to do to get there.*

EXERCISE #2—INVENT A JOB

If you could have any job in the world, what would it be? Don't worry
about the possibility of ever finding that job—make it up! Invent it. Write
it out. It may spark you to think of how to create that job in real life.

EXERCISE #3—IF YOU HAD A MILLION

If you had a million dollars (or maybe ten million) but still had to work,
what would you do?

　　When I asked myself this question, I decided I'd like to continue
doing what I was doing at work, but would like to write a book on job
hunting because I felt I had something to say. And here is that book.

　　People often erroneously see a lack of money as a stumbling block
to their goals. Think about it: is there some way you could do what you
want without a million dollars? Then do it!

EXERCISE #4—YOUR FORTY-YEAR PLAN

If you could be doing anything you wanted five years from now, what would it be? How about ten years from now? Twenty years from now? OK —now try thirty and forty years from now. Why not!

Write down, in the present tense, the way your life is right now, and the way you see yourself at each of the time frames listed above. This exercise should take no more than thirty minutes to an hour. Allow your unconscious to tell you what you will be doing in the future. Just quickly comment on each of the questions listed below, and then move on to the next. If you kill yourself off too early in the process (say, at age sixty), push it ten more years to see what would have happened if you had lived. Then push it another ten, just for fun. Now, relax and have a good time going through the years. Don't think too hard. If you like, have a friend ask you the questions:

What is your life like right now?
- Who are your friends? What do they do for a living?
- What is your relationship with your family, by however you define "family"?
- Are you married? Single? Do you have children? (Please list their ages.)
- Where are you living? What does it look like?
- What are your hobbies and interests?
- What do you do for exercise? How is your health?
- What kind of work are you doing?
- What else would you like to note about your life right now?

Finish the exercise—at least to past age eighty. Do you like the future you have imagined for yourself? If not, why not? If you don't like it, change it. It's *your* future. Make it what you want.

Some people feel locked in by their present circumstances. Many say it is too late for them. But a lot can happen in five, ten, twenty, thirty, or forty years. It's all in the way a person looks at life. I've had clients in their early forties who were waiting for the Grim Reaper. But I've had others—in their seventies—who were making plans and telling me that I ought to be doing more with *my* life. Compared with some of these seventy-year-olds, I looked as though I was standing still.

A lot can happen to you over the next few decades—and *most* of what happens is up to you. If you see the next few decades as boring, I'm sure you will be right.

Pick your own vision of the future, and be as sure as you can be that it is what you really want. If it is what you want, chances are you will find some way to make it happen.

SELF-ASSESSMENT SUMMARY

Summarize the results of all the exercises. This information will help define the kind of environment that suits you best, and will also help you brainstorm some possible job targets. Finally, it can be used as a checklist for job possibilities. When you are about to receive a job offer, use this list to help you objectively analyze it.

WORKSHEET

1. What I need in my relationship with my boss:
   _____

2. Job satisfiers/dissatisfiers:
   Satisfiers:
   _____

   Dissatisfiers:
   _____

3. Most important job-related values:
   _____

4. Interests:
   _____

5. The threads running through the Seven Story analysis:
   Key accomplishments: _____
   Motivators/satisfiers: _____
   My role: _____
   The situation: _____
   The subject matter: _____

6. The top six or seven specialized skills from my work experience:
   _____
   _____
   _____
   _____
   _____
   _____
   _____

7. From the Forty-Year Plan or Obituary or Ideal Job:
   Where I see myself in the long run:
   _____

   What I need to get there:
   _____

8. My basic personality and the kinds of cultures it will fit:
   _____

BRAINSTORMING POSSIBLE JOBS

> Why am I trying to become what I don't want to be? What am I
> doing in an office, making a contemptuous, begging fool of myself,
> when all I want is out there, waiting for me the minute I say I know
> who I am!
> —ARTHUR MILLER, *Death of a Salesman*

You are now ready to brainstorm job possibilities using the information
you have gathered about yourself. It will require a leap of faith, as well as
the help of your friends. Use the form on page 64.

1. Across the top of the page, list the following elements as they apply
   to you. Use as many columns as you need for each category.

   - Your basic personality
   - Specialized skills
   - Long-range goals
   - Work experience/areas of expertise
   - Interests
   - Role/environment/subject matters
   - Education
   - Values

Here is one person's list of column headings across the top: (personality)
outgoing; (three different interests—takes three columns) environment,
computers, world travel; (specialized skills) use of PC; (from Seven Stories
exercise) enjoy being part of research group; (from Seven Stories exercise)
interest in Third World countries; (from Forty-Year Plan) head up not-for-
profit organization; (education) master's in public policy; (work experience) seven years marketing experience. This takes up ten columns across
the top.

2. Down the side of the page, list possible fields, functions, or positions
   that rely on one or more of these elements. At this point, do not
   eliminate anything. Write down whatever occurs to you. Ask your
   friends and family for new job possibilities that make sense for you.
   Do library research and talk to lots of people for other ideas. Open
   up your eyes and your mind when you read or walk down the street.
   Be open and observant and generate lots of possible jobs. For example, combine marketing with environmental, or computers with research and Third World countries. What kinds of jobs occur to you
   and your friends? Write down whatever anyone suggests. A particular suggestion may not be exactly right for you, but it may help you
   think of other things that *are* right.

3. Analyze each job possibility by checking off across the page those elements that apply to that job. For example, if the job fits your basic personality type, put a check mark in that column. If it uses your education or relies on your past experience, put check marks in those columns. If it fits into your long-range plans, put a check mark there.

4. Any job that relies on only one or two elements is probably not appropriate for you. Certain elements are more important to you than others, so you must weigh those more heavily. Those jobs that seem to satisfy your most important elements are the ones you will list as some of the targets to explore in Chapter 9: How to Target the Job You Want. Also list positions that would be logical next steps for you in light of your background.

Agnes has been a marketing/merchandising/promotion executive in the fashion, retail, and banking industries. Her only love was retail, and her dream job was working for one specific, famous fashion house. Perhaps she could actually get a job with that fashion house, but what kind of job could she go for after that? The retail and fashion industries were both retrenching at the time of her search, although she could probably get a job in one of them. She needed more targets, and preferably some targets in growing industries so she would have a more reasonable career path.

In addition to the retail and fashion industries, what other industries could Agnes consider? In the banking industry, where she had been for only three years, some of the products she promoted had been computer-based. In combining "computers" with "retail" we came up with "computerized shopping," a new field that was threatening the retail industry. Computerized shopping and related areas were good fields for Agnes to investigate. What about something having to do with debit cards and credit cards or Prodigy—all computer-based systems aimed at retail? Or what about selling herself to banks that were handling the bankrupt retail companies that she was so familiar with? We came up with twenty areas to explore. Agnes's next step is to conduct a Preliminary Target Investigation (which you will read about next) to determine which fields may be worth pursuing in that they hold some interest for her and there is some possibility of finding a job in them. At this point she has an exciting search lined up—one with lots of fields to explore and one that offers her a future instead of just a job.

BRAINSTORMING POSSIBLE JOBS

In far right-hand column, add total check marks across.

Possible jobs
(List down the left.)   Job elements (List across the top.)

PRELIMINARY TARGET INVESTIGATION

Fresh news is got only by enterprise and expense.
—OLIVER WENDELL HOLMES

Facts are friendly. Facts that tend to reinforce what you are doing
and give you a warm glow are nice, because they help in terms of
psychic reward. Facts that raise alarms are equally friendly,
because they give you clues about how to respond, how to change,
where to spend the resources.
—IRWIN MILLER, FORMER CEO, CUMMINS ENGINE CO.
The Renewal Factor

Although it takes up only a paragraph or two in this book, Preliminary
Target Investigation is essential. Agnes's investigation will probably take
only a few weeks because she is high in energy and can devote full time
to it. She has to test her ideas for targets in the marketplace to see which
ones are worth pursuing. As she researches at the library, and by meeting
with people in her fields of choice, she will refine those targets and perhaps develop other ones. Then she will know where to focus her job
search, and the search will be completed much more quickly than if she
had skipped this important step.

People who conduct a Preliminary Target Investigation while employed sometimes take a year to explore various fields while they continue
in their old jobs. If you are not at all familiar with some of the job targets
you have selected, do some Preliminary Target Investigation *now* through
library research (see Chapter 13) and networking (see Chapter 16). You
will find that some targets are not right for you. Eliminate them and conduct a full campaign in those areas that seem right for you and which offer
some reasonable hope of success.

Whether you are employed or between jobs, Preliminary Target Investigation is well worth your time and a lot of fun. It is the difference
between blindly continuing in your old career path because it is the only
thing you know, and finding out what is really happening in the world so
you can latch on to a field that may carry you forward for many, many
years. This is a wonderful time to explore—to find out what the world
offers. Most job hunters narrow their job targets down too quickly, and
wind up later with not much to go after. It is better for you emotionally as
well as practically to develop *now* more targets than you need so you will
have them when you are actively campaigning. If, on the other hand, you
do not have the inclination or time to explore, you can move on. *Just
remember, you can come back to this point if your search dries up and you
need more targets.*

FINAL THOUGHTS

> Resolve to be thyself and know that he who finds himself loses his
> misery.
> —MATTHEW ARNOLD

Sometimes we get so caught up in the path we are on that we think we
have no choice. We forget what we would rather be doing. It is easy to
lose sight of what would make us happy. We forget we have made choices
that have brought us to where we are.

Approach job hunting with an open mind—be open to the possibilities available to you. It is only by going out into the world and testing your
ideas that the possibilities present themselves. Explore. Don't rush to take
a job just because it is something well known to you.

> The purpose of knowledge, and especially historical knowledge, is
> understanding rather than certainty.
> —JOHN LUKACS, *A History of the Cold War*

Although your motivated skills do not change, keep reexamining them so
you can see how they fit into various situations in your changing world.
You will always fit in because your motivated skills adapt themselves to
new situations and new possibilities.

Expect to be surprised. And think of surprise as a pleasant thing,
because it adds interest to your life. Every move you make will open a
new range of possibilities.

The step you are now taking is one that can alter the direction of
your life. If you are aware, it can have as much or as little effect as you
want it to have. If it turns out to be a mistake, you can move on.

This is not the last step: it is a transition. The next step is a preparation for the one after that. In the future, it will rarely be possible to say,
in concrete terms, "I want to be this for the rest of my life." The past is
over and is subject to a new interpretation depending on the situation you
are now in and where you want to go from here. It's your story, and it is a
story you make up as you go along. You don't know how the story will end,
and the ending really doesn't matter. What matters is that you are living
your life, enjoying the *process* of living. It's a journey, not a battle.

OPTIMISM EMERGES AS BEST PREDICTOR TO SUCCESS IN LIFE

"Hope has proven a powerful predictor of outcome in every study
we've done so far," said Dr. Charles R. Snyder, a psychologist at
the University of Kansas. . . . "Having hope means believing you
have both the will and the way to accomplish your goals, whatever
they may be. . . . It's not enough to just have the wish for

something. You need the means, too. On the other hand, all the skills to solve a problem won't help if you don't have the willpower to do it."
—DANIEL GOLEMAN, *The New York Times*, December 24, 1991

How many cares one loses when one decides not to be something but to be someone.
—COCO CHANEL

CHAPTER 8

HOW TO DECIDE WHAT YOU WANT TO OFFER

The fastest way to succeed is to look as if you're playing by other people's rules, while quietly playing by your own.
    —MICHAEL KORDA

YOUR MOTIVATED SKILLS and your dreams help you set your long-term direction. In order to go somewhere, you must know where you are right now. In this chapter, you will look down and see where your feet are. You will become more pragmatic. What have you done so far in your life? What do you have to offer the world?

WHAT DO YOU HAVE TO OFFER?

In deciding what you *want* to offer, first list all you *have* to offer—a menu to choose from. When you go after a certain kind of position, emphasize those parts that support your case. If you decide, for example, to continue your career in the same direction, you will probably focus on your most recent position and others that support that direction.

Someday you may decide to change careers—most of us will have to. Or if most of your adult satisfactions have occurred outside your job, you may want to change something about your work life. If you decide to change careers, activities outside your regular job may help you make that change. Twelve years ago, when I was interested in changing from computers to advertising, I offered as proof of my ability the three years I had spent at night promoting nonprofit organizations. My portfolio of press coverage for those organizations was my proof. Later, when I wanted to work as a career counselor, my proof was my many years' experience in running The Five O'Clock Club at night, the seminars I had given on job hunting and career development, and so on. When I wanted to continue working in business management, I simply offered my on-the-job experience in making companies profitable.

If you have available the entire list of what you have to offer, you can be more flexible about the direction you want to go.

HOW TO STATE YOUR ACCOMPLISHMENTS

Present what you have to offer in terms of accomplishments. Tell your "story" in a way that will provoke interest in you and let the "reader" know what you are really like. Accomplishment statements are short, measurable, and results-oriented. We each handle the situations in our work lives in different ways. What problems have you faced at work? How did you handle them? What was the effect on the organization?

Some of us are project-oriented and others are process-oriented. If you are project-oriented, you will tend to take whatever is assigned to you, break it into "projects" in your mind, and then get those projects done. You like to solve problems, and you get bored when there are none. Your accomplishments will state the problems you faced, how you solved them, and the impact you had on the organization.

On the other hand, if you are process-oriented, you like to run the day-to-day shop. You can be trusted to keep an existing situation running smoothly, and your accomplishments will reflect that. You like stable situations and systems that work. You will state that you ran a department of so many people for so many years.

Work on this exercise now. Write down your current or most recent position. State your title, your company name, and list your accomplishments in that position. Do not worry right now if you do not like your job title, or don't even like your job. Later on, we will change your title to make it reflect what you were actually doing, and we can emphasize or deemphasize jobs and responsibilities as you see fit. Right now, get down on paper all of your accomplishments. Then we will have something to work with.

A project-oriented accomplishment could look like this:

- Designed and directed a comprehensive and cost-effective advertising and sales promotion program that established the company as a major competitor in the market.

A process-oriented accomplishment could look like this:

- Reviewed ongoing market performance of investor-owned utility securities. Used multiple equity valuation techniques. Recommended redirection of portfolio mix to more profitable and higher-quality securities.

After you have completed your accomplishment statements for your present or most recent position, examine the job before that one. State your title, your company name, and list your accomplishments.

Work on as many accomplishments as make sense to you. Some people cover in depth the past ten years. If you can, cover your entire career, because you never know what may occur to you, and you never know what may help you later. In doing this exercise, you may remember jobs you had completely forgotten about—and pleasant and satisfying accomplishments. Ask yourself what it was about that job that was so satisfying. Perhaps it is another clue about what you might do in the future.

Do not wish to go back to your youth. What was challenging then will probably not satisfy you today. Look for the *elements* of those early jobs that satisfied you. These elements should be compared with your list of motivated skills to determine lifelong interests.

You will feel better after you have completed this exercise. You will see on paper all that you have to offer. And your accomplishments will be stated in a way that will make you proud. Discipline yourself to do this exercise now, and you will not have to do it again.

After you have listed your work experiences, list accomplishments outside work. These, too, should be short, measurable, and results-oriented. These outside experiences can help you move into a new field. In fact, that's how I and many others have made career transitions. By volunteering to do advertising and public relations work at night, I developed a list of accomplishments that helped me move from computers to advertising. In those days, my outside experience went like this:

- Walnut Street Theatre Gallery
  Planned, organized, and promoted month-long holography exhibition. Attendance increased from less than one hundred visitors per month to over three thousand visitors during the month of this exhibition.
- YMCA
  Handled all publicity for fund-raising campaign. Consulted with fund-raising committee on best techniques for them to use. Received plaque in recognition.
- United Way
  Received four United Way awards for editorial work in 1979; two awards the prior year. Spoke at the United Way's Editor's Conference.

- Network for Women in Computer Technology
  Chair of the Program Committee.

Later, career counseling became my volunteer work, and that eventually helped me move into the field I am now in. In the early days, my outside experience was stated like this:

- Organized and ran The Five O'Clock Club.
  Conducted weekly groups as well as individual counseling. Trained people in career decisions, marketing techniques, and practice interviewing. Brought in outside lecturers.

I also listed the organizations for which I had done job-hunting seminars, and stated my relevant work experience—such as when I was a training manager.

Here are a few accomplishment statements from various higher-level professionals. I put them in the context of a complete job so you can see how to bullet and sub-bullet. Everyone can use this technique of bulleting and sub-bulleting on a résumé:

VICE PRESIDENT OF MARKETING SERVICES 1985–1987
- Contributed to 3 consecutive years of record 9.7% growth.
- Developed marketing and sales **training programs for 5,000 employees.**
  - Program changed "hard sell"/reactive selling to consultative and entrepreneurial approach.
  - Program shifted selling culture and positioned company for growth in the '80s.
- **Repositioned subsidiary** by redesigning logo, signage, brochures, direct-mail solicitations, and collateral materials.
- Introduced customer satisfaction measurement program that provided feedback to 1,100 branch operations and produced changes in operational procedures.

This example is written the way it would appear on a résumé, a topic that will be covered in depth later. For now, note that certain parts are underlined so the reader cannot miss them. Underlining makes the résumé more scannable. If you want the reader to know that you have developed training programs, does it hit the reader's eye? If you are proud of having repositioned a subsidiary and think it may be important to your next employer, can he find it on your résumé? You will not have to think about highlighting your résumé until it is completely put together. For now, just know that it will be an option later.

International Rescue Committee, Thailand   1980–1981
Educational Programs Coordinator

Directed all educational programs in Thailand's second-largest Cambodian refugee camp, with a population of 35,000.
- Managed a budget of $300,000 and an international staff of 550.
- Conceived of and introduced programs which resulted in both a 250% expansion of participants and national recognition in fund-raising literature.
- Negotiated regularly with the Thai government and the United Nations.

Depending on the positions this job searcher is going after, these accomplishments may be included or not. They may, for example, be unimportant for ten years, and later on become important again, depending on his job target.

Vice President, Chief Budget Officer   1988–1989
Major Not-for-Profit

Reported to Chief Financial Officer. Staff of 50 in two cities. Joined management team of new CEO and CFO to implement a more results-oriented culture in a non-profit environment.
- Coordinated annual corporate budget of $500 million expenses. Introduced top-down approach, PC modeling and budget programs.
- Developed cost allocation computer system to transfer over $200 million in indirect back office expenses.
- Projected program costs, including . . .
  - Correcting cost allocations to collect over $2 million in additional annual revenues.
  - Saving program $3 million in potential cost overruns.
  - Developing product costs for future programs, as a member of product development teams.
- Improved financial systems and information flow:
  - Streamlined financial reporting, **reduced cycle by 5 days.**
  - Presented strategic plan to upgrade financial systems.

Her job was basically a process-oriented job: getting things to run smoothly, reducing the reporting cycle. Process-oriented jobs can still be presented in terms of accomplishments.

Curator, <u>Penobscott Museum</u>   1971–1974

Organized all major exhibitions (5 to 6 per year) and their accompanying catalogs.
- Developed educational programs supplementing these exhibitions.
- Reorganized and cared for Museum's collection of paintings, sculptures and graphics.
- Organized special films, concerts, and lectures at Museum.
- Maintained an extensive speaking schedule, promoted public and community relations.
- Supervised the activities of curatorial, library, and installation assistants.

A person working for the government who wants another government job has to be low key in stating his accomplishments. He can't brag, for example, about the famous criminals he has captured. However, the following résumé went on to list Harold's extensive certifications and commendations (which took up an entire page), followed by all of his specialized training and courses, which took another page, followed by his education and then outside activities that showed he was a good citizen (Cubmaster, etc.). It is easy to see that he has always been an outstanding performer.

Only the basic résumé portion is presented here so you can see how he understated his accomplishments. Do not worry about the résumé length at this point. We will get to that in Chapter 11. For now, focus on listing *all* of your accomplishments. By the way, Harold's résumé helped him get the major promotion he wanted.

HAROLD R. GREENBERG

---

15 Haverbrook Drive
Cash-in-Hand, NV 14555

Summary of Qualifications

Career State Investigator having 19 years experience;
over 14 years with the Division of Criminal Justice.

Extended diversified exposure both conducting and supervising investigation into the areas of Economic Crime, Organized Crime, and Official Corruption.

Since 1976, was a Division Instructor and representative to groups interested in the subject of various types of financial-related crimes, their detection, investigation, and prosecution.

Professional Experience
State Division of Criminal Justice, 1974–present
Office of the Attorney General

Supervising State Investigator of the   1986–present
Organized Crime and Racketeering Bureau
Conduct both financial and non-financial investigations of allegations concerning Organized Crime and Official Corruption.

Special Prosecutions Section   1981–1986
- Assigned to this section to investigate allegations of organized crime and official corruption.
- Specialized in financial implications.
- Investigations conducted in most part with State Police and allied agencies.

Mayor Fraud Unit   1974–1981
  Senior State Investigator
  State Investigator

- Conducted primarily financial-related investigations.
- Investigations involved areas such as:
  - bank fraud and embezzlements,
  - securities fraud (stocks, bonds, commodities and other investment schemes),
  - insurance fraud (including reinsurance fraud),
  - taxation frauds (including income taxation),
  - sales and use tax,
  - excise taxes (i.e., motor fuels and employment taxes),
  - unemployment fraud conspiracies, and
  - other various schemes and offenses.
- Conducted investigation on individual and supervisory basis with Division personnel, and with allied governmental agencies as necessary.

State Law Enforcement Planning Agency-   1971–1974
Executive Office of the Governor
  Audit Supervisor
  Auditor
- Established audit procedures and audit programs.
- Conducted audits.
- Supervised 5 staff auditors on statewide basis.

Internal Revenue Service   1970–1971
  Internal Revenue Agent—Field Audit
- Conducted audits of individuals, partnerships and corporations as to Federal Income Taxes.

State Treasury, Division of Taxation   1969–1970
  Auditor-Accountant: Field
- Began as auditor-accountant trainee in corporate tax bureau.
- Then assigned as Field Auditor responsible for individual audits of corporations as to state taxes.

Here are a few accomplishment statements from various lower-level professionals:

- Designed and coded two COBOL programs.
- Able to take on major projects and handle them from initiation and planning through implementation and follow-up. For example: . . . ("Major" can apply to anyone. The accomplishment was major in light of that person's level.)
- Administered the entire _____ system from receipt of information through acknowledgment, analysis flow, and final entry into the computer system.
- Monitored status of departmental projects.

- Collected, analyzed, and assembled data from reports and printouts into meaningful logs and charts for manager's use.
- Achieved 140% growth in assigned account responsibility: from $90,000 to $230,000 in one year. Accounts were previously declining at a 35% rate annually.
- Finished in top three in both advanced and basic sales training classes.

The following accomplishments are stated in the context of a complete job so you can see how they might look when finished.

Senior Paralegal   **1975–1983**
Burstein, Kleinder and Feld, PC
- Trained, directed and **supervised four support employees.**
- Administered, coordinated and ran secured loan transactions.
- Served as liaison to clients and attorneys; wrote detailed progress reports.

This is a process-oriented job: administering and coordinating.

Office Manager/Chiropractic Assistant   **1986–1989**
Dr. James Taylor

One-person office force for this busy chiropractic office.
- Transcribed own correspondence.
- Set up Leading Edge Word Processor.
- Assisted doctor with exam preparation.
- Billed patients, maintained patient files, answered phones, ordered medical and office supplies, handled appointments.

Another process-oriented position.

Brevard Elementary School, Parent Volunteer   **1979–1988**
- Assisted teachers with proofreading/grading students' creative writing assignments.
- Coordinated/edited newspapers for two class groups.

Debbie's volunteer work shows that she has the experience necessary to do that next job.

Federated Department Stores, Rich's Department Stores   Atlanta, Ga.
Sales Assistant   Summer 1984
- Sold merchandise in various departments and resolved complaints.
- Balanced daily accounts and prepared displays.

Summer jobs can count, too. Include anything on your résumé that makes you look appropriate for that next position.

Editor/Public Relations Manager, Outboard Marine Corp.   **1968–1969**
- Edited company magazine and handled company P.R. duties.
- Obtained publicity through most national trade magazines.
- Coordinated free-lance artists and writers around the country in producing special on-the-spot application stories about the company's products.
- Distributed innovative ideas and encouragement/promotional letters to dealers.
- Attended meetings and conventions.
- Assisted in advertising campaigns, such as photography of products.

This job happened a long time ago, but the details are important to what this career changer wants to do next.

POLISH UP YOUR ACCOMPLISHMENT STATEMENTS

This is *your* chance to brag—everyone else does.

Rework the wording of your accomplishment statements. Think of how they will sound to the reader. Do not "tell all." Make the reader want to meet you to find out more.

In addition, rephrase your accomplishments to make them as independent as possible of the particular environment you were working in. Make your accomplishments seem useful in other companies or even other industries.

Here is an accomplishment statement as originally written:

> Compared the changes in various categories of revenue to the changes in various categories of labor. Plotted results on a scatter diagram to show the relationships.

This is so boring. What were you really doing and why? Look at what you did as if you were an observer rather than the grunt working on something day in and day out. What were the results of your efforts?

Here is the same accomplishment statement reworked:

> Defined the factors that influence profitability in professional service firms. Resulted in launch of major reorganization of company's largest division.

Sounds better, doesn't it? The first example sounds like a person who is technical and adds up numbers all day—which is what this project was. The rewrite sounds like a person who knew what he or she was doing, had some say in how it was done, and was aware of the impact on the organization—perhaps even pushed for the changes that took place in the company. The new wording makes the reader want to meet this person to learn new insights.

Here is another "before-and-after" example. The first one was not bad:

Investor Business Manager, Middle East, Africa Division 1986–1987
- **Reinvigorated risk taking; improved credit practices** during rebuilding of business in the Gulf region. Managed relationships with selected investors.
- Helped **modernize and strengthen risk management** in various functions of the European division by leading a group critique of risk management issues.

In the rewrite, the job hunter thought more about what he *really* did in the job, which became the main focus, with the actual details of the job subordinate to that.

Manager, Middle East Investor Business, Middle East, Africa Division 1986–1987

Redefined the opportunities in and helped rebuild Gulf region business after years during which the company perceived high risks and low profitability. Had operating centers in 5 countries, 400+ staff.
- **Redirected marketing** to focus on clients' needs as investors.
- **Reinvigorated risk taking** *and* improved credit practices.
- **Improved profitability.**
- Designated a **senior credit officer** and Division Risk Manager.

When writing your accomplishments:

- *Focus on results,* as opposed to the process you went through. Focus on the effect your actions had.
- *Use quantitative measures* when possible. If the quantity doesn't sound important, don't use it.
- *Show the part you played* in whatever happened to your company. If the company grew from $50 million to $200 million, were you an observer or did you have something to do with it? What was your key accomplishment?
- Don't say what you did. *State the magnitude and the effect* it had. For example, if you say you "started up a new computer system," that statement could apply to anyone at any level. What effect did that computer system have on the company? Rework your accomplishment to say:
  "Developed spreadsheet program to highlight salary inconsistencies within range. Resulted in a more equitable personnel system and savings of $100,000 a year."
  or:
  "Solely responsible for the development of a computerized system that resulted in a new way to analyze accounts. Resulted in $2 million profit improvement and the renegotiation of key accounts."

Now go back and rework your accomplishment statements.
Other areas to list:

Skills and equipment. If you are in a technical job, you may want to list the equipment you are familiar with, such as computers or computer languages or software, and perhaps foreign languages you know.

Books or articles written; speeches delivered. One important example implies that you have done more. If you have addressed the United Nations, do not mention the speech you gave at a neighborhood meeting.

Organizations. List organizations you've been active in that are related to the work you may be seeking. If you list too many, the reader may wonder how you will have time for work.

HOW YOU WILL USE YOUR ACCOMPLISHMENT LIST

Your list of key accomplishments will help you interview, write cover letters, and prepare your résumé. It is the raw material for the rest of your job hunt. In fact, you may refer to this same list for years to come.

These are the key selling points about you—the things that will make you different from your competition. They will whet the appetite of the reader, so he or she will want to meet you. The purpose of a résumé or cover letter is not to tell what you did, but to get interviews. During the interview, you can elaborate on what you did.

CASE STUDY: THOMAS WARREN
We all have trouble stating our accomplishments

Take a look at Tom Warren's before-and-after résumés on pages 80–82. He stated his accomplishments in a pretty standard way: he listed the jobs he's had and what he did in each. The problem is that his résumé does not address what Tom *really* did in each job. For example, in the last job on the page, he states that he managed eight Manhattan bank branches. We had already completed his Seven Stories exercise, so I knew there was more to his personality than this. Here is how our discussion went:

KATE: *Tom, do you want to manage bank branches?*

TOM: *Not a chance. I hate branch management.*

KATE: *But your accomplishments position you, among other things, as a branch manager.*

TOM: *That's what I did in that job.*

KATE (trying to provoke him): *But this sounds so boring to me. What did you really do in that job? What is it you brag to your wife that you did?*

TOM: *Kate, you don't understand. That job was important.* **I turned around the largest, problem-ridden branch business the company had.**
KATE: *I don't see that on your résumé. Let's put it on there.*

We also rewrote his other accomplishments.

KATE: *Now, what kinds of things would you like to do next?*
TOM: *I really want to build major businesses or turn around problem brands.*
KATE: *Have you done those things before?*
TOM: *Yes, I definitely have.*
KATE: *Then let's put that in your summary. It will dramatically increase your chances of getting to do those things again. Let's not make them search through your résumé to figure out that you can do these things.*

We will cover the summary portion of your résumé in more detail in Chapter 11. For now, think about what you've really done. For most people, the problem is not that they stretch the truth on their résumés; the problem is that they don't say what they've *really* done.

Figuring out what you've really done is much more difficult than simply reciting your job description. That's the importance of doing the Seven Stories exercise. It helps you step back from a résumé frame of mind so you can concentrate on the most important accomplishments of your life (in terms of what you really enjoyed doing and know you also did well). Then the exercise helps you think about each accomplishment in terms of what you *really* did: what led up to the accomplishment, what was your role, what gave you satisfaction, what was your motivation, and so on.

We added those parts to Tom's résumé and left the rest alone. In fact, the parts we added are the only ones that really matter—so those parts are highlighted and the rest become the background. You will see more of these strategies in Chapter 11: How to Develop Your Résumé.

Now Tom has a good sales piece—one that truly reflects what he's done. You can see that Tom's new résumé tells a completely different story than his previous one and positions him for the kind of job he'd like to have next. This new résumé is a strategic document. It looks ahead, not back. It is aimed at what he would like to do next, and states those things in his background that support what he wants to do. In addition, it highlights those areas that were the most satisfying to Tom. Now he has increased his chances of finding a new job in which he can repeat or build on those satisfying experiences.

When you write down your accomplishments, think about your future and those parts of your accomplishments you may want to emphasize, and think about what you've *really* done.

"BEFORE" RÉSUMÉ
THOMAS WARREN

2343 Fifth Avenue
New York, New York 11000

Home: 212-333-4444
Business: 212-555-1111

PREMIERBANK   1978–Present

International Institutions Group   1987–Present
Director of Electronic Banking

Responsible for support and development of all interbank payment and information systems.

- Developed and market tested a new off-line funds transfer product.
- Upgraded and repositioned existing worldwide on-line payment system.
- Created line-wide repricing plan to maximize target customer penetration.
- Developed strategy to integrate payment, information and securities products.

New York Retail Bank   1985–1986
Director, Special Marketing Group

Responsible for growth and profitability of the New York Bank's $13 billion consumer portfolio. Managed new product development, pricing and sales promotion.

- Developed, positioned and introduced the PremierBank Investment Portfolio, PremierBank's first mass-market integrated investment product. Created new portfolio selling concept to incorporate it into the branch sales process.
- Established more efficient PremierBank core account promotion tactics.
- Developed new investment savings product.
- Created unique research method to guide new product development.

Senior Area Director, Financial District   1985

Managed eight Manhattan branches with $31 million net revenue and $1.2 billion total footings. Responsible for total branch performance, including sales, service, control, revenue and expenses.

- Put new management team in place in three key branches.
- Reversed balance declines by revitalizing business account marketing.
- Established distribution strategy and plan for World Trade Center marketplace, including customer and business offsites.
- Developed a high net worth tailored credit program for area with $2MM–$3MM annual revenue potential.
- Initiated regional staffing efficiency analysis which significantly improved branch productivity.

"AFTER" RÉSUMÉ
THOMAS WARREN

2343 Fifth Avenue   Home: 212-333-4444
New York, New York 11000   Business: 212-555-1111

SUMMARY

Innovative financial services marketer with ten years at PremierBank and heavy package goods product management experience. Created new products. Built major businesses. Turned around problem brands. Strong strategic thinker and team builder.

Areas of Expertise

- Product Management
- New Product Development
- Sales Management

- Electronic Banking
- Branch Banking
- Market Analysis

PREMIERBANK   1978–Present

International Institutions Group   1987–Present
Director of Electronic Banking
Created a multiyear business plan to restore PremierBank's leadership in interbank electronic payments through the worldwide rollout of superior off-line payment products.
Responsible for support and development of all interbank payment and information systems.

- Developed and market tested a new off-line funds transfer product.
- Upgraded and repositioned existing worldwide on-line payment system.
- Created line-wide repricing plan to maximize customer penetration.
- Developed strategy to integrate payment, information and securities products.

New York Retail Bank   1985–1986
Director, Special Marketing Group
Created the New York Retail Bank's first effective way to package and sell its diverse investment product line.
Responsible for growth and profitability of the New York Retail Bank's $13 billion consumer portfolio. Managed new product development, pricing and sales promotion.

- Developed, positioned, introduced PremierBank Investment Portfolio, the bank's first mass-market integrated investment product. Created new selling concept to incorporate it into the branch sales process.
- Established more efficient core account promotion tactics.
- Developed new investment savings product.
- Created unique research method to guide new product development.

Senior Area Director, Financial District   1985
Reorganized and redirected a large, problem-ridden branch business to restore balance and revenue growth.
Managed eight Manhattan branches with $31 million net revenue and $1.2 billion total footings. Responsible for total branch performance, including sales, service, control, revenue and expenses.

- Put new management team in place in three key branches.
- Reversed balance declines by revitalizing business account marketing.
- Established distribution strategy and plan for World Trade Center marketplace, including customer and business offsites.
- Developed a high net worth tailored credit program for area with $2MM–$3MM annual revenue potential.
- Initiated regional staffing efficiency analysis which significantly improved branch productivity.

IF YOU THINK YOU HAVEN'T DONE A THING WITH YOUR LIFE

Many people are intimidated when they see other people's accomplishments. They think they have none of their own. Chances are, you aren't thinking hard enough about what you have done. As you can see from Tom's example, even obviously accomplished people struggle to express what they have done.

If you think you haven't done much, think again. If you are reading this book, we already know that you are competent, ambitious, and intelligent. Even the lowest-level clerks have accomplishments they are proud of. At all levels in an organization, people can be presented with problems and figure out how to handle them.

Don't compare yourself with others, and don't worry about what your boss or peers have thought of what you have done: maybe they did not appreciate your talents. Brag about what you have done, anyway—even though your boss may have taken credit for the work, and even though you may have accomplished it with the help of others. Think of problems you have faced in your company. What did you do to handle them? What was the result for your company? Think of an accomplishment. Write it down. Then pare it down until you can show the reader what you handled and the impact it made.

Finally, don't say anything negative about yourself. Don't lie, but don't hurt yourself either.

In this chapter, you were to write down everything you've done so that it will serve as a menu you can draw on, depending on the kinds of jobs you are going after. You also saw how people struggle to develop well-written accomplishment statements. In the next chapter, we will become more focused: your goal during your search process is to start out thinking broadly, and then focus.

> The next thing most like living one's life over again seems to be a recollection of that life, and to make that recollection as durable as possible by putting it down in writing.
> —BENJAMIN FRANKLIN

CHAPTER 9

HOW TO TARGET THE JOB YOU WANT

I always wanted to be somebody, but I should have been more specific.
—Lily Tomlin

YOU ARE ON your way to finding your place in the world. In Chapter 7, you made a list of your motivated skills and what you want in a job, and then you brainstormed a number of possible job targets that might fit in with your enjoyable accomplishments and/or fit into your vision of your future. Some of these targets may be very long term. In Chapter 8, you thought about what you would be willing to offer. (You took it an extra step by stating this as accomplishments.)

Now we will work on firming up your job targets. You will do some preliminary research on each target (Chapter 13) through the library and by talking to people to see if these areas still interest you and are practical. Then you will *focus* by selecting two, three, or four areas to concentrate on, based on what appeals to you and what you think you have that is marketable. Then you will conduct a thorough campaign aimed at each area. Because each campaign takes a lot of work, it is best if we spend some time refining your targets.

SELECTING JOB TARGETS—YOUR KEY TO JOB HUNT SUCCESS

As we have seen, selecting a job target means selecting a specific geographic area, a specific industry or company size, and a specific position within that industry. A job target must have all three.

Select your targets. Conduct a campaign aimed at each. Concentrate your energies and you increase your chances for success.

Approach each target with an open mind. Commit to a target, but only as long as it makes sense. You can change your mind after you find out more about it. It makes no sense to strive to be a ballerina after you find you have absolutely no ability as a dancer. Commitment to a target lets you discover your real possibilities and increases your chances of landing a job of your choice. The unsuccessful ballet student may have something else of great value to offer the world of dance—such as the ability to raise funds or run a ballet company.

THE RESULTS OF COMMITMENT

Commitment increases the chance that you will come across clearly and enthusiastically about the industry and the position you seek; it will help you do a thorough job of networking the chosen area, of investigating and being knowledgeable about the area, of conducting a thorough search, and of being successful in that search.

If the result of your initial commitment is that you realize a job target is not what you thought it would be, you have resolved the issue and can move on.

Jim, a marketing manager, had targeted four industries: environmental, noise abatement, shipping, and corporate America, a backup target in case the other three did not work. He conducted an excellent search aimed at the environmental target, an area he had always wanted to explore. It was only after a brief but committed job search that he found the environmental area was not for him: the people in it were different from what he had expected. He would not be able to do the things he had imagined he would do there. That target no longer interested him. The noise abatement and shipping industries, however, were very exciting to him and he found a good match for himself. Later, his exploration of the environmental area paid off. He was employed by a shipping company in the containment of oil spills.

Commitment to a target means you'll give that target your best shot —and results in a better job hunt than if you had no target at all.

TARGET A GEOGRAPHIC AREA

Targeting a geographic area is usually the easiest part of the targeting process. Some people decide that they want to work near their present homes, while others decide that they would be willing to move where the jobs are. Are you willing to move anywhere? Is a small town and a big city the same to you? Would you move to the coast? To Arizona? Would you rather be near your family? If you want to stay where you are now, target that area as your first selection—and you'll have a better chance of getting offers there. If you really care about where you live, *target it*.

Think about where you stand on this. You will be assigning yourself an impossible task if, for example, you want to be an export manager but want to work only in a geographic area where there are no export management positions. If you must live in a particular area, be realistic about the kinds of jobs open to you there.

Resolve this issue. Then you will know if you'd be willing to change your target industry so you can live where you want, or change your geographic area so you can work in the industry or function that interests you.

TARGET AN INDUSTRY AND A FUNCTION WITHIN THAT INDUSTRY

Many people say they don't care what industry they work in. When pressed, they usually have stronger opinions than they thought.

If you think *any* industry would be OK for you, let's find out. Would you work in the not-for-profit sector? If so, where? In education? A hospital? How about government? A community organization? Does it matter to you?

Would you work for a magazine? A chemical company? The garment industry? How about a company that makes cardboard boxes? Or cheese? Does it matter to you?

Does it matter if the company has forty employees? What about forty thousand? Four hundred thousand? Does it matter to you?

YOU'VE SELECTED A TARGET IF . . .

. . . you can clearly state the industry or company size you'd be interested in, your position within each industry, and some guidelines regarding geographic location.

For example, if you're a junior accountant, you may already know that you want to advance in the accounting field. You may know that you want to work for a small service company as an assistant controller in the geographic area where you are now living.

If you have clearly selected your targets, then you can get on with finding interviews in your target area. To do that, you would conduct a campaign in your target area. (Job hunt campaigns are covered in Section III.)

Here is one person's target list:

By geographic area:

- Washington, D.C.
- New York City

By industry:

- Book publishing
- Magazine publishing
- Advertising
- College Administration (weak interest)
- Administration of professional firms (weak interest)
- Nonprofit associations
- Direct marketing companies

By function:

- Business manager/General manager—publishing
- International controller
- Corporate-level financial planning analysis
- General v.p. finance/General manager—nonprofit organizations

OTHER ISSUES YOU MAY WANT TO CONSIDER EVEN IF YOU HAVE A TARGET

Does the style of the company matter to you? Would you rather be in a fast-paced, dynamic company with lots of headaches or one that's more stable, slow paced, with routine work as the norm? Which would you prefer?

What kind of people do you want to work with? Friendly people? Sharp, challenging people? People interested in making a fast buck? People who want to make the world a better place? Think about it. You may have said before that you just want a job—any job—but is anything still OK with you?

If you want to be in sales, for example, would it matter if you were selling lingerie or used cars or computers or large office building space? What if you were selling cats? Rugs? Butter? Saying you want "to be in sales" is not enough.

Let's take it a step further. If what appeals to you about being a salesman is that you like to convince people, why not be a politician? Or a clergyman? Or a doctor? Or if what appeals to you is money, why not become a trader? Or a partner in a law firm? Remind yourself where your heart lies.

CASE STUDY: WILLIAM
Finally—an organized search

William wanted a job—just about any job he saw in the want ads. He spent months answering those ads. He thought he was job hunting, but he wasn't. He was simply answering ads for positions for which he was unqualified. William didn't stand a chance.

After a long time, William gave up and agreed to follow The Five O'Clock Club system. At first he resisted because, like so many job hunters, he did not want to "restrict" himself. William thought that focusing on only two or three job targets would limit his opportunities and lengthen his search. He wanted to be open to whatever job came his way.

Many job hunters, like William, simply want a job. But William needed to put himself in the position of the hiring manager: Why would he want to hire William? In his cover letters, William took the "trust me" approach. He did nothing to prove his interest in the industry, the company, or even the position he was applying for. His credentials matched the ad requirements only with the greatest stretch of the imagination.

A shotgun approach like William's may lead to a job offer, but it may also lead your career in a direction that is not what you would have preferred. Later, you may find yourself back in the same boat again—wondering what to do with your life, wanting to do almost anything but what you are doing, hoping your next job will miraculously be in a field that will satisfy you.

William's basic problem was not that he wanted to change careers, but that he didn't know what he wanted to do. He was willing to do anything—anything except focus on a specific area and go after it.

William eventually narrowed himself to two targets he was truly interested in. Then he worked to find out his chances for getting jobs in those fields. William did the exercises in Chapters 7 and 8, and came up with this list to focus his search:

What I want in a job:

- A challenge in meeting new situations/variety.
- A complex situation I can structure.
- Something I believe in.
- A chance to express my creativity through my communication skills.
- A highly visible position.

- An opportunity to develop my leadership and motivational skills.
- Sole responsibility for something.

What I have to offer (that I also want to offer):

- Enthusiasm for the company's basic mission/purpose.
- Penetrating analysis that finds the "answer."
- The ability to synthesize diverse parts into a unified whole.
- An ability and desire to be in new/untested situations.
- Effective in dealing with many kinds of people.
- Strong oral and written communication skills.

Goal: A small or medium-sized organization where I can feel my impact:

- Service
- Health care
- Human care
- Science
- Academia and learning
- Human understanding

Description of targeted areas:

- Targeted geographic areas:
  - Major East Coast cities or locales:
    - New York
    - Philadelphia
    - Boston
    - Baltimore
    - Washington

- Targeted industries:
  - First priority is health care:
    - Pharmaceuticals companies
    - Biotechnology companies
    - Hospitals
    - Maybe research labs
  - Second priority is not-for-profit community organizations

- Targeted positions:
  - marketing/competitive analysis
  - organizational positioning
  - operations planning

William's first campaign was aimed at pharmaceuticals companies. He discovered what they looked for in new hires, and how he could get a position. In addition, he pursued his second objective: not-for-profit community organizations.

The result: As usual, a career transition takes time. William discovered he could make a transition into the pharmaceuticals industry, but decided not to take the backward step that would require. He learned of a job being created in a not-for-profit organization. Although he was not qualified for this position, he knew he could handle it, and it matched the list of what he wanted.

William went through the steps described in Chapter 2, to convince his prospective employer he could indeed handle the job and was eager to have the chance to do it. This was difficult because the other candidates were better qualified than William—they had been in this kind of job before. For William, it was a career change.

William decided to write a number of proposals. To write them, he first needed to do research, which would not be easy. After some library research, he called the heads of development at six major not-for-profits. He told them he was hoping to get a position at a certain organization, and wanted some ideas of how he could write a proposal of what he would do if he were hired.

Amazingly, his sincerity won the day. All six gave him information over the phone. Because he had done library research, William was able to ask intelligent questions. He wrote a proposal, stating in his cover letter that he had spoken with the heads of development at major not-for-profits, and asked for another interview. It would be nice if that were all it took: William got another interview, but was rejected a *number* of times. Yet he continued to do research, and eventually showed enough fortitude and learned enough that he was hired.

The position was just what he wanted: a brand-new marketing research position at a major not-for-profit organization. He would head his career in a different direction and satisfy his motivated skills. His career was back on track, under his own control. And he's still with the organization today.

SELECT *YOUR* TARGETS

The only difference between caprice and a lifelong passion is that the caprice lasts a little longer.
—Oscar Wilde

List your targets in the order in which you will conduct your search. List first the one you will focus on in your first campaign. If you are currently employed and have time to explore, you may want to select as your first target the most unlikely one. (Job hunters sometimes want to target areas they had only dreamed about before.) Concentrate on it and find out for sure if you are truly interested and what your prospects are. If it doesn't work, you can become more realistic.

On the other hand, if you must find a job quickly, concentrate first on the area where you stand the best chance of getting a job—perhaps the field you are now in. After you are settled in your new job, you can develop yourself in the area that interests you in the long run. Remember, it's OK to take something less than your ideal job; just keep working toward your dreams.

Someone who made this work is Nat, who wanted to work for a Japanese company. He thought the Japanese culture suited his temperament. Yet Nat was forced to take a job at another company because the Japanese process was slow (approval had to come from Tokyo). Still, Nat kept pursuing the position with the Japanese firm.

Eventually, his dream job came through—at much more money than he had been making. The Japanese company realized that Nat's personal style, uncommon in America, meshed with Japanese management methods. Nat, his new job, and his new employer were a good fit. Despite many obstacles, Nat pursued his dream and got it. And it was worth it in job satisfaction and in having some say over what happened in his own life.

If you are targeting a geographic area different from where you are now, be sure to conduct a serious, complete campaign aimed at that target. For example, you will want to contact search firms in that area, do library research, perhaps conduct a direct-mail campaign, and network. Use the work area below to plan your targets.

TARGET SELECTION

Target #1:
   Geographic area: _____
   Industry or company size: _____
   Position/function: _____

Target #2:
   Geographic area: _____
   Industry or company size: _____
   Position/function: _____

Target #3:
    Geographic area: _____
    Industry or company size: _____
    Position/function: _____

MEASURING YOUR TARGETS

You've selected three to five targets to focus on. Will they be enough to get you an appropriate job?

Let's say, for example, that your first target aims at a small industry (ten companies) containing small companies for which you could fill a top management post. Each of these companies has one position that would be appropriate for you. Chances are, those jobs are filled right now. In fact, chances are there may be no opening for a year or two. The numbers are working against you. But if you have targeted *twenty* small industries, each of which has ten companies for which you could fill a top management post, the numbers are more in your favor. On the other hand, if one of your targets has a lot of positions that may be right for you, the numbers are again on your side.

Let's analyze your own search and see if the numbers are working for or against you. Fill out the following information on your own target markets. You will probably have to make an educated guess about the number of positions. A ball park figure is all you need to get a feel for where you stand.

For target #1:
    Geographic area: _____
    Industry or company size: _____
    Position/function: _____

How big is the market for your "product" in this target?
    A. Number of companies in this target market: _____
    B. Number of probable suitable positions in the average
    company in this target.   _____
    A × B = Total number of positions appropriate for me
    in this target market: _____

For target #2:
    Geographic area: _____
    Industry or company size: _____
    Position/function: _____

How big is the market for your "product" in this target?
    A. Number of companies in this target market: _____
    B. Number of probable suitable positions in the average company in this target: _____
    A × B = Total number of positions appropriate for me in this target market: _____

For target #3:
    Geographic area: _____
    Industry or company size: _____
    Position/function: _____

How big is the market for your "product" in this target?
    A. Number of companies in this target market: _____
    B. Number of probable suitable positions in the average company in this target: _____
    A × B = Total number of positions appropriate for me in this target market: _____

RULE OF THUMB

A target list of two hundred positions results in seven interviews which result in one job offer. Therefore, if there are less than two hundred potential positions in your targets, develop additional targets or expand the ones you already have. Remember that when aiming at a target of less than two hundred, concentrated effort will be required.

Sometimes, however, one company by itself may be enough. What if a very qualified secretary wanted to work for a regional telephone company? What are the chances she would find a job there? A regional telephone company may have *thousands* of secretaries, and a qualified person would certainly be able to find a job there within a reasonable time frame. Sometimes a *company* can be a target.

In a tight job market, however, you will probably need to *expand your job hunting targets*. If you are searching only in Chicago, or only in the immediate area where you live, think of other geographic areas. If you are looking only in large public corporations, consider small or private companies, or the not-for-profit area. If you are looking for a certain kind of position, what other kinds of work can you do? Think of additional targets for your search, and focus on each target in depth.

In the next chapter, you will learn how to position yourself for each of these targets. That way, when you go after a target, you will have a better chance of looking appropriate to the people in each target area.

Live all you can; it's a mistake not to. It doesn't so much matter what you do in particular, so long as you have had your life. If you haven't had that, what have you had? What one loses one loses; make no mistake about that.
  —HENRY JAMES
    The Ambassadors

Our doubts are traitors,
And make us lose the good we oft might win
By fearing to attempt.
  —WILLIAM SHAKESPEARE
    Measure for Measure

PART THREE

KNOWING THE RIGHT PEOPLE

HOW TO GET INTERVIEWS IN YOUR TARGET AREA

(IF YOU ALREADY HAVE INTERVIEWS SET UP, GO TO PART FOUR.)

*. . . Until one is committed there is hesitancy, the
chance to draw back, always ineffectiveness.
Concerning all acts of initiative (and creation), there
is one elementary truth, the ignorance of which kills
countless ideas and splendid plans: that the moment
one definitely commits oneself, then providence moves
too.*

*All sorts of things occur to help one that would
never otherwise have occurred. A whole stream of
events issues from the decision, raising in one's favor
all manner of unforeseen incidents and meetings and
material assistance, which no man could have
dreamt would have come his way.*

*I have learned a deep respect for one of Goethe's
couplets:*
Whatever you can do, or dream you can, begin it.
Boldness has genius, power and magic in it.

　　　　　　　　　　　　　—W. H. MURRAY

CHAPTER 10

POSITIONING POWER FOR A JOB CHANGE

There is nothing like a dream to create the future.
    —VICTOR HUGO

FEEL STUCK IN your present position? Peel off your old label, slap on a new one, and position yourself for something different.

Whether you're a branch manager who wants to go into commercial lending, or an operations person who dreams of being a trainer, the challenge you face is the same: you have to convince people that, even though you don't have experience, you can handle the new position.

It's a little like show biz: you play the same role for years and then you get typecast. It can be difficult for people to believe that you can play a different role. To move on to new challenges, you have to negotiate into the new job by offering seemingly unrelated skills as an added benefit to the employer. The key to these negotiations is "positioning" yourself.

POSITIONING

Simply put, positioning yourself means stating your skills and qualities in a way that makes it easy for the prospective employer to see you in the new position.

You may want to stay in your present company. In that case, you are positioning yourself to the person in charge of hiring for the particular department you want to enter. Or, you may want to go to a new company or even a new industry. In this case, you are positioning yourself to a new employer. Either way, the steps are the same:

1. Decide what skills and qualities your prospective employer wants.
2. Search your background to see where you have demonstrated skills that would apply.
3. Write a "position statement" and use it as the basis for your résumé.
4. Use the position statement to sell yourself in an interview.

Your position statement says it all. It should sell your ability, experience, and personality. It brings together all your accomplishments.

The rest of your résumé should support the position statement. For example, if the statement says that you're a financial wizard, the résumé had better support that. Remember, it is completely within your control to tell whatever story you want to tell. You can emphasize certain parts of your background and deemphasize others.

Thinking through your position statement is not easy, but it focuses your entire job hunt. It forces you to clarify the sales pitch you will use in interviews. A position statement is not the statement many people put on their résumés. They say they want "a challenging job in a progressive and growth-oriented company that uses all my strengths and abilities." That says nothing at all, and it doesn't do you any good.

Let's consider a few examples of statements that will work for you.

CASE STUDY: ALBERTO
Pursuing the dream job

Alberto, a client-relationship manager at a major bank, has handled high-net-worth clients for more than twenty years. He is taking early retirement and thinking about a second career. Two directions interest him: one, a job similar to what he has done, but in a smaller bank; or, the job of his dreams—working as one of the top administrative people for a high-net-worth family (such as the Rockefellers), handling their business office, and perhaps doing some things that involve his hobbies over the years, staffing and decorating.

If Alberto were to continue on his current career path and go for a position as a relationship manager at a smaller bank, he would highlight the years he has worked at the bank. His position statement, if used in his résumé, would look something like this:

> Over 20 years handling all aspects of fiduciary relationships for Premier-Bank's private banking clients. Successfully increased revenue through new business efforts, client cultivation, and account assessment. Consistently achieved fee increases. Received regular bonus awards.

To pursue his "dream" job, Alberto's regular résumé will not do. He has to reposition himself to show that his experience fits what his prospective employer needs. His position statement should read like this:

Administrative manager with broad experience in running operations. In-depth work with accountants, lawyers, agents, and so on. Over 20 years' experience handling all aspects of fiduciary relationships for PremierBank's private banking clients (overall net worth of $800 million). Expert in all financial arrangements (trust and estate accounts, asset management, non-profit, and tenant shareholder negotiations).

His résumé would focus on his work outside PremierBank that would interest his prospective employer: first his work with the apartment building of which he was president for fourteen years, and then the post he held for ten years as treasurer of a nonprofit organization. Finally, Alberto would highlight the work he had done at PremierBank that would be of interest to his prospective employer, such as the account on which he saved a client $300,000 in taxes.

These different positionings would require different résumés. You can see Alberto's final résumé in Chapter 11: How to Develop Your Résumé.

CASE STUDY: CLYDE
Ready to take charge

Clyde had worked in every area of benefits administration. Now he would like to head up the entire benefits administration area—a move to management. His positioning statement:

14 years' experience in design and administration of all areas of employee benefit plans, including five years with Borgash Benefits Consultants. Advised some of the largest and most prestigious companies in the country. Excellent training and communications skills. MBA in Finance. An effective manager who delivers consistent results.

CASE STUDY: JACK
From supporting to selling

Jack wants to move into sales after being in marketing support. He has been an executive in the sales promotion area, so his position statement stresses his marketing as well as his management experience:

10 years' progressive marketing and managerial experience. Devised superior marketing strategies through qualitative analysis and product repositioning. Skillful at completing the difficult internal sale, coupled with the ability

to attract business and retain clients. Built strong relationships with the top consulting firms. A team player with an enthusiastic approach to top-level challenges.

Notice how he packages his experience running a marketing department as sales. His pitch will be, "It's even more difficult to sell inside because, in order to keep my job, I have to get other people in my company to use my marketing services. I have to do a good job, or they won't use me again."

Jack lacked a position statement on former résumés. If you do not have a position statement, then your position, by default, is the last position you held. With this statement, however, the employer would receive the résumé and say, "Ah-ha! Just what we need—a salesperson!"

CASE STUDY: ELLIOTT
Making a career change

Elliott had been in sports marketing years ago, and had enjoyed it tremendously. However, he had spent the past four years in the mortgage industry, and was having a hard time getting back into sports marketing. The sports people saw him as a career changer—and they saw him as a mortgage man. Even when he explained that marketing mortgages is the same as marketing sports, people did not believe him. He was being positioned by his most recent experience, which was handicapping him.

When a job hunter wants to change industries—or go back to an old industry—he cannot let his most recent position serve as a handicap. For example, if a person has always been in pharmaceuticals marketing, and now wants to do marketing in another industry, his résumé should be rewritten to emphasize *generic* marketing, and most references to pharmaceuticals should be removed. Then the person is more likely to be seen as a marketer who can market in other industries.

In Elliott's case, the summary of qualifications in his new résumé helps a great deal to bring his old work experience right to the top of the résumé. In addition, Elliott has removed the word "mortgage" as much as possible from the description of his most recent job, so his title at the mortgage company stands out more than the company name, and he has gotten rid of company and industry jargon, such as the job title of segment director, because it is not something easily understood outside of his company.

"Before" Résumé

Elliott Jones
421 Morton Street
Chase Fortune, KY 23097

Professional Experience

Sears Mortgage Company   **1987–present**

Vice President, Segment Director, Shelter Business

- Director of $4.6 billion residential mortgage business for the largest mortgage lender in the nation.
- Organized and established regional marketing division for largest mortgage lender in nation, a business which included first and second mortgages, and mortgage life insurance.

SportsLife Magazine   1985–1987
Publisher and Editor

- Published and edited the largest consumer health and fitness magazine and increased circulation 175%.

and so on . . .

"After" Résumé

Elliott Jones
421 Morton Street
Chase Fortune, KY 23097

Summary of Qualifications

Fifteen-plus years of domestic and international senior management experience in the **leisure/sporting goods industry;** multibrand expertise specializing in marketing, new business development, strategic planning, and market research.

Proven record of identifying customer segments, developing differentiable products, communication strategies, sales management, share growth, and profit generation.

Business Experience

Sears Mortgage Company   1987–present

VICE PRESIDENT, BUSINESS DIRECTOR
Residential Real Estate Business

- Business Director of a $4.6 billion business with overall responsibility for strategic planning, marketing, product development, and compliance.
- Consolidated four regional business entities into one; doubled product offerings and initiated a unique direct mail, market research, and merchandising effort. Grew market share 150 basis points and solidified #1 market position.
- Developed and executed nationally recognized consumer and trade advertising, public relations, and direct response programs.

- Structured a product development process that integrated product introductions into the operations and sales segments of the business.
- Organized and established regional marketing division for largest mortgage lender in nation, a business which included first and second mortgages, and mortgage life insurance.

SPORTSLIFE MAGAZINE   1985–1987
Publisher and Editor

- Published and edited the largest consumer health and fitness magazine and increased circulation 175%.

and so on . . .

Notice that the description of what Elliott did for the mortgage business is now written generically—it can apply to the marketing of *any* product. With his new résumé, Elliott had no trouble speaking to people in the sports industry. They no longer saw his most recent experience as a handicap, and he soon had a terrific job as head of marketing for a prestigious sporting goods company.

If you need to move into a new industry or profession, state what you did generically so people will not see you as tied to the old.

BRING SOMETHING TO THE PARTY

When it comes down to negotiating yourself into a new position, seemingly unrelated skills from former positions may actually help you get the job.

For example, some of my background had been in accounting and computers, when I decided to go into counseling. My chief financial officer (CFO) experience helped me ease into that career. I applied at a ninety-person career counseling company and agreed to be their CFO for a while —providing I was also assigned clients to counsel. They wanted a cost accounting system, so my ability to do that for them was what I "brought to the party." I was willing to give the company something they wanted (my business experience) in exchange for doing something I really wanted to do (counseling executives).

Combining the new with the old, rather than jumping feet first into something completely new, is often the best way to move your career in a different direction. You gain the experience you need in the new field without having to enter at the entry level. Equally important, it is less stressful because you are using some of your old strengths while you build new ones.

Coming from a different background than the one to which you are applying can also give you a bargaining chip. If you are looking at an area where you have no experience, chances are you will be competing with people who do have experience. You can separate yourself from the competition by saying, "I'm different. I have the skills to do this job, and I can also do other things that these people can't do." It works! Examples of positioning (summary) statements are listed below. Others appear in the chapter on résumés. Positioning statements go at the top of your résumé and set the tone for the rest of it. They are usually under the heading "Summary of Qualifications."

SAMPLE POSITIONING STATEMENTS

Summary of Qualifications

INTERNATIONAL HUMAN RESOURCES EXECUTIVE
Policy Development   Organizational Planning   Management Training

Over 15 years experience in international human resources environments. Solid capabilities in strategic planning, policy formulation, management development, succession planning, and recruitment.

Major accomplishments in improving productivity through executive development, management training, business development, and strategic planning. Additional skills in providing technical and professional assistance to start-ups in international markets.

Below is the summary from a résumé for someone who thinks he might like to explore his interest in sports as a career change. His other résumé focuses on his computer experience.

Summary of Qualifications

A lifetime involvement in competitive sports: participation, administration, and promotion. Ongoing relationships with corporate sponsors and local governments. Personal connections with TV, radio and newspapers to bring events to the public. Work closely with the U.S. Cycling Federation. Manage cycling championships. Won over 100 races, including 3rd place 1989 Olympic trials. Former President of HGSC. Annually promote the largest race in New York. Persuasive, detail-oriented manager who overcomes obstacles to successfully complete projects.

Here are two more examples:

EXECUTIVE with 23 years of diversified experience in international and domestic markets. Includes ten years of P&L responsibility for businesses in Europe, Africa, Middle East, and Far East. Extensive experience in Latin and South America. Earlier experience in financial and manufacturing functions. Special skills in:
- Managing businesses to turn around performance and achieve full potential;
- Developing and implementing viable long-range plans, including marketing, product, operations, financial, and acquisition/divestiture strategies;
- Analyzing and controlling all aspects of business to reduce costs and improve profits.

EXECUTIVE having 17 years of senior management experience with multinational natural resources/mining/materials companies. Ten years with full P&L responsibility. Extensive earlier experience in line management, operating, and technical positions. Special skills in:

- Managing businesses to improve financial performance and provide for growth;
- Staffing and motivating to improve individual and group performance;
- Marketing to increase markets, market share, and profitability;
- Optimizing operations to enhance return on investment.

Remember Tom Warren from a few chapters back? The following summary first states what Tom is (an innovative financial services marketer) and then backs it up with two proofs: his position with a prestigious institution and his packaged-goods experience. The summary does not simply state what he's done; it highlights those things Tom would like to do next. He *enjoys* creating new products. He *likes* building major businesses. He *wants* to turn around problem brands.

SUMMARY

Innovative financial services marketer with ten years at PremierBank and heavy package goods product management experience. Created new products. Built major businesses. Turned around problem brands. Strong strategic thinker and team builder.

Areas of Expertise

- Product Management
- New Product Development
- Sales Management

- Electronic Banking
- Branch Banking
- Market Analysis

Here are two summaries for the same person. In the first, he targeted being president of another company. He used the second résumé to get board directorships and consulting work. The two examples show a simple change of focus. The body of both résumés is the same.

You also may sometimes want to make a slight change in your summary to change its focus. But don't get carried away and change your résumé every time you turn around.

President, Chairman, Chief Executive Officer

known for repositioning and turning around
major manufacturing businesses of 12,000–28,000 people . . .

. . . through strategic analysis, unrelenting focus, major cost-cutting, and the development of high employee morale and commitment.

Director/Management Advisor

- Former President, Chairman, Chief Executive Officer
- known for repositioning/turning around major manufacturing businesses . . . of 12,000–28,000 people . . . through strategic analysis, unrelenting focus, and major cost-cutting.
- As Chairman of the Tri-State Association, led the resuscitation of this organization.

This job hunter wants to highlight the type of medical sales she has been in. Her most recent position was in another area of medical sales that she does not want to get into again.

11 years of medical sales experience ranging from medical instruments to pharmaceuticals.

A "producer" who analyzes the situation and quickly achieves a strong increase in sales. Known for excellent organizational and interpersonal skills. Thorough; high in initiative and innovation. Enthusiastic, consistent, dedicated performer with high standards. An achiever who meshes well with highly visible, high-level medical personnel. A seasoned professional adaptable to new markets, new product lines.

In the next summary, the job hunter emphasizes his accounts receivable background to differentiate himself from other credit and collections managers. He has also worked for three recognized companies, and wants to stress that as well. The bulleted accomplishments pull from his background things that happened a while back—things the reader might not notice right away in his résumé. If you have done things in the past you want the reader to notice, consider including them in your summary. If you have worked for companies that are worth bragging about, put them in your summary.

Summary of Qualifications

Credit Manager / Credit and Collections Supervisor with strong Accounts Receivable background. Over 20 years experience in finished goods and services.

- ARK Financial   • MAINLINE Industrial Credit   • Citizens & Southern
- Supervised 3 credit analysts and 3 collectors.
  - Train workers to become independent, high-quality producers.
  - Trained people for A/R, credit, and collections positions.
  - Regularly selected by management to break in new people (because of knowledge of job content as well as systems).
- A troubleshooter . . .
  . . . selected to turn around problem clients, problem accounts, problem teams.
- Personable: get along with management, clients, staff, and salespeople.

Your summary is the most important part of your résumé. If it positions you incorrectly, your résumé becomes a handicap. What's more, you will use a paraphrase of your summary in your cover letters. A good summary is worth the time it takes. Here are more for you to study:

Director/Curator/Art Adviser
10 years museum experience and 10 years in business management.

- P & L responsibility in both museums and for-profit organizations.
- 7 years as an owner manager.
- Directed staffs of up to 70.
- Independently managed major retail/wholesale complex and handled urgent projects from conception to execution.
- Accomplished projects through established long-term social and professional relationships.
- A resource person, problem solver, troubleshooter, and creative turn-around manager.

SUMMARY OF QUALIFICATIONS

CEO/COO
with strong marketing/finance background
Create, grow, and turn around diverse businesses in U.S. and overseas.

Industry experience includes:

- Transportation & Airlines
- Manufacturing; Computer Hardware
- Financial Systems & Bnkg
- Publishing, TV

Sample accomplishments:

- Built the largest credit card business in the world in only 4 years.
- At Delta, with a severe strike and fuel shortage, was brought in to **turn around the U.S. marketing operation.** Within days, created a whole new image.
  — Put plan together within 2 weeks, and **within 3 months division was at an all-time high** and had largest profit ever, with no change in spending.

Find the unique solution (financial, marketing, business niche)
for every business problem.
Install long-term direction, financial controls, and staffing.

EVP of Operations
for major service businesses

AMERICAN EXPRESS   IBM   GENERAL MOTORS

Managed staffs of 6,000 to 15,000 people
and budgets of $0.5 to $1.5 billion
in broad-gauge, multiple functions.

- Turned around large organizations to:
  — Deliver increased customer satisfaction.
  — Get costs out of the business with minimal disruption.
  — Improve employee morale.
- Motivated large organizations to deliver uncommon performance.
  — Solicited full employee involvement.
  — Sped the flow of information and decisions up and down the chain.
- Managed meaningful part of a team that won the Malcolm Baldridge Award.
- MBA, Harvard; undergraduate degree, Columbia.

A strategist who knows how to implement.
Manage large, geographically dispersed customer service organizations.
Deliver large-scale computer systems.
Strong record of delivering balanced results.

SUMMARY OF QUALIFICATIONS

Senior Information Executive
Managed all technology areas: Applications, Systems, & Operations

- CIGNA
- CARGILL, INC.
- SEARS, ROEBUCK & CO.

- Brings a **business perspective** to technology management in tough industries: financial services, publishing, retail.
- Strong **technology background:** Integrated systems, client server, telecommunications, LAN's international networks, open systems, HELP desks, CASE tools, automated operations, customer support.
- **A leader:** Produce the quality product needed by the senior management team.
- Worked with CEO's of major corporations. Strong executive presentation skills.
- MBA, Columbia; B.S., Electrical Engineering.

An information executive with strong financial skills.
An integral part of the senior management team.
A leader who gets major work accomplished.

HUMAN RESOURCES MANAGEMENT

Administration Recruiting Employee Relations Training

Broad-based Human Resources generalist background with leading financial institution, Big-6 Accounting firm, Retail Management company, and Fortune 25 multi-industry corporation. Special strengths in employment practices, EEO/AA, recruiting, and training. Innovative and resourceful problem-solver, at best in turnaround situations. Possess initiative, determination, and excellent consultative skills.

> *Headed revamped recruitment and staffing efforts in Financial Controller's and Sales Management departments.*

> *Managed EEO departments and resolved major compliance reviews and potential class action issues.*

> *Developed and implemented "Human Resources Information Systems" covering Benefit programs, Payroll Administration, Government Compliance, and Pension reporting.*

SUMMARY

Senior International Business Executive.
Start-ups, turnarounds and shutdowns.

- Business Analysis
- People Management
  - International Operations
  - Risk Management
  - Strategic Planning/Organizational Structure

- 14 years international business experience.
- Operations in over 20 countries.
- Part of team to get changes in international regulations.
- Skilled at setting up effective organizational structures.
- An acute observer of existing systems of operations. Go to core of the problem and quickly resolve it.
- Conducted orderly reallocation of large numbers of people.

SENIOR CORPORATE FINANCE ORIGINATOR
with broad background in structuring and distribution
- BANK OF ENGLAND   • RCA CREDIT   • DAIWA

- Recognized for developing and maintaining strong client relationships.
- Highly experienced marketer with well-developed presentation, communications, and consultative selling skills.
- Thorough grounding in credit, corporate finance tools and techniques, debt/equity structures, and other financial products/services.

Someone interested in a career continuation:

Financial and administrative executive. Eighteen years in the communications industry. Domestic as well as international experience. Have consistently made a dramatic contribution to business results.

A hospital administrator interested in management consulting (which requires a personality quite different from what the reader may expect from hospital administrators. Therefore, the personality traits were considered more important than the accomplishments, in this case):

Articulate, energetic, innovative, and resourceful. A Master's Degree in Nursing is coupled with **over 15 years hospital management experience in clinical administration and consulting.** Successfully directed institutional projects incorporting management information systems and analysis, budgeting, and quality assurance. Worked with all levels of management. Created a climate that enhanced productivity and cooperation.

This approach works whatever your level in a company. Let's take a lower-level example. A secretary produced this one:

Four years of executive secretarial experience coupled with continuing college education. A solid history of **excellent work relationships,** both with the public and with internal personnel at all organizational levels. **High in initiative and energy,** with strong ability to exercise **independent judgment.** Excellent **writing skills.** Trustworthy and discreet.

A few more:

SUMMARY OF QUALIFICATIONS

18 years proven project management experience
PC computer systems, Training and Education, PC-based business solutions
A PC problem-solver, developer, and troubleshooter

- Designed, developed, and managed state-of-the-art PC-based training tools that significantly enhance training experience and performance of participants.
- Managed the development of unique, highly marketable real time computerized simulation.
- 18 years of teaching, training, and adult education.
- During two-year period, managed company's first PC center devoted entirely to learning a fundamental new technology.
  — hired and managed instructor staff.
  — trained over 500 professionals of all levels in first year of operation.
  — taught classes in Lotus, WordPerfect, Dbase, and DOS.

SUMMARY OF QUALIFICATIONS

10 years Purchasing Management Experience
Budget of $25 million

International sourcing and purchasing experience
An experienced International Trade Show Manager

Areas of Expertise include:

- International, Domestic Purchasing
- European Sales Mgmt.
- Payroll, Personnel Mgmt.
- Advertising, Promotion Mgmt.

- Trade Show Mgmt.
- European Account Development
- Manufacturing
- Warehouse and Inventory Control

- Maintenance Supervision

We've made a lot of progress: you've developed your accomplishments as well as your summary statement. In the next chapter, we'll put it all together.

> History records the successes of men with objectives and a sense of direction. Oblivion is the position of small men overwhelmed by obstacles.
> —WILLIAM H. DANFORTH

> It is a tragedy that most of us die before we have begun to live.
> —ERICH FROMM
> *For the Love of Life*

> Never let the seeds stop you from enjoying the watermelon.
> —The family maid in *Made for Each Other*,
> starring James Stewart and Carole Lombard

HOW TO DEVELOP YOUR RÉSUMÉ

. . . for while history does not teach that honesty, in this world, is
the best policy, it surely teaches that dishonesty ultimately is the
worst policy.
—JOHN LUKACS
    A History of the Cold War

YOUR RÉSUMÉ IS the equivalent of a sales brochure. It is
not supposed to tell every detail, but to grab someone's attention, entice
him, spark his interest. Later on, the interviewer can use it to sell you to
someone else. It speaks for you in your absence.

Your résumé also softens the reader. It predisposes him to think of
you in a certain way. When you meet, the reader has a preconceived
notion about you. Tailor your résumé to make the impression you want.
Most people never consider using their résumé to create a certain impression of themselves; they simply write down their work experience. Job
hunters who think of their résumé as a tool for communication tend to be
more effective than those who play it safe and use a bland approach. Your
credentials and experience are only one half of what you are selling. Your
style and personality are the other half.

Your résumé can serve as a guide to the interview. If you highlight
certain areas in your résumé, the interviewer cannot help but ask about
them. If you play down or even leave out certain things, you reduce the
chances of having the interview center on those areas.

This chapter will present some new thoughts on résumé writing. Use
what you want. Some ideas may suit your style; others may not. On the
other hand, if you have not been as successful as you would like, you may
want to try a style different from what you have been using.

WHAT HAPPENS TO YOUR RÉSUMÉ

Make yourself necessary to someone.
—RALPH WALDO EMERSON

Your résumé crosses the desk of someone. This person was not looking to hire, but something about your résumé or cover letter struck a responsive chord in him. If one of your achievements fits the reader's problems at the moment, you may be called in.

The reader says to his or her secretary, "Ask this person to come in for a chat, but be sure to say that we have no openings." You are called in for an exploratory meeting.

In most cases, there truly is no specific job opening. If the chemistry is right, and if things progress smoothly, however, a position may be developed for you. This happens more often than the average job hunter may realize—and is the ideal scenario. A position created for you has the best chance of being a successful and satisfying one. You could slant it toward your motivated skills.

It's important to realize that your résumé—your brochure about yourself—*will be looked at for only ten seconds*. You must make that ten seconds worthwhile. The reader will usually look at the top of the first page, and perhaps glance at the rest. You want the reader to see your opening paragraph—your summary—and other parts that you want to stand out. If something sparks the reader's interest, he or she may spend a little more time on your résumé.

YOUR RÉSUMÉ IS COMPLETELY UNDER YOUR CONTROL

An unlearned carpenter of my acquaintance once said in my hearing: "There is very little difference between one man and another, but what little there is, is very important." This distinction seems to me to go to the root of the matter.
—WILLIAM JAMES, "The Importance of Individuals"

You have complete control. Determine exactly what will hit the reader's eye on each page, and the impression you want the reader to have of you. For example, you may want to appear as a person with experience in a certain background. Be sure to mention that area in your summary and highlight it in the body of your résumé. You may want to stress your long-term managerial experience, or your technical expertise. Your résumé can show that you are the kind of person who constantly comes up with new ideas and implements them, or solves problems for the company.

Tell the reader outright the kind of person you are. Most résumés focus on credentials, but with so many qualified people vying for the same position, a résumé with personality is more readable and stands out. Résumés that are detached and cold are not as effective as those that seem more human. Résumés and cover letters should be alive and enthusiastic.

What you say predisposes the reader to see you in a certain way. If, for example, you describe yourself as dynamic, you will be treated that way. You do not have to come across as dynamic in the interview. If you seem in the interview truly to be that way, do not be surprised if the interviewer happens to mention just how dynamic you are.

This is your story. It is one you want to be proud of. Don't be boring about it.

JOB OBJECTIVE

> They are able because they think they are able.
> —VIRGIL

In developing your résumé, your job target must be clearly in your mind. Major changes in your target may require different résumés. Minor changes will not.

With your target in mind, go through the accomplishment statements you developed in Chapter 8. Select those that support your job objective, and leave out those that do not support it.

If the accomplishments that best support your objective occurred a long time in the past, select excerpts from them and put the excerpts in your summary. This will make it easier for the reader to see that you have had that experience.

Have your target clearly in mind before you develop your résumé—but don't put it on your résumé. Your résumé can include you or exclude you from the hiring process. A "job objective" makes it seem as if you want a specific position. Even if you are open to other positions, it may seem that you are not. On the other hand, if you know exactly what you want, and if there are plenty of jobs with the title you are going after, then perhaps you should put a job objective on your résumé.

Career changers are often not sure what they want to do. But you need a résumé just to talk with people. Develop a résumé and use it to "test market" yourself—to find out if your target market thinks you have a chance. A more focused, polished résumé will grow out of this process.

YOUR SUMMARY STATEMENT

> In differentiation, not in uniformity, lies the path of progress.
> —LOUIS BRANDEIS

The position statement you developed in Chapter 10 becomes the summary statement in your résumé. It sets the tone and highlights the theme —the threads that bind your accomplishments. Your summary statement describes what makes you qualified and yet different from others who may be aiming for the same position.

The summary statement goes at the top of your résumé, after your name, address, and phone number. It brings all your accomplishments together. If in your summary statement you want to say that you are a financial wizard, your accomplishment statements must support this.

Consider underlining what you want the reader to see. Remember, the reader scans the underlined parts—which make the résumé easier to read—and then reads the rest of the summary. When highlighting is used throughout the résumé, the reader will tend to focus on those areas first. If underlining makes you uncomfortable, don't use it. But it is very effective.

THE FORMAT

> I don't like work—no man does—but I like what is in work—the chance to find yourself.
> —JOSEPH CONRAD

Your résumé should be attention-getting in an understated way, and readable. Lines of type that go clear across the page from one margin to the other are difficult to read. Use bulleted accomplishments to break up the text.

Your résumé should be as long as it has to be, and no longer. Cut and cut until you cannot cut any more. You do not care if anyone ever reads your entire résumé; he probably won't read it all, whether it is two pages long or five. You want him simply to stop at your résumé and spend more than ten seconds on it, so perhaps he will call you in.

My own résumé happens to be three to four pages long—I feel it has to be to say what I want in the way I want to say it. I could cram it into two pages—but instead I make it attractive and readable, and use as many pages as necessary.

I get *lots* of interviews, even though interviewers almost invariably tell me that my résumé is too long. One thing *everyone* knows about job hunting is that a résumé should be no longer than two pages. Years ago, that made sense. People stayed in one job or one company for a very long time. But now people change jobs more often, and a simple listing of jobs can sometimes take an entire page. Many people mistakenly think a shorter résumé is more likely to be read, so they force a lot of information into one completely unreadable page. It is better to have a longer résumé that is scannable and readable. But remember, no matter how long or short your résumé is, the average reader will look at it for only ten seconds.

TEST YOUR RÉSUMÉ

> I applied to banks. I have never seen men on Wall Street in such complete agreement on any issue as they were on my application. A few actually laughed at my résumé.
> —MICHAEL LEWIS
>   *Liars Poker*

You need to test what you have written in the marketplace. First, show your résumé to a friend. Ask him to describe in ten seconds how the information comes across. If your friend describes you the way you wanted to come across, then your résumé is presenting you properly. If you come across as having expertise in a field that you did *not* want to highlight, then your résumé needs to position you more properly. The most valuable comments are *strategic* in nature. If your friend wants you to change the third word on the second page, *it will not help you get a job*. But if he tells you that you come across as a junior accountant, when you actually headed up a division of a company, that is valuable feedback. Or if you come across as a salesperson, when you hate sales, that is valuable. It is important for you to know if you come across as being at a higher or lower level than you are.

PHONE

List a daytime phone number. If you have an answering machine, you can list the number as "213-555-1212 (message)"; interviewers will then expect to leave a message but not talk to you. Do the same if you use the number of a relative who is taking messages for you. Or consider using an answering service, which can be reasonably priced. By doing so, you can call for your messages and not worry about missing them. Within reasonable limits the service can be instructed to receive your messages in a manner calculated to enhance your campaign.

JOB TITLES

You must be honest in stating your job title, and sometimes that means *not* using the title your company gave you. Use a title that accurately reflects the job you held—one commonly understood outside your company. For example, if your company calls you a "Programmer C," is that a high-level programmer or a low-level one? It would be better to call yourself a junior programmer or a senior programmer—titles that make more sense to the outside world.

I had a client whose job title was "marketing representative," yet what she did was market analysis. Since she was applying for positions in market analysis, the title was holding her back—and it was also misleading: until she agreed to change her title and make it more honest, readers thought she was in sales.

REPORTING RELATIONSHIPS, COMPANY DESCRIPTIONS

Sometimes your reporting relationship gives a good indication of your level of responsibility. If it helps, put it in. For example, you could say, "report directly to the president."

It may help to put in parentheses what your company does. For example: "Complex, Inc. (a computer software company)." Again, if it helps, put it in.

HIGHLIGHTING OR UNDERSTATING JOB TITLES

Look at the first job listed on your résumé. Which is more important to the *reader*, your job title or the name of your employer? Decide which you want the reader to notice for each position. You do not have to be consistent: in one case, it may be your title; and in another, say, if you're looking within the same industry, it may be the name of your employer. Or you may want to highlight both or play down both.

Emphasize or deemphasize by using caps, underlining, boldface, and positioning on a page. I list one job that was a bore for me at the bottom of page two of my résumé. Both my title and the name of the company are written in upper- and lowercase. Nothing stands out, and most interviewers don't ask me about that job.

Here are some examples of highlighting:

Assistant Researcher, ACME CORPORATION
Assistant Researcher, **ACME CORPORATION**

ASSISTANT RESEARCHER, Acme Corporation
ASSISTANT RESEARCHER, Acme Corporation

This practice is effective and not offensive. It helps in the readability and the dynamism of your résumé. When it's done correctly, the interviewer will tend to talk about what *you* want to talk about.

RANK YOUR ACCOMPLISHMENTS

Within each job, list first the accomplishment most important to the *reader*. If your most important one is listed last, the reader may never get to it.

WHERE TO SPEND YOUR ENERGY

On the first page—especially the summary.

HOW TO DECIDE IF YOU SHOULD PUT SOMETHING INTO YOUR RÉSUMÉ

Always use this philosophy: if it helps your case, put it in. If it does not help your case, leave it out.

Let's take the example of a person's age. The accepted practice is not to give a clue in your résumé about your age, but the reader will try to guess how old you are anyway. If, for example, you leave out your years of graduation, it will make your age look like an issue, and the reader may guess that you are older than you are. When I was applying for management positions years ago, my résumé made me sound younger than I actually was—I had worked for a few years before completing my undergraduate work. It helped my case to put my date of birth in my résumé, because I wanted employers to know how old I really was.

Look at your own situation to see if putting something in would help your case or not. And remember, it is not always best to follow the rules.

USE THE LANGUAGE OF YOUR TARGET MARKET

Restate your background in terms your target market will understand. Do not use the lingo of your industry or your company. For example, if you want to switch from education to a training position in the corporate world, remember that corporate life does not have "teachers"; it has "trainers" or even "instructors." Consider using these words instead. Do not expect the reader to translate the terminology. Make it easy for him to see how you fit in; let him see that you understand his business.

If you have worked for a major corporation, do not use the company jargon. Use words generally understood in your target market.

Think about how you want to position yourself to the reader, the story you are trying to tell, and how you can make sure the story comes across successfully.

IS THIS RÉSUMÉ GOOD OR BAD?

Take a look at the sample résumés coming up. You'll see that it is difficult to judge whether a résumé is good on its face. You need to know the direction in which the job hunter is trying to go, and which areas of his background should be emphasized to get him there.

People show me résumés all the time and ask me to tell them quickly if the résumés are good or bad. Usually, the ones that have no summary statement are not very good. And those written with lots of large block paragraphs are difficult to read (the messages get lost in the middle of those paragraphs). But other than that, I frankly cannot tell if a résumé is good or bad. I need to know more about the person and his or her goals in writing the résumé. How did this person want to position himself? *If the résumé positions him the way he wants to be positioned, it's a good résumé. If it doesn't, it's not.*

CASE STUDY: WALLY
OK for kids

The approach Wally used in his résumé used to be OK for someone just getting out of school: he stated a career objective, which was followed by his education and then a historical listing of his work experience. Today we live in an age of sound bites and résumé overload. It would have taken the reader too long to figure out what level Wally was at, the important things he had done, and where he might fit in.

Wally's "after" résumé has a summary, which makes it easy for the reader to figure out exactly what Wally does and his level. What's more, the reader gets a feel for Wally's personality: "an innovator with people, processes, and equipment." Wally's old résumé told us nothing about his work style. Finally, the résumé is scannable. It is now two pages, but the reader is more likely to notice the things Wally thinks are important.

"BEFORE" RESUME

WALLACE M. PETERSEN Height: 5'10"
20 Midwood Road Weight: 185 lbs.
Strathmore, New Jersey 05555 Birth date: Dec. 22, 1954
Telephone: 609-555-3412 Married—3 children

CAREER OBJECTIVE: To gain a position with a firm that offers a challenging opportunity, which utilizes a background of actual press work combined with supervisory responsibilities and an opportunity for advancement.

EDUCATION: CAMDEN COLLEGE, Blackwood, NJ
Associate Degree in Business Administration
Major: Business Management; Elective: Two years of Spanish

EXPERIENCE: BUCKMASTER ASSOCIATES, Ivytown, PA
Dec. 1989 to present Responsible for creating a web printing operation, which involved traveling the country to locate, negotiate, purchase, erect and manage the operation, which consisted of two web presses, one sheet-fed press, and a prep room, which included an Opti-copy Camera-Imposer. Other duties included negotiating with vendors for best supplies and prices and building a competent work force, which stressed high production *and* quality with low operating cost. Very successful and efficient.

Oct. 1982 to PONTIAC PRESS, INC., Philadelphia
Dec., 1989 BERTRAM COMMUNICATIONS, INC., subsidiary

Hired initially to operate Pontiac's 4 unit, 2 folder Harris Press, after demonstrating the ability to motivate press crews and substantially increase production in a union environment, appointed to direct and manage the pressroom operations of a new experimental plant. It is widely known to have been an outstanding success.

Reason for leaving: Entire plant being moved to New York.

Dec. 1981 to A. D. WEINSTEIN LITHOGRAPH
Oct. 1982 Hollywood, FL

Pressman with extensive Heat-set background on Harris M-1000, M-200, ATF, and Hantscho, all with double four-color (8 units) Butler and Wood Splicers, Tec and Offen Dryers, Combination and Double Former Folders, Sheeters, and one Ribbon Folder.

Reason for leaving: Huge loss in accounts would have meant major pay cut.

"After" Resume

Wallace M. Petersen

---

20 Midwood Road
Strathmore, New Jersey 05555
Residence: 609-555-3412

Summary of Qualifications

**Web Press Supervisor/Manager
with 20 years' experience
and an emphasis on quality and productivity.**

- **A hands-on supervisor.** Inspire workers' pride in quality/quantity of their work.
  - Train workers to become independent, high-quality producers.
  - Select/retain the best: self-starters with an eye on quality and productivity.
- An innovator with people, processes, and equipment:
  - Regularly develop **timesaving and cost-saving methods.**
- A **strong negotiator** for both equipment and supplies. Substantial savings.
- Proficient in **rebuilding equipment.** Reduced machine downtime and costs.

Professional Experience

Web Operations Manager   1989–present
Buckmaster Associates **(specialized exclusively in printing for other printers)**

Set up and managed a web press operation. Company formerly had none.

- **Built a competent work force:** stressed high production *and* quality/low cost.
  - As **printers for the trade,** our customers demanded the highest quality at a price where they could still make a profit reselling our work.
- Built from the ground up cost-effective, highly productive web printing operation.
  - Engineered the entire setup, determined the equipment needs, and negotiated the purchase of used equipment.
  - Hired/managed daily operations of this **20-person shop** with two 36″ <u>web presses, one sheet-fed press, and a prep room.</u>
- Researched nationally to locate, select, negotiate, and purchase equipment.
  - Oversaw reconditioning/rebuilding/assembling of 7 printing units, 2 folders, 5 splicers, and 2 counter-stackers. Made it operational within 2 months.
  - **Saved $300,000** versus the price of already refurbished equipment.
  - To produce the highest-quality work, supervised the erection of two 36″ web presses, and one sheet-fed press to **tolerances of 1/1000ths of an inch.**
- Designed the prep room for good work flow **(Opti-copy Camera-Imposer,** plate burners, light tables, plate processors). **Saved $200,000.**
- Negotiated with vendors for prices usually given only to very large companies.
  - **Saved $500,000** per year.

Web Manager/Working Supervisor　　　　　　　　　　1982–1989
Bertram Communications, Inc., subsidiary of **Pontiac Press, Inc.**

Set up and managed web operations as working supervisor.
- **Payback on investment accomplished in only 14 months.**
- Developed a highly motivated work force.
  - The plant regularly attracted visitors who wanted to observe the operation.
  - The cleanliness of the workplace inspired pride in the workers.
- Produced **high quality** work. Work formerly done on sheet-fed presses because of quality requirements was done on web at a tremendous cost savings.
- Developed **innovative** press folder **techniques** and conversions.

Reason for leaving: Entire plant moved to New York.

Pressman, A. D. Weinstein Lithograph　　　　　　　　1981–1982
- Extensive Heat-set background on Harris M-1000, M-200, and Hantscho, all with double four-color (8 units) Butler and Wood Splicers, Tec and Offen Dryers, Combination and Double Former Folders, Sheeters, and one Ribbon Folder.
- A. D. Weinstein is almost exclusively a publication printer producing products such as *Time* magazine, *Cosmopolitan, Good Housekeeping, Eastern Review,* etc.

Reason for leaving: When mail rates went up, company could no longer compete.

Working Supervisor, Macmillan Publishing Company　　　1976–1981
Hired as Pressman's Helper. **Promoted to lead four-color Pressman at age 23.** After 3 years, promoted to Working Supervisor.

Experience on Harris 845 with 4 units, Harris V-25 with 7 units, 4 butlers, 4 pass dryer and chill tower, combination folder, three knife trimmers, Martin Tensimatic unit, in-line glueing system. Four-color process work on publication and newspaper supplements. Experienced on coated offset, and newsprint paper.

Assistant Pressman, Acme Printing Company　　　　　　1974–1976
Hired as Flyboy of Goss Community five-unit press. Promoted to Asst. Pressman.

EDUCATION

Associate Degree in Business Administration, Camden College, 1975
Major: Business Management; Elective: Two years of Spanish

CASE STUDY: JEFFREY
Starting over

Jeffrey had spent seventeen years selling a certain product. His entire career was based on it. Now that product no longer existed, and the clients he had developed over the years were worthless. Jeffrey would have to start from scratch in another area.

When Jeffrey did his Seven Stories exercise, a number of things became clear:

- He liked to sell rather than simply manage salespeople. He wanted to be a "producing manager" in his next position.
- Repeatedly, he had taken businesses from zero and developed them into something substantial; Jeffrey was gong to have to do this again —but in a field very different from the one he had been in. We decided to make this the theme in his new résumé. To make it stand out even more, we underlined it in the summary and emphasized it throughout: **Proven record of building customer relations and business revenues in a short time frame.**

One other consideration was that in Jeffrey's industry, there were many unsavory people. Jeffrey wanted to work for someone who was ethical. Therefore, the last line of his summary statement lets employers know which side of the fence he is on. Furthermore, the personal information at the end lets them know that he is a good family man, retired from the Marines, and so on.

Jeffrey had actually never job hunted before, and therefore his résumé had never been tested. At first he was resistant to having a résumé that was longer than one page. On Wall Street, "everyone's résumé was one page long."

I explained that a one-page résumé worked just fine on Wall Street in good times, when people were looking to hire. But when times were tough, a person has to do everything he can to separate himself from his competitors. If everyone else had a certain kind of résumé, that was argument enough to have something that was better.

Jeffrey found himself a new job that not only paid the high base he had made before, but he also got an equity position in the new company. What's more, his search took him only two months. A résumé that positioned him properly helped his search along, and his background was no longer a handicap.

"Before" Résumé

JEFFREY LUCAS
Street Address
New York, New York 11000
Business: 212-555-1111
Home: 212-333-4444

BUSINESS EXPERIENCE:

1986–Present	Manager U.S. Government Securities Sales and Trading, GlitzBank, London.
1983–1986	President GlitzBank Securities Markets Inc., a NASD-registered broker dealer and wholly owned subsidiary of GlitzBank operating U.S. government securities sales offices in five major U.S. cities.

1979–1983	Salesman and Manager of GlitzBank Mortgage-Backed Securities Sales Team covering top-tier U.S. thrifts and mortgage banking companies.
1976–1979	Sales Manager for GlitzBank Private Banking Services for high-net-worth individual clients in the New York metropolitan region.
1973–1976	Manager GlitzBank Investment Selection Service and IRA Rollover products ($25MM equity portfolio).
1971–1973	Relationship Manager, GlitzBank Private Banking Dept. ($20MM loan portfolio)
EDUCATION:	B.S., Finance, Rutgers University, 1966; Credit Analysis Program, GlitzBank, 1972; T.E.P., Darden School, University of Virginia, 1979; Registered Series 3, 7, and Municipal Securities Principal
PERSONAL:	U.S. Naval Aviator, Major USMCR (retired) Married, 4 children

"AFTER" RÉSUMÉ

JEFFREY LUCAS

Street Address
New York, New York 11000

Home: 212-333-4444
Business: 212-555-1111

SUMMARY OF QUALIFICATIONS

17 years experience with GlitzBank in sales of financial services. 8 years in the fixed income market covering major institutional customers in the U.S. and Europe. **Proven record of building customer relations and business revenues in a short time frame.** A strong producing manager who is demanding but reasonable and easy to deal with. Sets high standards of customer service, integrity, and professionalism.

PROFESSIONAL EXPERIENCE

GLITZBANK 1971–Present

Institutional Bond Sales 1988–Present
Team Leader
- Mortgage Backed Securities coverage of major U.S. mortgage bankers.
- U.S. governments, options, and MBS sales to key London customers.

GlitzBank Investment Bank, London 1986–1988
Producing Manager, U.S. Government Securities Sales and Trading
- Directed 6 salespeople and 2 traders (London and Zurich).
- Distributed government, MBS to customers in Europe and Middle East.

Regional Sales Manager 1983–1986
- In charge of 5 U.S. institutional sales offices—**60 people.**
- Distributed government, municipal, and MBS across the U.S.
- **Grew the business from $2 to $15 million in revenues in 3 years.**
- Made GlitzBank the first dealer with an effective regional network.

GlitzBank Mortgage Backed Securities   1979–1983
Producing Manager
- Personally opened up 10 top-tier U.S. thrifts and mortgage banking institutions.
- Created a business and customer base that didn't exist prior to 1980.
- **Grew volume from 0 to $13 billion in 2 years.**

GlitzBank Private Banking Services   1977–1979
Sales Manager
- Directed 5 salespeople in marketing and trust and investment services to high-net-worth individual clients in the New York metropolitan region.

Business and Portfolio Manager   1973–1976
- Directed investment decisions on individual accounts aggregating to a $25 million equity portfolio.
- Designed and launched GlitzBank's IRA Rollover and Keogh products.
- Supervised advertising, direct mail, and telemarketing promotional efforts.

GlitzBank Private Banking Department   1971–1973
Relationship Manager
- Cross-sold and delivered banking and investment services to high-net-worth individual clients.
- Built a $20 million loan portfolio.

EDUCATION
B.S., Finance, Rutgers University, 1966
Credit Analysis Program, GlitzBank, 1972
Executive Program, Darden School, University of Virginia, 1979
Registered Series 3, 7, and Municipal Securities Principal

PERSONAL
U.S. Naval Aviator, Major USMCR (retired)
Married, 4 children

CASE STUDY: ALBERTO
Changing careers

In the chapter on positioning yourself, Alberto made a doubly successful career move: he went from the for-profit to the not-for-profit sector, which is a major industry switch, and he changed the kind of work he was doing as well, going from relationship management to administration. This is exactly what he wanted—and is exactly the way his résumé positioned him.

The thought process Alberto used is exactly the same thought process you will have to use every time you want to change careers. You will decide what your target is, pull from your background everything that makes you look appropriate to that target market, and then write a summary that positions you for that target. Here are the two résumés used for his search, one aimed at staying as a relationship manager in banking, and one aimed at administrative work in the not-for-profit sector.

Administrative Résumé

M. ALBERTO TERLIZZI

71 South 44th Street   Home: (212) 555-1111
New York, NY 10001   Office: (212) 555-0000

SUMMARY OF QUALIFICATIONS

An administrative manager with broad experience in running operations. In-depth work with accountants, lawyers, agents, and so on. Over 20 years experience as a trust officer handling all aspects of fiduciary relationships for PremierBank's private banking clients (175 families with overall net worth of $800 million). Expert in all financial arrangements (trust & estate accounts, asset management, nonprofit, and tenant shareholder negotiations), as well as real estate matters. Have worked with New York's most prestigious law firms. Extensive experience in staffing.

PROFESSIONAL EXPERIENCE

PREMIERBANK—PRIVATE BANKING DIVISION   **1960–PRESENT**

Relationship Manager

Responsible for overall management of 175 family relationships having an overall net worth of $400 million. Coordinated trust, investment-advisory, custodial, and banking services. Coordinate cotrustees, attorneys, accountants, and beneficiaries.

- Saved family $3 milliion in taxes with innovative estate planning method.

- Developed a complete estate plan for a family whose financial arrangements were in disarray: They had archaic wills and no tax planning in the event of death. Resulted in their having appropriate wills, trusts for children, investment account for wife with gifted securities, and a new attorney and accountant.

- Broad knowledge of discretionary powers, fiduciary accounting, tax applications, and investment requirements.

- Reviewed complex financial situations, weighing options vis-à-vis income payments, gifts, and estate impact. As liaison between family members, attorney, and advisors, formulated annual financial programs saving one client $30,000 annually in taxes.

- As consultant to a wealthy family in jeopardy of losing $600M income flow and having U.S. assets attached, analyzed all accounts determining precise options available.

President, 71 SOUTH 44TH STREET CORPORATION INC.   1973–Present

- **Run a premiere building—set very high standards.**

- Closely direct the managing agent and superintendent, who oversee a staff of 7 serving a 38-unit apartment building. Resulted in minimum turnover of staff; priority attention from managing agent.

- Screen all prospective tenant shareholder applicants as to financial and personal qualifications. Instituted a new way of dealing with applicants that avoided lawsuits, while maintaining apartment quality.

- As President, interface with board of directors on matters of policy, building maintenance, operating expenses, and revenues. With Treasurer, chart anticipated capital improvements and budget appropriately.

- Act as liaison with outside counsel.

- Recommended and implemented an innovative revenue concept resulting in greater financial security for the corporation.

Treasurer, THE LOGOS SOCIETY OF NEW YORK   1972–Present

- **Very much improved the solvency of this organization.**

- Manage operating budget, and track sources of all revenue and expenditures, both operating and capital improvements.

- Coordinate in-house and outside accountants. Monitor all legal and financial matters concerning gifts, legacies, and other actions affecting the organization, including contracts.

- Oversee all investments and real estate matters. Sold old headquarters, and recommended the sale of abutting property, which resulted in financial solvency.

- Monitor staffing requirements. Put in retired businessman to better run the clinic and allow doctors to serve clients.

- Individual fund-raising resulted in two $100,000-plus legacies.

- Work with lawyers on publishing contracts, leases, other matters.

EDUCATION

New York University	Graduate Courses: Business Law Accounting, Corporate Management	1962
St. Crispin University	BA, Business Admin./Economics	1959

Banking Résumé

M. ALBERTO TERLIZZI

71 South 44th Street
New York, NY 10001

Home: (212) 555-1111
Office: (212) 555-0000

SUMMARY OF EXPERIENCE

Over 20 years experience handling all aspects of fiduciary relationships for **PremierBank's private clients (175 families with overall net worth of $800 million).** Successfully increased revenue through new business efforts, client cultivation and account assessment. Consistently achieved fee increases resulting in bonus awards. Work well with high-net-worth individuals.

PROFESSIONAL EXPERIENCE

PREMIERBANK—PRIVATE BANKING DIVISION   1960–PRESENT

RELATIONSHIP MANAGER—Private Banking Division   1972–Present
TRUST OFFICER—Investment Management Group   1965–1972

Handle all aspects of fiduciary relationships for private banking clients: 175 families with overall net worth of $800 million.

- As a seasoned account officer, assigned the most difficult, time-consuming accounts that presumably had the lowest potential. Turned the accounts around. Achieved fee increases. Received bonuses.
- Recently gained an $18 million will appointment one week before person's death. Generated $350,000 fee.
- Saved family $3 milliion in taxes up front by the use of an innovative estate-planning method.
- Developed a complete estate plan for a family whose financial arrangements were in disarray: They had archaic wills and no tax planning in the event of death. Resulted in appropriate wills, trusts for children, investment account for wife with gifted securities, and a new attorney and accountant.

AREAS OF SPECIAL COMPETENCE

<u>Client Relations</u>

- Identified 50 cases (20% of account base) where client dissatisfaction existed. Identified problem areas through one-on-one contact. Instituted aggressive service campaigns and quarterly review meetings. Within two years gained confidence of 96% of dissatisfied customers. Obtained $26MM in new business and retained a vulnerable $10MM account.
- Recognized importance of interfacing with several hundred attorneys, acccountants, and financial advisers. Maintained high profile through constant contact and briefings. Won their esteem. Resulted in a greater working compatibility, efficient decision making, and new business. In one instance, obtained a $60MM acccount relationship.

<u>Consulting</u>

- Reviewed complex financial situations, weighing options vis-à-vis income payments, gifts, and estate impact. As liaison between family members, attorney, and advisers, formulated annual financial programs, saving one client $30M annually in taxes.

- In capacity as a consultant to a wealthy family in jeopardy of losing $600M income flow and having U.S. assets attached, analyzed all accounts, determining precise options available. Evolved a plan through the use of assignments and off-shore corporations to preserve income and assets.

Analysis and Planning

- Evaluated requests for special payments of capital assets and income. Processed and documented approximately 75 requests annually, with 100% of recommendations accepted.
- Developed improved alternatives to outdated operational procedures. Formulated a new plan for handling over 1,500 telephone requests during a 2-month period. Coordinated with Operation Department to establish direct customer wire into central information center, eliminating 5,000 unnecessary calls. In another instance, developed form letters reducing expense in responding by 95%.
- Analyzed 260 accounts for substandard fees. Developed a strategic plan to align revenue with services. Aggressive action and persistence resulted in fee increases, adding $200M to revenues annually.

EDUCATION

New York University	Graduate Courses: Business Law Accounting, Corporate Management	1962
St. Crispin University	BA, Business Admin./Economics	1959

ASSOCIATIONS

Director of cooperative apartment building President of Board in 1979. Operating budget $650M.	1973–Present
Director of The Logos Society of New York Served as Vice President. Treasurer in 1978. Operating budget $1M.	1972–Present

---

RÉSUMÉS FOR PEOPLE WITH "NOTHING TO OFFER"

The same strategy holds true even for those who have not worked in a very long time, or who have never worked at a full-time job.

> No one knows what he can do til he tries.
> —PUBLILIUS SYRUS
> *Maxims*

Recent college graduates, housewives, and those with very little or very low level work experience often feel as though they have nothing to offer. They think if they had better experience, they would have no trouble writing a résumé.

They are wrong. Even the most highly accomplished executives have a great deal of difficulty preparing their own résumés. Résumé preparation is a skill just as marketing or finance is a skill, and it is not something executives have to do every day on their jobs.

You are probably not competing with high-powered executives. Therefore, it doesn't matter that you haven't run a division of six hundred people. If you had run that division, you'd have other problems in preparing your résumé. It's better for each of us, no matter what our experiences, to think that we have done OK considering where we came from. Our experiences have made us what we are today, and that's not so bad. We should be thankful and be proud of whomever we are, and make the most of it. We should *each* strive—executive, young person, housewife— to uncover our special gifts and contributions, and let the world know about them.

On a national TV program, I was once asked to take an "ordinary housewife" and develop a résumé for her. It was promoted as something akin to magic: can Kate make this nothing into someone? The producers picked a woman who had been at home for twenty years—that would be a good one! Sight unseen (just like magic), I phone interviewed the woman and developed a great résumé for her.

Afterward, people said it wasn't fair: we should have picked someone who *really* had nothing to offer. Of course, in real life, most housewives are not sitting home doing nothing for twenty years. When a counselor helps a person, the counselor can find the things that person has to offer. Every housewife, every young person, has *done* things. With an open mind and the right help, they can present these things well in a résumé.

THE PROCESS

Prior to show time, I spent one hour on the phone with Angela, the "ordinary housewife," who'd had no preparation. You, however, may want to prepare by doing some of the exercises listed below. If you have trouble doing them, don't worry: you can do them together with a counselor.

1. List the kind of field(s) you think you would like to go into. **If you know the kind of field you would like to go into, that would be great. Let your counselor know.** If not, a counselor can still help you do a fine résumé.

2. **List all the work you have ever done,** before your marriage (or school) or during it. (We left out the dates on the work Angela had done many years earlier.) We want that experience to still count. It does not matter whether you earned money doing this work. For example, Angela "helped out" in her daughter's store. She didn't get paid for it, but it added a lot to her résumé.

3. List all the **volunteer work** you have done—for your church, school, for neighbors and friends. What are the things you find yourself doing again and again? For example, do you find you are always baking cakes for parties or baby-sitting or making items for church or school fairs? List these things.

4. Think of the things you have done that you **enjoyed doing and knew you did well**—whether or not you earned money doing them, and no matter what other people thought. Think of things that happened before as well as during your marriage or school years.

5. List any **organizations you have belonged to and any courses you have taken. List your most important personality traits.**

6. List your **most important hobbies, pastimes, or interests.** Perhaps, for example, you enjoy needlepoint. We had one group member whose passion was bowling—she not only bowled, but she also scheduled tournaments. She was able to make a résumé out of it, and she got a job with a bowling association.

Housewives and young people often feel as though they have nothing to offer. That's OK. Still, try to list everything, no matter how silly it seems. Then **set up an appointment with your counselor (even if you haven't done the exercises).** If you don't have a counselor, use Angela's résumé as a guide.

These are essentially the same exercises the executives do. Again, the Seven Stories exercise is the key to uncovering those things you enjoyed doing and also did well—and would like to do again. But the exercise is helpful in uncovering other things as well. Through the exercise, you will find out:

- what you have done that you are proud of. In the sample résumés that follow, each person has found something to be proud of, whether it's earning money to get through school or helping a daughter in her shop.

- personality traits that will separate you from the competition, such as the ones noted in the summary statement of Larry's résumé—productive, self-motivated, and so on—which appears on page 130.

- how to look at your work, school, and volunteer experiences objectively. In Larry's example, he spent a great deal of time analyzing the job he had. This analysis gave his résumé a lot of meat.

Even young people with no "real" work experience, or housewives who have been out of the work force for a long while, can develop strong résumés—if they can think about their experiences objectively.

And, as with executives, the experiences have to be "repositioned" to fit the target market. For example, Angela said she had helped her daughter in the store. The fact is, Angela was alone in the store most of the time. Therefore, she was "managing" the store. And when she went shopping with her daughter for things to sell in the store, they were not "shopping" but "buying."

Give it a try. With a little help and an open mind, you, too, can develop a résumé that truly reflects your skills.

> There's always a struggle, a striving for something bigger than yourself in all forms of art. And even if you don't achieve greatness —even if you fail, which we all must—everything you do in your work is somehow connected with your attitude toward life, your deepest secret feelings.
> —REX HARRISON
> as quoted in *The New York Times*

LAWRENCE A. DiCAPPA
1112 Vermont Lane
Downingtown, PA
(215) 555-1111

SUMMARY OF QUALIFICATIONS

<u>Extensive product knowledge</u> is coupled with <u>creative</u> ideas for product applications and a <u>solid history of sales success.</u> A proven ability to <u>develop sales potential in new market areas.</u> Strong analytical and planning skills, combined with the ability to coordinate the efforts of many to meet organizational goals. <u>Productive</u> and <u>efficient</u> work habits without supervision. Self-motivator and high energy.

PROFESSIONAL EXPERIENCE

A <u>solid background in sales and product experience.</u>
Additional <u>supervisory, as well as training, experience.</u>

EMPLOYMENT HISTORY

Telephone Sales Representative, AMP Special Industries   June 1988–Present

- <u>Achieved 140% growth</u> in assigned account responsibility, from $90,000 to $230,000 in the year 1989. Accounts were previously declining at 35% annually.
- <u>Developed a complete marketing program where none previously existed.</u> Program now serves as a guide for new hires and future departmental growth.
- <u>Set up and established new territory by</u>:
  — Devising a technique for <u>introducing the sales concept and then the product.</u>

— <u>Designing an introductory call script</u>—is now a standard for the department.
— Developing a <u>strategy for attacking and penetrating a customer master list.</u>
— Serving as product specialist and trainer for six new hires.
— Developing <u>complete managerial outline</u> for continued growth and success of the department.
- Finished in top three in both advanced and basic sales training classes.

Office Manager, American Excelsior Company   1984–1988
(approximately two years full-time while attending college)
- <u>Responsible for internal sales service.</u>
- <u>Purchased 70%</u> of company's <u>raw materials.</u>
- <u>Managed work flow</u> for an office of five personnel.
- <u>Coordinated the workload</u> of warehouse and trucking personnel in arranging shipments of customer orders via company-owned fleet and common carriers.

EDUCATION

B.S., Business Administration, Drexel University, Philadelphia, PA, 1988
Major: Marketing, <u>4.0 Average in Field of Concentration</u>

<u>65% of total college expenses were earned through full- and part-time employment.</u>

Housewife's Name

1234 'XYZ' Street
City, New York 11999
516-555-3456

Summary of Qualifications

The **most important highlight of your experience is placed first.** This is followed by your other experiences and skills. Perhaps you are an excellent administrator or organizer, work well with all kinds of people, or have some other special experience. Think of the best way to express your strengths.

Professional Experience

Job title or function you performed   dates or years
Company or organization name, or project your worked on

- List here some of the things you did, <u>whether or not you were paid.</u>
- **Think about what you *really* did, whether or not it was your job to do it.** It's *very* difficult to think about this yourself. A counselor can help you develop a résumé that reflects you. Your résumé will follow this format.

Another job title or function you performed   dates or years
Company or organization name, or project you worked on

- A list of things you did, **whether or not you were paid for them.**
- If the work you did was not for an organization, but was for family or friends, that's OK. We can make a résumé out of those experiences also. Example:

PTA   1976 to present

- Angela thought her PTA experience was useless. Her résumé now reflects her efforts. A counselor can do the same for you. Do *not* compare your experiences with Angela's. Comparing yourself with someone else will prevent you from thinking about those things you truly did well, enjoyed doing, and are proud of.

- Instead, **think only about yourself:** What do *you* enjoy? What are you good at? What do you do again and again? "Cater" parties for friends? Stage raffles for your church or synagogue? Have you held posts in an organization? What do others say about your work? What do *you* think? Talk, and put it down on paper.

- You are proud of your husband and children. Instead of talking about their accomplishments, talk about yours. You may be used to building them up instead of yourself. But we are trying to get *you* a job, so let's talk about you. Give it a try. Believe it or not, *everyone* comes out with a good résumé.

Coursework

List here any courses you have taken if they are appropriate.

Angela Salerno

1234 'XYZ' Street, City, New York 11999
516-555-3456

Summary of Qualifications

9 years experience in office management and the fashion industry. 10 years as an officer or committee member for a not-for-profit organization. A thorough, conscientious, and hard worker who meets deadlines and gets the job done. Works well with others, including management, peers, and the public.

Professional Experience

Salesperson/Store Manager (Part-time)   1½ years
Propaganda Boutique, **(top-of-the-line women's clothing)**
- As Assistant Buyer, went to showrooms, selected clothing and accessories.
- Managed the store. Dealt with the public. Handled complaints.

Office Manager   3 years
Micro-Ohm Corporation
Office Manager for a 30-person company.
- Kept books, did the payroll, answered the phones.
- Regular contact with clients and employees. Worked closely with President.

Bookkeeping Department
Lansing Knitwear (Also modeled clothing)   2 years
Chase Manhattan Bank   3 years

PTA 1976 to present

Over the course of 13 years, served as Vice President and on every Committee.

- Received **Certificate of Appreciation** for outstanding service and dedication.
- As **Vice President** (2 years)
  — Substituted for President. Attended Board meetings of all Committees.
- With members of the **InternationalCommittee,**
  — **Researched foreign countries.** Visited consulates. Recruited speakers.
  — **Held special events** to represent each country to the students. Served foreign foods, gave out flags, or whatever was appropriate for that country.
- As a member of other committees,
  — **Recruited various speakers** to address the students.
  — These included a nutritionist, a computer expert, a Chinese cook, experts on drug and alcohol abuse, and so on. Also had **state senators and representatives** come in to address parents' concerns.
- As PTA Liaison, regularly meet with the Principal, Department Heads, and faculty. Meetings are held to update the PTA, and to ask questions of the faculty.
- Serve as a delegate to other schools as a representative of the PTA.

RÉSUMÉ CHECKLIST

1. Positioning:
- If I spend <u>10 seconds</u> glancing at my résumé, what are the ideas/ words that pop out? (specific job titles, degrees, company names):

  _____

- This is how I am "positioned" by my résumé. Is this how I want to be positioned for this target area? Or is this positioning a handicap for the area I am targeting?

2. Level:
- What *level* do I appear to be? Is it easy for the reader to guess in 10 seconds what my level is? (For example, if I say I "install computer systems," I could be making anywhere from $15,000 a year to $200,000 a year.)

3. Summary statement:
- If I have no summary statement, I am being positioned by the most recent job on my résumé. Is that how I want to be positioned?
- If I have a summary, does the very first line position me for the general kind of job I want next?
  - Is this followed by a statement that would elaborate on the first statement?
  - Is this followed by statements that would prove how good I am or differentiate me from my likely competitors?
  - Have I included a statement or two that would give the reader an indication of my personality or my approach to my job?

4. Accomplishments:
- Within each job, did I list historically what I had done, or did I state my accomplishments with an eye to what would interest the reader in my target area?
- Are the accomplishments easy to read?
  - Bulleted rather than long paragraphs.
  - No extraneous words. Accomplishments tell *what* I did, but usually I will tell them *how* I did it during the interview.
  - Action-oriented.
  - Measurable and specific.
  - Relevant. Would be of interest to the readers in my target area. Either the accomplishment is something they would want me to do for them, or it shows the breadth of my experience.

5. Overall appearance:
- Is there plenty of white space? Or is the information squeezed so I can get it on one or two pages?
- Is it laid out nicely—so it can serve as my marketing brochure?

6. Miscellaneous:
- Length: Has extraneous material been eliminated?
- Writing style: Can the reader understand the *point* I am trying to make in each statement? (If I am hoping the reader will make a conclusion from what I have said, have I actually told the reader outright what that conclusion is?)
- Completeness: Is all important information included? Are all dates accounted for?
- Typos: Is my résumé error-free?

I told Reginald what I had learned: that in order to get something you had to look as though you already had something.
> —MALCOLM X
> *The Autobiography of Malcolm X* as told to Alex Haley

CHAPTER 12

PRECAMPAIGN PLANNING

It is circumstance and proper timing that give an action its character and make it either good or bad.
—AGESILAUS II

BOY! YOU HAVE done a lot of work so far. In Chapter 9, you selected three or four targets after conducting a Preliminary Target Investigation, and ranked them so you know which one you want as your first campaign, your second, third, and fourth. You have also developed a preliminary résumé for the first campaign. Now we will plan your *entire* job hunt, just as you would plan any other project. A planned job search will save you time. You will be able to tell what is working and what is not, and change what you are doing accordingly.

Take a look at the chart on the next page. It is a conceptual view of the job hunt process. There are no time frames for a phase. For some people, the Evaluation Phase can be as short as ten minutes. For others, it can take years. The time each step takes depends on you and the situation you face.

Do every step, and spend the length of time required for your situation. That time is not wasted. It will save time later because your effort will be organized.

Your campaigns aimed at each target will overlap. You will start one campaign, and when it is in full swing, you will start campaign number two. Each campaign will be condensed, and your total job search will be *shorter* following this approach than if you conducted all of the campaigns together.

EVALUATION PHASE
- Motivated abilities
- Work-life requirements
- Key accomplishments

TARGETING PHASE
- Ranked job targets
- Overall job hunt plan

CAMPAIGN #1 (for target #1)
- Campaign strategy
- Research of the field
- Résumé preparation
- Search firm contact
- Research of specific companies
- Research through networking
- Interview training
- Direct-mail campaign
- Ads answered
- Quality control checkpoint
- Job interviews/negotiations
- Assessment of job interviews
- Thank-you notes & follow-up
- Reassessment of situation

CAMPAIGN #2 (for target #2)
- Campaign strategy, research, résumé preparation, etc.

WEEKLY GROUP MEETINGS (2 hours)

PERSONAL DEVELOPMENT (3 hours)

CAMPAIGN #3 (optional)

*** = Quality control checkpoints. Is your campaign on target?**

WHAT A JOB HUNT LOOKS LIKE

NOTE:
*You can get a job
at any point
in a campaign.*

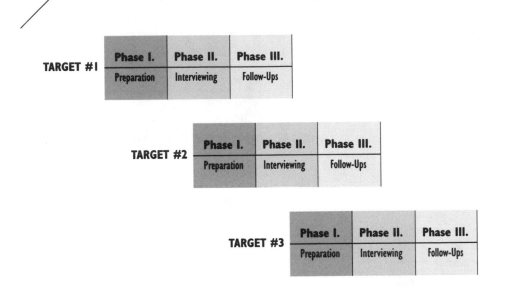

Each campaign has three phases. The first phase is Preparation; the second is Interviewing; the third is Follow-Up. Each phase should be given equal weight. *During the Preparation Phase*, you:

- research and make a list of the companies you want to contact
- develop your Two-Minute Pitch and your cover letters
- make sure your résumé makes you look appropriate to your target
- plan your strategy for getting interviews (through networking, direct contact, search firms, and ads)

When you are in the Interview Phase of campaign one, you may start campaign two.

CASE STUDY: JIM
An Organized Search

Jim, the marketing manager mentioned in Chapter 9, had targeted four industries: environmental, noise abatement, shipping, and corporate America, which was a backup target in case the other three did not work. Jim had selected thirty companies in the environmental area, and began to contact them. When he met with an environmental company, he could mention that he had "just met yesterday with another environmental company, and this is what we discussed. What do you think?" *Focusing* on one target at a time can give you credibility and information. Jim can mention other companies he is speaking with, and let a prospective employer know that he is truly interested in that industry. Focus also saves him time. It takes so much time to develop a good pitch, cover letter, and résumé that it only makes sense to sell yourself to a *number* of companies. It's too difficult to try one pitch one day and then a completely different pitch the next. It's better to completely test one pitch and have it down pat. That's why you can start your second campaign when you are in the interview phase of the first campaign.

Furthermore, a condensed campaign allows you to test what is wrong and drop what is not working. Job hunters who go after lots of different targets at the same time usually do not develop a great pitch for any one of them, and cannot tell what is working and what is not.

Jim dropped his first target—the environmental industry—except for following up on two possibilities that seemed promising. He also came up with a number of possibilities from his second and third targets. In the end, he got one job offer from each target, and never started his fourth campaign, corporate America, which he was not interested in anyway. In addition, Jim followed up on serendipitous leads, which also could have yielded something. But a focused search was the core of his campaign, with serendipitous leads on the side.

A focused campaign is shorter, even though you're zeroing in on only one target at a time (until you are in the follow-up stage, where you are following up on *all* of your targets, and generating more leads in each of them). Many executives who follow a targeted approach can cover four targets in depth in two months. And many executives have that next position within two and a half to four months!

THE TIMING OF YOUR CAMPAIGNS

> The distance doesn't matter. Only the first step is difficult.
> —MME. DU DEFFAND

In the next chapter, you will plan the strategy for getting interviews in your first campaign. Implement that campaign right away. When you are midway through it, start your second campaign—even if you do not think you will need it.

When you start your first campaign, you will be full of hope. Your résumé will be great, and you will be talking to lots of people. Some will tell you that you should have no problem finding a job. They are being sincere. But job offers dry up. What once seemed like a sure thing does not materialize.

There seem to be phases and cycles in each campaign—there is the initial rush, the long haul, the drought, followed by the first poor job offer and the later better offers. After a letdown, job hunters can lose momentum. They sometimes think they will *never* find a job.

If, however, you have already started that second campaign, you will know that those cover letters are in the mail working for you. You stand a chance of getting some response from the second campaign. You will do better in the interviews from your first campaign because you will not feel so desperate. Your second campaign backs you up.

Your second campaign could include additional people in the same target market as the first. (Do more research and get more names.) It could be a variation of your first target market (a related field or a related industry) or a new target.

I have had clients start a second campaign even when they were in the final negotiation stages of the first. Those negotiations went better, and helped them land the job because they had the comfort of knowing that the second campaign was in the mail.

If, perchance, your first campaign does *not* work, you will not lose momentum if you are already in the midst of your second—or perhaps even preparing to start your third. It is better not to lose momentum.

> Everything comes to him who hustles while he waits.
> —THOMAS A. EDISON

CUSTOMIZE YOUR CAMPAIGN

Think of yourself as a corporation. Given equal economic conditions, certain corporations thrive while others fail. Successful companies adjust their approaches to the changes in the economy. And even when the economy is at its worst, certain companies come up winners.

In many respects, job hunt management resembles the management of a company. The economy has changed dramatically over the past several years; times are more competitive—for companies and for job hunters. Whether you are managing a company or managing your own career, adjust the techniques you use.

Statistics show that certain techniques work better than others in the aggregate. Consider what might be best for you *and* your situation. The hiring system works differently in different industries and in different companies. Remain flexible: do what works in the industry and the profession you are interested in.

In addition, do what works for your personality. For example, certain job hunters phone company executives rather than using the written approach of a direct-mail campaign. What if you are the sort (as I am) who finds it difficult to make calls to people with whom you have had no

contact? Or what if you are currently employed and find that heavy use of
the phone is out of the question for you? Or it may be that the industry
you are approaching considers this technique an arrogant way to do business.

This same rule applies to the techniques you will find in this book.
Use what you want. Do what works for *you*.

A CAMPAIGN TO PROMOTE YOURSELF—JUST LIKE PROMOTING A PRODUCT

> In soloing—as in other activities—it is far easier to start something
> than it is to finish it.
> —AMELIA EARHART

Airlines run promotional campaigns to get passengers to fly with them.
Computer software companies use their promotional efforts to get people
to buy their software. You will conduct a promotional campaign to generate interest in your "product."

You and an airline go through the same steps to market your respec-
tive products:

• *An airline analyzes the market to determine the kinds of people
who are interested in its product, the number of potential customers, and
how much need there is for the product.* Analyze your market to determine
the kinds of companies that could be interested in you, and the number of
companies and the number of positions in your field of interest. Find out
how much demand there is for your services in your target market.

• *An airline defines itself by its features,* such as the kind of seating
it has, the cities it flies to, and so on—and it also defines its personality or
style. For example, an airline may say it represents the "friendly skies"
or is the "only way to fly." Or it may define itself as a bargain or as an
exclusive carrier.

Define yourself not only in terms of your skills and experience, but
also in terms of your style and personality. There are many qualified
people for each position, just as there are a number of airlines offering the
same kinds of planes going to the same cities. The difference between the
airlines is not in their basic product, but in their personality and the way
they go about their business.

You and your competition will often be equally well qualified. The
difference will lie in your style and in the way you go about your business.
One main difference in Wally's "before" and "after" résumé in Chapter
11 is that the "after" résumé has personality. It highlights Wally's "ability
to inspire workers" and says that he is an "innovator with people, processes, and equipment." Let *your* personality come through.

- *An airline test markets what it has decided to offer.* If the test results are poor, the airline changes either its basic product (such as its number of seats) or offers the same product in a way that is more attractive to the target market. It could also decide to withdraw from that target market.

Test what you have decided to offer. If it is not of interest to your target market, change what you are offering, the way you are offering it, or the image you are projecting. For example, you can change what you are offering by getting more experience or training in a certain area. You change your image by looking different or by highlighting a certain aspect of your personality that is of interest to your target market. Or you may change your promotional techniques.

On the other hand, you may decide to withdraw from that market. Perhaps it is inappropriate for you. An example is when you find your target market is in the middle of major layoffs. If you can help turn the company around, you have a chance. If you are comparable to the people it is laying off, consider a different target.

Some people pick a target and stick with it no matter what, but you need flexibility and common sense to figure out what may be going wrong in your campaign. You may need more experience, or you may need to present yourself differently. Or it may be that there is no hope of obtaining an offer in certain markets. No matter how much you may want to work for a foundation, for example, there may not be many positions available. Then, even the best job hunting techniques will not help you. Change your target.

- *An airline assesses its competition and so will you.* Who is your competition and how well do you stack up in your basic qualifications? What can you offer that is different?

- *An airline asks itself if the timing is right for a campaign it may be planning.* Consider if the timing is right for what *you* want to offer a particular market. Sometimes there is a great demand for lawyers or engineers, for example, and at other times there is a glut in the market. When the oil business was booming, there was a demand for people in that field. Aerospace engineers could once name their price. You can easily find out the level of demand by testing what you want.

- *An airline asks itself if it is worth it*—if it can afford to do what it would take to offer its product to a certain market. It decides if its return will be adequate, and it makes sure this venture will satisfy other company needs and support company objectives.

Ask yourself if it is worth it. You may find that a field is not what you thought it was: perhaps the pay is too low or the hours too long. Or the field may not fit with your long-term goals. Or it may run contrary to your motivated skills or values, or what you want in a company or a position. You can lower your expectations or you can look elsewhere.

• *There is one major difference between what you and the airline have to offer:* the airline has a lot of planes and a lot of seats, but there is only *one* of you. Be particular about whom you sell your services to. Get a couple of potential offers so you can make a comparison and select what is best for you.

WEEKLY GROUP MEETINGS

> Throughout life our internal lives are enriched by the people we have permitted to touch us.
> —GEORGE E. VAILLANT
> *Adaptation to Life*

Not everything can be covered in a book. Meeting every week with people like yourself can be a tremendous help. They will become familiar with your job search and can give you feedback on your efforts. The experiences of other people can teach you what to do when the same things happen to you. In the group, you can trade stories and techniques, and network with one another.

Believe it or not, weekly group meetings are *fun* and a respite from the discouraging job of job hunting. They can spark you on: your own situation seems less hopeless. You feel that if they can do it, you can, too.

Being in a group with your peers can be more effective than one-on-one counseling with a "pro." A group can take risks that a counselor cannot. For example, even if you have been unemployed for a while, the group may suggest that you do not take a position because it is not right for you. You can easily ignore the advice of the group if you want. A counselor has to be more careful about giving advice that can adversely affect a person's financial situation. Your peers have more freedom to discuss your needs and to give a variety of "free" advice.

In one of my groups there was a dynamic public relations man who had been unemployed for two months. The group came to know him well. He received a job offer to do public relations work for a conservative dental firm. When he told us about the offer, the look on his face clearly showed how unhappy he felt about it. Everyone knew that this would not be the right job for him, and the group discouraged him from taking it.

A few weeks later, he received another job offer—this one from a dynamic company in San Francisco. The company had been searching to fill this position for more than six months, and it was thrilled to find him. So was he: for him, the job was the chance of a lifetime.

TIME FOR PERSONAL DEVELOPMENT

> There is no music in a "rest," Katie, that I know of: but there's the making of music in it. And people are always missing that part of life—melody.
> —JOHN RUSKIN

If you happen to be unemployed, welcome to the club. Some unemployed people think they don't deserve any fun at all. But it is difficult to job hunt for a full forty hours a week.

If you have only thirty hours of work to do, you may spread it out to fill forty hours. With too much time on your hands, you may take longer than usual to write a memo or make a phone call or an appointment. You may stretch things out so you will always have "something to look forward to." You will wind up stretching out your search.

Wasting time is itself not the bad part. The bad part is losing your flow of adrenaline. Better to spend thirty-seven hours a week searching for a job and making those hours *intense*—just as you would in a real job —and then rewarding yourself with three hours of fun that week.

During a period of unemployment, I indulged myself by going to auction houses and spending the time it takes to study furniture. Auctions aren't crowded during the day, when everyone else is working. I never regretted the time I spent there. I felt I would never have that luxury again. I worked hard at my job hunt and felt I deserved a break—so do you.

But you don't deserve too much of a break. One of the worst things a person can do is start off his or her unemployment with a "well-deserved" vacation. Sometimes the job hunt never gets started. The momentum never builds. Instead, why not look for a job and take two weeks off after you have landed it? If you are unemployed, don't punish yourself, but don't overindulge yourself, either.

Job hunting is a job in itself, hard work that can be discouraging. But since you have to do it, you might as well have fun. You will meet interesting people who may become new friends. And you will learn a lot. That's not so bad.

> The world presents enough problems if you believe it to be a world of law and order; do not add to them by believing it to be a world of miracles.
> —LOUIS BRANDEIS

CHAPTER 13

HOW TO FIND THE INFORMATION YOU NEED

> The knowledge of the world is only to be acquired in the world, and not in a closet.
> —PHILLIP DORMER STANHOPE,
>   Earl of Chesterfield

MANY PEOPLE TEND to bypass the research phase of their search. They prefer simply to get interviews. This makes their search haphazard, lacking in direction. They cannot assess where they are in the search or what they may be doing right or doing wrong. They can also waste a lot of time.

THE INFORMATION YOU NEED

> Information gathering is the basis of all other managerial work, which is why I choose to spend so much of my day doing it.
> —ANDREW S. GROVE, *High Output Management*

In addition to developing a list of the companies in your target area, think of the other information you will need during your search. Much of the information can be divided into three general categories:

1. Industry or profession information
2. Company information
3. Job information

1. Industry/profession information:
- What are the industry/profession trends? What is marketable?
- What are the hot issues right now?
- What companies are in this industry? Where do people in this profession work?

- Which companies should I be talking to right now?
- Which are the best ones? What ones should I stay away from?
- Whom should I talk to, by name, at each company? What are his or her hot buttons? What is of interest to him at this time?
- What skills are hot or current? What are the buzzwords in this industry or profession?

2. Company Information:
   For each company, or for a specific company:
- What is the company culture like?
- What is it like to work there?
- What are the growing areas of the company?
- How is the company organized?
- What problems is it facing?
- Who are the strongest competitors?
- How does it stand versus the competition?

3. Job Information:
- What are the normal requirements for someone in this job? What does the company normally look for?
- What are the typical job duties?
- What does this job usually pay?
- How do I compare with others who would want this job?
- What are the job possibilities for someone like me?
- What do I have that's marketable?

NETWORKING VS. LIBRARY RESEARCH

Some people avoid research. Others spend all their time on research and avoid networking: they would rather not talk to anyone. Good research is accomplished both through networking interviews and through library and other research. It is not a good idea to try to get all of your information through networking. In this competitive market, research before a networking interview so you will get the most out of the interview and not irritate the interviewer.

WHY IS RESEARCH IMPORTANT?

> You don't just wait for information to come to you.
> —ROBERT H. WATERMAN, *The Renewal Factor*

Research is a solid way to develop a list of your target companies; then you can decide how to contact them and can measure your progress against this list. Research will improve your networking and interviewing skills, and increase your confidence during interviews. You will create a good impression, and look like an insider rather than like someone who is trying to break in. Research will give you an edge over your competition and help you decide which company to join.

LIBRARY RESEARCH

Find a university or big-city library that's conveniently located and has an extensive business collection. You will not be completely on your own: librarians are often expert at helping job hunters, so plan to spend some time with the business reference librarian. Be specific: tell the librarian what you are looking to accomplish. Get comfortable with the environment. Spend time using the reference books. Photocopy articles you can read at home.

Most job hunters need to set aside at least two full days strictly for library research. As you research, you will get a better feel for your target market. As you record information, the people you list will begin to seem more real to you, and you will write better cover letters and do better in your interviews. Lots of companies will not interest you, and you will not include them on your list. While you research, you will think of other organizations to contact and possible job targets.

Be organized about it: do not spend your time reading everything of interest in the library. Remember that you are there to do a job. Do it.

SELECTING INDUSTRIES AND PROFESSIONS

If you are not sure of the industry or profession you want to pursue, spend two days researching it. Where would you like to work: in a public or private corporation (what size?), not-for-profit (government agencies, foundations, groups to help people in need, policy analysis groups, professional and trade groups, arts institutions, academia, hospitals or other health care organizations), elsewhere? In which geographic area do you want to work?

To research professions, you can use the *Dictionary of Occupational Titles*, the *Occupational Outlook Handbook*, the *Encyclopedia of Careers & Vocational Guidance*, and trade publications and magazine articles about various professions.

One of my favorite reference books is the *Encyclopedia of Business Information Sources*. It lists industry fields, such as "oil" or "finance" or "real estate." Under each are listed the most important periodicals, books, and associations devoted to that field, so I can quickly research any field in depth. The U.S. Department of Labor also reports on various industries and professions.

AFTER SELECTING TENTATIVE INDUSTRIES OR PROFESSIONS

Once you've identified industries, tell the librarian the particular industry you are interested in. Also look at trade publications for information on the industry; you may find company names and the names of principals only sporadically, or they may have a listing in an annual issue. Use the Standard Industrial Classification (SIC) code to identify specific companies to target within the geographic area you have chosen. Look in reference books such as the *Million Dollar Directory, Standard & Poor's, Fortune* magazine, *Forbes*, the *Business Index*, or *Directories in Print*.

Do not neglect to research small businesses. Consider the INC magazine 1000 or simply be alert to small companies that get publicity or that you may hear about. Ask the librarian if there is a directory of some of these fledgling industries.

TAKING NOTES

Copy down the company name, address, phone number, size (number of employees and sales), and other relevant information (such as business type if you are not familiar with the company). Then list the names and titles of all the people you think you may want to contact.

Make note of three to five people in larger organizations who are two levels higher than you are, and perhaps the names of one or two in smaller organizations. *Many* people in one organization may be in a position to hire or recommend you. In larger companies, often the manager of one group has no idea that another manager may be considering developing a new position or replacing someone.

If you are uncomfortable writing to all three to five people at once, write to one or two, wait for rejection letters, and then write to a few more. People listed in general directories have a lot of people writing to them because their names are so readily available. Therefore, consider a targeted mailing, which takes more research per company but increases your response rate.

In a smaller organization, such as a company of two hundred people or less, the company head is likely to know of all potential openings. Who is in charge of the job openings? The president? Perhaps the general

**LIST OF
COMPANIES TO CONTACT**

> **List companies within this industry and the names
> of the people you want to contact at each company.**

For target # _____:
   Geographic area: _____
   Industry or company size: _____
   Position/function: _____

Company Name, Address, Phone	Contacts and Titles	Date & Method	Inter-view Date	Follow-up Dates

Contact Method:
**N = Networking; D = Direct Mail; S = Search firm; O = Other;
A = Advertisement; also show "R" if résumé given—such as "NR"**

manager? Note both names so you can write to both at once, or one first and the other later. Although names in smaller companies are tougher to come by, these people don't get as many letters as those in large companies.

If you are able to work in many industries, get a sense of those that are growing and also fit your needs. Make a long list of the companies that interest you. Call each one for an annual report or company literature (you can easily call thirty companies in half an hour or so). Find articles on each industry or company.

Your effort is only as good as your list. Bill had a list of sixty companies, but most were out of state and he had no intention of relocating. Only eight were within his geographic target.

Make sure your list contains companies or industries you are at least somewhat interested in. Then you'll know you are contacting eight good ones—not sixty that aren't worth your time. If you know the real size of your target, you may decide to make contact through a different technique, such as a targeted mailing with a follow-up phone call.

OTHER WAYS TO GET A LIST OF COMPANIES/PEOPLE IN YOUR TARGET AREA

You could buy the subscriber list from a trade magazine, use an industry directory or a local business publication that provides listings of companies (such as *Crain's* in New York, Chicago, and other cities), contact local chambers of commerce, or research magazine articles that cover certain industries. Do not forget the Yellow Pages as a great source of companies in your local area. To investigate certain fields, consider taking a course or contacting a professor or other professional who may be an expert.

ASSOCIATIONS

Associations are an important source of information. If you don't know anything at all about an industry, associations are often the place to start. They tend to be very helpful, and will assist you in getting the jargon down so you can use the language of the trade. The *Encyclopedia of Associations* lists a group for whatever field you are interested in. For instance, if you are interested in the rug business, there's a related association.

Call them. If they have lots of local chapters, chances are there's one near you, and it will be a great place to network. Call the headquarters, and ask them to send you information and the name of the person to contact in your area. Then call that person, and say you are interested in the association and would like to attend its next meeting. If there is no local chapter in your area, associations can still send you information. They are often very helpful over the phone, and they also have resources you may find useful.

Associations usually have membership directories, which they will sell you. They often publish trade magazines and newspapers that can update you on the business, such as the important issues facing the industry and notices about who's been hired and who's moving (perhaps you should talk to the people you read about). They may even have a library or research department, or a PR person you can talk to. Often they sell books related to the field.

An association's annual meeting is a very quick way to become educated in a field. These meetings are not cheap, but you will hear speakers on the urgent topics in the field, pick up literature, and meet lots of people.

Join an organization related to the field that interests you. Networking is expected. When you meet someone you think may help you, ask if you can meet on a more formal basis for about half an hour.

You can write to members, or network at meetings. If you want to contact them all, you either can continue to network or conduct a direct-mail campaign.

THE PRESS

Read newspapers with your target in mind, and you will see all kinds of information you would not have otherwise. Contact the author of an article in a trade magazine. Tell him how much you enjoyed the article and what you are trying to do, and ask to see him just to chat. I've made many friends this way.

MAILING LISTS

You can rent lists from direct-mail houses or magazines. For example, one job hunter contacted a computer magazine and got the names of companies that owned a specific kind of computer in his geographic area. It was then easy for him to contact all of the companies in his area that could possibly use his skills.

CHAMBERS OF COMMERCE

Quasi-governmental groups such as regional economic development groups and chambers of commerce have lots of information on companies in their area. If you are doing an out-of-town search, a chamber of commerce is often a good place to start.

HOW TO RESEARCH THROUGH NETWORKING

Networking is a great research tool. Once you have tentatively selected industries or professions, do additional research through networking to find out their buzzwords and to refine your Two-minute Pitch to that industry or for that field. People you meet through networking can introduce you to their customers, vendors, other companies of interest, current and former employees, competitors—you name it. Networking at this point may also uncover other possible targets, which you can simply add to your list of targets or research later.

While networking you may be able to get a list of people in your targeted field—perhaps an association membership list. For example, if you are interested in personnel, you may be able to get the membership list of a personnel group. Or perhaps someone will invite you to an association meeting and you can get a list that way.

Integrate your target list into your networking. That is, ask your networking contacts if they happen to be aware of the companies on your list. What are their impressions of these companies? Do they know someone you should contact there? You can also research by going to meetings where the speaker or the attendees are people who should know people in your targeted area.

ALUMNI DIRECTORIES AND ASSOCIATIONS

Think about your old school ties. Your college may have an alumni directory with a listing of where people work or what they do for a living. It is usually considered acceptable to call people on the basis of having gone to the same school they did.

IN CONCLUSION

Be creative when figuring out where the information might be or who may have it. Then go after it. Remember, do not skip the research portion of your job hunt.

> Figure out what you need to know and assume the data is out there somewhere. It usually is. Make an educated guess about where to look. Or network to find out where it might be.
> —MARK CARSMAN
>   career consultant

> A man only learns in two ways, one by reading, and the other by association with smarter people.
> —WILL ROGERS

CHAPTER 14

HOW TO CONDUCT A CAMPAIGN TO GET INTERVIEWS

The codfish lays ten thousand eggs,
The homely hen lays one.
The codfish never cackles
To tell you what she's done.
And so we scorn the codfish,
While the humble hen we prize,
Which only goes to show you
That it pays to advertise.
—ANONYMOUS

AN OVERVIEW OF THE STRATEGY FOR YOUR FIRST CAMPAIGN

If the only tool you have is a hammer, you tend to see every
problem as a nail.
—ABRAHAM MASLOW

BY NOW, YOU have done preliminary research (through networking and at the library) to determine which of your targets are worth a full campaign. You now also have a complete list of companies you would like to contact *in each of those target areas*, and, ideally, the *specific names* of the people you want to meet in each company. Direct all of your energy toward reaching them. Plan how to contact them to get plenty of interviews in your target area. Stay open to serendipitous leads, but do not let them form the basis for your search.

There are four basic techniques for meeting people in each of the areas you have targeted for a full campaign. In the following chapters, you will learn more about them. They are:

- networking (Chapter 16)
- direct contact (direct mail, targeted mail, walk-in, cold call) (Chapter 17)
- search firms (Chapter 18)
- answering ads (Chapter 19)

Do not think of these as techniques for getting *jobs*, but as techniques for getting *interviews*. After the interview, think about what to do next to keep the relationship going (Chapter 20) or perhaps to turn the interview into a job offer (Chapter 21).

Only 5 to 10 percent of all job leads are through search firms; and another 5 to 10 percent are through ads. You do not have much control over these leads: you have to *wait* for an ad to appear, and *wait* for a search firm to send you on an interview. Both networking and direct contact are *proactive* techniques you can use to get interviews in your target market. In networking, you contact someone simply by using someone else's name. In direct contact, you contact someone directly—usually after you have done some research and know something about him or her. Networking and direct contact complement each other and gain added effectiveness when used together. You may start your campaign with either direct contact (if you know your target area very well) or with networking (to research an area you don't know well or to find a way to contact people), and introduce the other technique as your campaign progresses.

Consider all four techniques for getting interviews, but spend most of your energy and brainpower on networking and direct contact.

SELECTING THE TECHNIQUES

> Do not be too timid and squeamish about your actions. All life is an experiment.
> —RALPH WALDO EMERSON

Select the techniques most appropriate for the industry or profession you are targeting, as well as for your own personality. Each technique can work, but the strength of your campaign lies in your ability to use what is best for your particular situation. Contact as many potential employers as possible and then "campaign" to keep your name in front of them.

Use all of the techniques to:

- learn more about your target area
- test what you are offering
- let people know you are looking
- contact people in a position to hire you

SEARCH FIRMS

If you are looking for a position that naturally follows your most recent one, you can immediately contact search firms. As I've mentioned, only about 5 to 10 percent of all professional and managerial positions are filled by search firms, so it would seem logical to spend only 5 percent of your effort on them. However, certain professions use search firms more than others do.

Contact reputable search firms that tend to handle positions in your target area. If you don't already have relationships with search firms, find the reputable ones through networking, by asking managers which search firms they use or recommend. Remember, search firms are rarely able to help career changers. (See Chapter 18 for more on search firms.)

ANSWERING ADS

Five to ten percent of all jobs are filled through ads. The odds are against you, so don't spend too much thought or energy on them. And don't sit home hoping for a response. Just answer the ad—so long as it sounds close to what you have to offer—and get on with your search. Maybe you'll hear from them—maybe you won't. (See Chapter 19 for the best way to handle ads.)

NETWORKING

> You must call each thing by its proper name, or that which must get done will not.
> —A. HARVEY BLOCK
> President, Bokenon Systems

Studies show that about 70 percent of all positions are filled through networking. This is partly because it is an effective technique, and partly because most job hunters mistakenly refer to talking to people as "networking," no matter *how* they wound up talking to them. For example, Pete just found a job. I asked how he got the initial interview. He said, "Through networking." When I asked him to tell me more, he said, "I'm an accountant, originally from Australia. There is an association here of accountants from Australia. I sent for a list of all the members, and wrote to all of them. That's how I got the job."

Pete got the job lead through a direct-mail campaign, *not* through networking. That's why the survey numbers are off, and that's why you should consider using every technique for getting interviews in your target market. You never know where your leads will come from.

Networking simply means getting to see someone by using another person's name. You are using a contact to get in. You want to see the person *whether or not they have a job for you.* This technique is essential if you want to change careers, because you can get in to see people even if you are not qualified in the traditional sense. To stay in the same field, you can network to get information on which companies are hiring, which are the best ones to work for, and so on.

Networking can lead you in directions you had not thought of, and can open up new targets to pursue. You can network to explore even if you are not sure you want to change jobs right now. What's more, it's a technique you can use *after* you land that new job, whenever you get stuck and need advice.

Networking is more popular today than ever before, and it is effective when used properly. But, depending on your target, it is not always the most *efficient* way to get interviews. Furthermore, it is getting a bad name because although people are constantly networking, they are doing it incorrectly. Learn how to network correctly (see Chapter 16), but combine targeted mailings (a direct-contact technique) with your networking when you are aiming at small companies or ones that have very few jobs appropriate for you. Networking your way into all of them could take forever. Also, directly contact other people when you would have great trouble getting a networking contact. If the direct contact doesn't work, you can always network in later.

When you combine direct mailing with networking, you can cover the market with a direct-mail campaign and then network certain sections of that market. Or you can network in to see someone, and then perhaps get a list of names you can use for further networking or a direct-mail campaign.

If you do not cover your market, you risk losing out. You may find later that they "just filled a job a few months ago. Too bad we didn't know you were looking." Be thorough. Let *everyone* in your target market know that you are looking.

DIRECT-CONTACT CAMPAIGNS

Writing directly to executives is a consistently effective technique for generating interviews. At least 20 percent of all jobs are found this way, and more jobs would result from this technique if more job hunters knew about it. You can write to lots of companies (direct mail) or a few (targeted mail). The techniques are very different.

Direct contact can save time. You can quickly test your target to see if there are job possibilities for someone like you. If you are familiar with your target area, you can develop your list, compose your letter, send it out, and start on your next target all within a matter of weeks. Most job hunters contact larger corporations, ignoring smaller firms. Yet new jobs are being created in smaller companies, so don't overlook them.

Direct contact is also the only technique that allows you to quickly contact *every* employer in the area that interests you. You are essentially blanketing the market. Networking, on the other hand, is spotty by nature: you get to see only those companies where your network knows someone. Direct contact is effective for an out-of-town job search. And this technique works whether you are employed or unemployed. It works for all job levels.

This technique is an effective one for career changers. You can state all the things that are positive about what you are offering, and leave out anything that does not help your case. Those things can be handled at the interview.

Direct contact can help you get in to see someone you know you cannot network in to see. Shelli, for example, wanted to see someone very senior in an industry in which she had no experience. But she knew the field would be a good fit for her—she researched the industry and figured out how her background could fit in. She targeted six companies, and was able to network into two of them. She knew she would not be able to network into the other four companies within a reasonable time frame: it would take her months to find someone who could only *possibly* help her get in to see the people she'd need to see.

Instead of networking, she researched each of the four companies, wrote to the senior people she was targeting at each company, and followed up with a phone call. Because of her presentation, three of the executives agreed to see her. This saved her many months in her search. Sometimes a targeted mailing can be *more* effective than networking in getting in to see important people. It takes more brainpower than networking, but you already have that.

Direct contact primarily involves targeted and direct mailing, but a junior person can also go from company to company to talk to personnel departments or store managers. So long as job hunters follow up, this technique can work. An executive client of mine used this technique effectively, by walking into a small, privately owned, prestigious store, speaking with the store manager to find out the name of the president, and then calling the president. It led to an executive position with that company. This was "direct contact" because he did not use someone's name to get in to see the store manager or the president. Even when I was very young, I used direct contact to get in to see virtually anyone I wanted.

Sometimes I had trouble getting in, but people eventually saw me because I usually had a good reason, did my homework, didn't waste their time, was sincere about why I wanted to see them, and was gently persistent. It suits my personality because I am shy about using someone else's name for the core of my effort, I am comfortable about putting my effort into research and writing, and I don't have the time it takes to see a lot of people who may not be right on target for me. As I go along, I network when appropriate.

Direct contact also includes cold calls, which can work for some personalities in some industries.

We will now focus on targeted mail and direct mail:

A **targeted mailing** is similar to networking. You target a relatively small number of people (say, fewer than twenty or thirty) and try to see all of them, *whether or not they have a job for you*. Instead of having a human contact, you *establish* your own contact through the research you do. The meeting is handled exactly the same as a networking interview.

Direct mail is used when you have a large number of companies to contact (such as two hundred or more). You would mail a brilliant package to all of them and expect seven or eight interviews from the mailing.

USING ALL OF THE TECHNIQUES

A good campaign usually relies on more than one technique to get interviews. Think of how you can divide up your target list. For example, if you have a list of two hundred companies in your target area, you may decide you can network into twenty of them, will do a targeted mailing (with follow-up phone calls) to another twenty or thirty, and do a direct-mail campaign for the rest. That way you have both blanketed your market and used the most appropriate technique to reach each company in your target area. In addition, you could also contact search firms and answer ads.

> Opportunities are multiplied as they are seized.
> —Sun Tzu, *The Art of War*

NETWORKING VS. DIRECT MAIL

Let's use the banking industry as an example.

You could easily network your way into a large bank. You could find someone who knew someone at a number of them. Each contact you'd make at a large bank could refer you to other people within that same bank—and that increases your chances of getting a job there. Since one person knows others within that organization, networking is efficient. You can meet many potential hiring managers within one company.

On the other hand, it may be difficult to network into smaller banks. Fewer of your friends will probably know someone there, because each small bank has far fewer employees. Each networking meeting would represent fewer jobs and fewer referrals within each bank. Referrals to other small banks would also generally represent fewer jobs than the larger banks have. It could take forever to network the same number of potential jobs at hundreds of small banks that could easily be covered by networking at large banks. Networking can be inefficient with smaller organizations, and you may find that you can't put a dent in the market.

You could contact smaller banks directly. They do not expect you to know someone who works there, so they are more open to intelligent mailings. They tend to get fewer contacts from job hunters. You could categorize the smaller banks in a way that makes sense to you—those strong in international banking, for example, or those strong in lending. Or you could categorize banks by nationality—grouping the Japanese banks, European banks, South American banks, and so on. Then you could *target each segment* with a cover letter customized for that market.

Decide which techniques are best for you. Think about how people tend to get hired within your target industry and profession. Also consider your own circumstances, such as whether you are currently employed, how much freedom you have to go on networking interviews, how much use you can make of the phone, and so on. You can always network your way into a few specific companies, but a great number is sometimes not possible.

Remember, networking requires a great deal of time and travel. Direct mail is often appealing to those who are working and must ration their interview and travel time.

A word of caution to very senior executives: Because of your extensive networks, you may be tempted to rely exclusively on them to find your next position. As extensive as they are, your contacts are probably spotty. You may be reluctant to do research, because you are used to having others do such things for you. Do your research anyway. Define your targets. List all of the companies in your target areas that are appropriate for you, and the names of the people you need to see in each of these companies. Most very senior executives skip this step, and get their next position serendipitously. That's just fine—if it is a position that is right for you. But many senior executives, in their eagerness to land something quickly, may land something inappropriate, beneath what they deserve, or nothing at all. If you have listed all of the people you should see in your target areas, you increase your chances of having a thorough campaign and you will not miss out on a good possibility for yourself.

If you can network in to see the people you should see in your target market, fine. But if you can think of no way to network in, contact them directly. You will get plenty of serendipitous leads, and meet plenty of people who have business ideas and want to form partnerships with you. These opportunities may be fine, but they are better if you can compare them with those you uncover through an organized search.

IN SUMMARY

Have a list of all the people you should meet in *each* of your target areas or, at the very least, have a list of all the companies in your target areas. Intend to contact all of them. Get meetings with people in your target area through networking, direct contact, search firms, and ads. Do not think of these as techniques for getting *jobs*, but as techniques for getting *interviews*. Plan how you can contact or meet the *right* people in *every* company in each of your target areas—as quickly as possible.

After the meeting, either keep in touch with networking-type contacts (regardless of how you met them) or think about what you can do next to *perhaps* turn the interview into a job offer.

GETTING POLISHED FOR A FULL CAMPAIGN

Before interviewing, be prepared: know exactly what you want and what you have to offer. In the next chapter, you will prepare your pitch to companies. Have your pitch ready even *before* you contact anyone—just so you are prepared. Read Chapter 23 on interviewing, and *practice*. Be a polished interviewer. Remember the cliché: "You don't get a second chance to make a good first impression."

After you have practiced interviewing, contact the people on your "hit list." Start with those who are less important to you, so you can practice and learn more about your target area. You will want to know, for example, your chances in that market and how you should position yourself.

After you have met with someone, follow up. This method works. Read Chapter 20: Following up When There is No Immediate Job, and Chapter 26: Planning Your Follow-Up. Once you have contacted a target area, contact it again a few months later. Keep following up on the people you meet.

Read magazines and newspapers. Attend organizational meetings. Keep abreast of what is happening in the field. Keep on networking.

A PROMOTIONAL CAMPAIGN TO GET INTERVIEWS

Sometimes I say to a client who is shy, "So far, you and I are the only ones who know you are looking for a job." Get your name out there. Get on the inside track. You must conduct a promotional campaign to contact as many potential employers as possible. "Campaign" to make sure they remember you.

Make a lot of contacts with people in a position to hire or recommend you. If there are sparks between you, and if you help them remember you, you will be the one they call when a job comes up. Or they can give you the names of others to contact. They may even create a job for you, if it makes sense.

The goal of your promotional campaign is to let the *right* people know what you are looking for. Some discussions will become job interviews, which will lead to offers. Get a lot of interviews so you will have a number of offers to consider. You want options.

Focus on getting *interviews* in your target area. People who focus on "getting a job" can get uptight when they interview. They do not think of themselves as "looking around" or "finding out what is out there." They act as if they are in a display case, hoping someone will buy them. They may accept the first offer that comes along—even when they know it is inappropriate—because they think they will never get another one.

If you aim to make lots of contacts and get lots of interviews, you are more likely to keep your perspective. If you are an inexperienced job hunter, talk to some people who are not in a position to hire you. Practice your lines and your techniques. Get experience in talking about yourself, and learn more about your target market. Then you will be more relaxed in important interviews and will be able to let your personality come through.

YOU ARE THE MANAGER OF THIS CAMPAIGN

> Begin at the beginning . . . and go on till you come to the end: then stop.
> —Lewis Carroll

You are in control of this promotional campaign. After reading this book you will know what to say, how to say it, and to whom. You will select the promotional techniques to use and when, and learn how to measure the effectiveness of your campaign.

You will also decide on your image. You can present any picture of yourself that you like. You present your image and credentials in your written communications—résumé, cover letters, and follow-up notes. You have *complete* control over what you put in them and how you present yourself.

How you act and dress also importantly affects your image. Look like you're worth the money you would like. Watch your posture—sit up straight. *Smile!* Decide to feel good and to feel confident. Smile some more. Smile again. Smiling makes you look confident and competent and gives you extra energy. It is difficult to smile and continue being down. Even when you are at home working on your search, smile every once in a while to give yourself energy and the right attitude to help you move ahead. This is true no matter what your level. Even executives are better off doing this as they go through their searches. The ones who cannot tend to do less well than those who can.

Whether direct contact or networking, search firms or ads, choose techniques most likely to result in a good response from your target— techniques appropriate to your situation. When you become expert, change a technique to suit yourself.

Modify your approach, or even abandon an effort that is ineffective. You want a good response from your promotional efforts. A "response" is an interview. A polite rejection letter does not count as a response. Some companies have a policy of sending letters, and some have a policy against them. Rejection letters have nothing to do with you. They do not count. Only interviews count.

This is a campaign to generate interviews. Your competition is likely to have polished presentations. Decide on the message you want to get across in the interview, and practice it. There are two kinds of interviews: contact ("networking") interviews, and actual job interviews. Do not try to turn every meeting into a job interview. You will turn people off—and lessen the chances of getting a job. *In the beginning, you are aiming for contact, or networking, interviews.* (See Chapter 16 for more information on networking interviews, and Chapter 23 for information on handling the job interview.)

When things do not work, there is a reason. Be aware and correct the situation. There is no point in continuing an unsuccessful campaign. Remember, when things go wrong—as they will—it is not personal. This is strictly business. It is a project. With experience, you will become better at managing your promotional campaigns to get interviews.

Labor not as one who is wretched, nor yet as one who would be pitied or admired. Direct yourself to one thing only, to put yourself in motion and to check yourself at all times.
    —MARCUS AURELIUS ANTONIUS
        Meditations

Although action is typical of the American style, thought and planning are not; it is considered heresy to state that some problems are not immediately or easily solvable.
    —DANIEL BELL, sociologist
        Daedalus, Summer 1967

CHAPTER 15

YOUR TWO-MINUTE PITCH: THE KEYSTONE OF YOUR SEARCH

Things which matter most must never be at the mercy of things which matter least.
— GOETHE

YOUR TWO-MINUTE PITCH is the backbone of your search—you'll use it in job interviews and networking, and in your cover letters. You'll be ready when someone calls and says, "So tell me about yourself."

Your "positioning" statement or résumé summary statement (see chapters 10 and 11) serves as the starting point for your two-minute pitch. Keep in mind:

- to whom you are pitching
- in what they are interested
- whom your likely competitors are
- what you bring to the party that your competitors do not

Don't tell your life story. Instead:

- Let this person know that you are competent and interested in the area he or she is interested in.
- Say things that are relevant.
- Come across at the right level.

If I had eight hours to chop down a tree, I'd spend six sharpening my ax.
— ABRAHAM LINCOLN

CASE STUDY: PHIL
Pitch for Target One vs. Pitch for Target Two

Here is a pitch Phil developed when he wanted a position in adult education:

> I have eighteen years experience in all aspects of education and training. I've set up and run training centers, and have hired and managed trainers. I've developed a variety of training programs—for stand-up training, video training, and computer-based training. I've developed the training materials, including the layout, the design, and the logo. I have trained over eight hundred people in individual and group programs, and have even designed and coded the student registration and grade reporting systems. I wanted to talk to you today because your company is known for its excellent training programs.

Phil met with a number of people in the training and education market, and things looked promising. But a friend knew Phil had another love: personal computers. In fact, the training centers Phil had set up and run were PC training centers. Phil's friend suggested he meet with Deirdre, who actually had a job opening. Phil was very excited about meeting Deirdre, and he and I met to prepare for this meeting.

When I asked Phil to do his two-minute pitch, he did the pitch you see above. However, Deirdre would be interested in Phil's experience with personal computers, not his background in education. How much did Phil know about PC's? A lot. "Why, I can make PC's dance," he said. "The only problem is that the hiring manager would probably want someone who could network them together, and I've never done that."

If your pitch—the way you position yourself—is wrong, everything else about your search will be wrong. Phil's first pitch is good if he wants to specialize in education, but terrible if he wants a job working with PC's. Phil needed a new pitch to suit this completely different target, and it would also be better if Phil had the experience Deirdre was looking for.

I asked Phil if he *could* network computers together, and he said, "Of course." Then why not quickly get the experience and have a stronger pitch for the interview? That night, Phil networked together the computers he had at home. Then he attended the meeting of a group that specialized in computer networking. Phil asked one of the members if he could go along on a computer networking call. Here was Phil's pitch only one week later:

> I have eighteen years experience in computers, specializing in PC's. I have built PC's from scratch, and I've done software applications programming on PC's. I also understand how important networking is. I've even networked together the PC's I have at home, and I belong to a group of PC

experts, so I always know who to call when tricky things come up. I can do anything that needs to be done with PC's. I can make PC's dance!

I'm excited about talking to you because I know your shop relies on PC's. I'd like to hear more about your plans and tell you some of the specific things I've done.

He'd managed to tailor his pitch to a specific situation. Both pitches are true about him. But each is *tailored to his target market*. In the first pitch, for example, he mentions that he has developed educational software. In the second pitch, the software application (education) is not important, but the fact that it was on a PC *is* important. Notice, however, that each pitch starts with a summary statement of how he would like the interviewer to see him, one as an experienced education expert and one as someone with PC experience.

Think through what you want to say to your target market—just as you did when you were developing the summary statement on your résumé. Think about whom you are talking to.

KNOW SOMETHING ABOUT THEM

If an interviewer immediately says, "Tell me about yourself," how will you know how to position yourself? If you don't know anything about why he is interviewing you or about the position he has in mind, you may say, "I'd be happy to tell you about myself, but could you first tell me a little about the kind of work you do here?"

WHAT POINT ARE YOU TRYING TO MAKE?

Most people write their two-minute pitch and rehearse it in front of a mirror. Say to yourself: What *point* am I trying to make? What impression do I hope they'll get about me?

Barbara had spent her life in the not-for-profit arena, and now wanted to teach grant writing. In her old pitch, she recounted the jobs she had held, and expected the listener to notice the parts of importance to them. When prodded, she admitted that the point she wanted to make was that she was seen as one of the best grant writers in the country. Her new pitch, which she used in her cover letters, started like this:

Would you like to meet someone who is seen as one of the "best grant writers in the country," and is also an excellent trainer?

I have been in the not-for-profit sector for almost two decades and have been able to attain grants for a variety of programs. For example, . . .

Ask yourself: What is the most important point I am trying to make? One client said, "I just want them to know that I have eighteen years experience in capital markets. Whether it's in aerospace or petroleum, metals and mining, or real estate—*my experience is in capital markets.*"

That's a great pitch. Why not tell them exactly that?

THEY WON'T "GET IT" ON THEIR OWN, SO JUST TELL THEM

Most job hunters think, I'll tell him my background and he'll see how it fits in with his needs. Usually, he *doesn't* see. Think about the point you are trying to make, and say it. If you have a conclusion you would like him to make about you, tell him what it is. Don't expect the interviewer to figure out something about you.

If you want him to see how all of your jobs have somehow been involved in international, say, "All of my jobs have somehow been involved in international."

If you want her to notice you have always moved wherever the company wanted, say just that. If you want her to know you have done things treasury executives rarely do, then tell her that. If you want her to see you have developed intensive product knowledge while handling various operations areas, say so. Do you want her to know that FORTRAN is your favorite language? Then don't say, "I have five years of FORTRAN experience." That's not your point. Do you want her to know that you can make computers dance? Tell her. Don't make her figure it out for herself. She won't.

Make your message so clear that if someone stops her and says, "Tell me about John," she will know what to tell the other person about you.

COMMUNICATING YOUR PITCH

Many people try to cram everything they can into their two-minute pitch, but people can't hear it. Think about those who are considered the great communicators today. We judge communicators differently from in the past. Today, our standards are based on the medium of TV. The best communicators speak on a personal level—the way people talk on TV. Whether you are addressing an audience or are on a job interview, cultivate a TV style—a friendly, one-on-one conversational style—not a "listing of what I've done" style.

The interviewer is assessing what it would be like to work with you.

Make your pitch understandable. Before people go to TV, they decide the three major points they want to make—what they want the audience to remember.

What do you want your "audience" to remember about you? Polish both your two-minute pitch and the two or three accomplishments that would interest this person. Prepare your pitch about each accomplishment the same way you prepared your two-minute pitch. For example, don't say, "I started out in this job as a trainer, where I traveled to x and y and worked on special projects, etc., etc., etc." if what you really want them to know is "That was a great assignment. My programs accounted for more than two thirds of the company's revenue." (Use a conversational tone. Speak normally.)

Many job hunters have pitches that are too heavy in content. For example:

> I have eighteen years experience in capital markets in airlines, real estate and petroleum, metals and mining, assessing customers' and prospects' financial requirements based both on the industry's point within the business cycle as well as the specific company's. I assess client credit, etc., etc., etc.

People can't listen to that. It needs some filler around the important words to resemble the way people really talk:

> I have eighteen years experience in capital markets—capital markets has always been my chief interest. I had this experience in three different areas, but the area where I spent the most time was in the airlines. I was also most recently involved in petroleum, metals and mining, and earlier on in my career, I was involved in real estate.

The new pitch is more conversational than a list, or simply getting all the facts out.

TWO MINUTES IS A LONG TIME. SHOW ENTHUSIASM

In this TV society, people are used to fifteen-second sound bites on the news. As the communicator, you have to engage the listener. Reinforce your main points. Don't say too many things. Sound enthusiastic.

If you are not a lively person, the least you can do is sit forward in your chair. I once did a magazine article on who got jobs and who got to keep them. I talked to the deans of business and engineering schools. I learned that the enthusiastic person was most likely to get the job. And the enthusiastic one got to *keep* the job later—despite the presence of more qualified people. Employers kept people willing to do anything to help the company.

Even more interesting is that this is true for senior executives. In my line of work, I sometimes have the opportunity to follow up when someone doesn't get a job. I am amazed by the number of times I was told (about people making from $150,000 to $600,000) that the applicant lacked enthusiasm: *He was managing 1,300 people, and I don't know how he did it. He just doesn't sound enthusiastic. How could he motivate his troops if he can't motivate me? Anyway, I don't know that he really wants the job. He didn't sound interested.*

Display enthusiasm. If you really want this job, act like it. It does not hurt your salary negotiation prospects.

As you practice, you will learn to see more of the job hunt process through the eyes of the "buyer"—the hiring manager. Instead of thinking only about yourself and what you want, you will think more about what the managers want and what you have that would be of interest to them.

In preparing for a meeting, use the worksheet "Summary of What I Have/Want to Offer." For each target area, you will need a different pitch —just as Phil did at the beginning of this chapter. And you will need to modify your pitch for various companies within that target. If your pitch never changes, you are not thinking enough about the person you are talking to.

SUMMARY OF WHAT I HAVE/WANT TO OFFER

For Target #1:

Geographic area: _____

Industry or company size: _____

Position/function: _____

Statement of why they should hire me (my two-minute pitch):

_____

3–5 accomplishments that would be of interest to hiring managers for this position/industry:

1. _____
2. _____
3. _____
4. _____
5. _____

3–6 personality traits appropriate to this position/industry:

_____

_____

_____

_____

_____

_____

Other key selling points that may apply even indirectly to this industry or position:

_____

_____

_____

_____

Any objection I'm afraid the interviewer may bring up, and how I will handle it:

_____

_____

CHAPTER 16

HOW TO NETWORK YOUR WAY IN

I use not only all the brains I have, but all I can borrow.
—WOODROW WILSON

NETWORK INFORMALLY BY talking to acquaintances who may know something about your target area. Network formally by contacting people at their jobs to get information about their company or industry. Networking is one way to find out what skills are needed where, what jobs may be opening up, and where you might be able to fit in. Networking used to be called "information-gathering interviews." Use the process *to gather information and to build new relationships.*

People will be more willing to help you than you might think *if* you are sincere about your interest in getting information from them, and *if* you are asking them appropriate questions that you could not find out the answers to through library research or from lower-level people.

If what you really want from them is a job, you will not do as well. At this point, you don't want a job, you want a meeting. You want to *develop a relationship with them*, ask them for information, tell them about yourself, see if they can recommend others for you to talk to, and build a base for contacting them later.

Before each meeting, write down the questions you sincerely want to ask *this specific person.* (If you find you are asking each person exactly the same thing, you are not using this technique properly.) Some examples:

THE INDUSTRY

- How large is this industry?
- How is the industry changing now? What are the most important trends or problems? Which parts of the industry will probably grow (or decline) at what rates over the next few years?
- What are the industry's most important characteristics?
- What do you see as the future of this industry five or ten years from now?
- What do you think of the companies I have listed on this sheet? Which ones are you familiar with? Who are the major players in this industry? Which are the better companies?

THE COMPANY OR ORGANIZATION

- How old is the organization and what are the most important events in its history? How large is the organization? What goods and services does it produce? How does it produce these goods and services?
- Does the organization have any particular clients, customers, regulators, etc.? If so, what are they like and what is their relationship to the organization?
- Who are your major competitors?
- How is the company organized? What are the growing areas? The problem areas? Which areas do you think would be good for me given my background?
- What important technologies does this company use?
- What is the company culture like? Who tends to get ahead here?
- What important challenges is the company facing right now or in the near future?

THE JOB OR FUNCTION

- What are the major tasks involved in this job? What skills are needed to perform these tasks?
- How is this department structured? Who reports to whom? Who interacts with whom?
- What is it like to work here? What is the company's reputation?
- What kind of people are normally hired for this kind of position?

- What kind of salary and other rewards would a new hire usually get for this kind of job?
- What are the advancement opportunities?
- What skills are absolutely essential for a person in this field?

REGARDING THE INTERVIEWER

- Could you tell me a little about what you do in your job?
- How does your position relate to the bottom line?
- What is the most challenging aspect of your job?
- What is the most frustrating aspect of your job?
- What advice would you give to someone in my position?
- What are some of the intermediate steps necessary for a person to reach your position?
- What do you like or dislike about your job?
- How did you get into this profession or industry?
- What major problems are you facing right now in this department or position?

You are also trying to build lifelong relationships. If a target area interests you, get to know the people in it and let them get to know you. It is unreasonable to expect them to "have something for you" just because you decided to contact them right now. Some of the most important people in your search may provide you with information and no contacts. Be sincerely grateful for the help you get, form a relationship that will last a lifetime, and plan to *recontact regularly the people you meet.*

Remember, you are not talking to people because "they might know of something for you." That technique rarely works. For example, if someone asked you if you happen to know of a position in the purchasing department in your old company, your answer would be no. But if they said, "I'm really interested in your former company. Do you happen to know *anyone* I could talk to there?" you could certainly give them the name of someone.

This is how people find jobs through networking. As time passes, the people you've met hear of things or develop needs themselves. If you keep in touch, they will tell you what's happening. It is a long-term process, but an effective one.

As you talk to more and more people, you will gather more and more information about business situations and careers you think you are interested in. And the more people you meet and tell about your career search, the more people who are out there to consider you for a job or a referral to a job when they know of one. But remember, they have to know you first. Networking allows you to meet people without asking them for a job and putting them on the spot. And the fact is, if they like you and happen to have a job that's appropriate for you, they will *tell* you about it—you will not have to ask.

People *like* to talk to sincere, bright people, and send on those who impress them. People will not send you on if you are not skilled at presenting yourself or asking good questions.

CASE STUDY: MONICA
Networking When You Don't Know Anyone

Monica moved to Manhattan from a rural area because she wanted to work in publishing. She found a temporary job and then thought of ways to network in a city where she knew no one. She told everyone she had always wanted to work in publishing and would like to meet with people who worked in that industry. She told people at bus stops, at church, and at restaurants. She read *Publishers Weekly,* the publishing trade magazine, to find out who was doing what in the industry, and contacted some people directly (see Chapter 17). She also joined an association of people in the publishing industry. At meetings, she asked for people's business cards and said she would contact them later. She then wrote to them and met with them at their offices.

Monica found that one of the best contacts she made during her search was a man close to retirement who was on a special assignment with no staff. There was no possibility of her ever working for him, but he gave her great insights into the industry and told her the best people to work for. He saved her from wasting many hours of her time, and she felt free to call him to ask about specific people she was meeting.

Over time, lots of people got to know Monica, and Monica got to know the publishing industry. She eventually heard of a number of openings, and was able to tell which ones were better than others. Monica is off to a good start in her new profession because she made lifelong friends she can contact *after* she is in her new job.

Using the networking technique correctly takes:

- time (because setting up interviews, going on them, and following up takes time)
- a sincere desire for information and building long-term relationships
- preparation

YOU ARE THE INTERVIEWER

In an information-gathering interview, *you* are conducting the interview. The worst thing you can do is to sit, expecting to be interviewed. The manager, thinking you honestly wanted information, agreed to see you. Have your questions ready. After all, you called the meeting.

THE INFORMATION-GATHERING OR NETWORKING PROCESS

1. Determine your purpose. Decide what information you want or what contacts you want to build. Early on in your job search, networking with people at your own level helps you research the field you have targeted. At this point in your search, you are not trying to get hired. Later, meet with more senior people. *They* are in a position to hire you someday.

2. Make a list of people you know. In the research phase, you made a list of the companies you thought you should contact in each of your target areas. You need lists of important people or companies you want to contact. Then, when you meet someone who tends to know people, you can ask if that person knows anyone on your list.

Now make a list of all the people you already know (relatives, former bosses and coworkers, your dentist, people at your church or synagogue, former classmates, those you play baseball with). Don't say you do not know enough appropriate people. If you know one person, that's enough for a start.

Don't discard the names of potential contacts because they are not in a position to hire you. Remember, you are not going to meet people to ask for a job, but to ask for information. These contacts can be helpful, provide information, and most likely have other friends or contacts who will move you closer and closer to your targets.

PEOPLE TO CONTACT IN EACH TARGET AREA

In Chapter 13, you made a list of companies you want to contact in each of your target areas. Now you want to get in to see the people at these and other companies.

For each target, list the names of people you know, or know of, or even generic names (such as "lawyers who deal with emerging businesses") who can help you in each target. Whether you contact them through networking or a targeted mailing, the meetings will all be networking meetings.

You will not be idly chatting with these people. Instead, you will have your pitch ready (see Chapter 15), and will tell them the target you have in mind. The target will include the industry or company size, the kind of possible position you would like, and the geographic area. For example:

"I'm interested in entrepreneurially driven, medium-sized private companies in the Chicago area. I would do well as a chief financial or chief administrative officer in that kind of company. Can you suggest the names of people who might have contact with those kinds of companies, or do you know anyone who works at that kind of company or a company on my list?"

Tell *everyone* the target you are going after—including people you meet on the train and at the barbershop. You never know who knows somebody.

Target #1	Target #2	Target #3	Other Names
			Such as: Dentist, hairdressser, neighbors

3. Contact the people you want to meet. Chances are, you will simply call (rather than write to) people you already know—those on your "People to Contact" list. In the beginning of your search, practice on people who know you well. If you say a few things wrong, it won't matter. You can see them again later.

But as you progress in your search, most of the people you meet should not be people you know well. Extend your network beyond those people you are comfortable with.

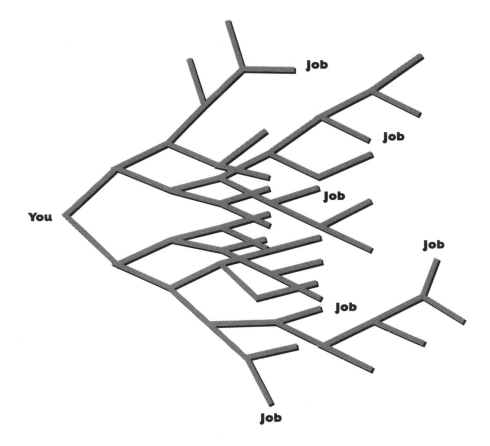

As you build your network of contacts (people you know refer you to people you don't know, and they refer you to others), you will get farther away from those people you originally began with. But as you go farther out, you are generally getting closer to where the jobs are. Be willing to go to even farther networking levels. Many people report that they got their jobs through someone six or seven levels removed from where they started.

You will probably want to contact by letter the people you do not know personally. Force yourself to write that letter and then follow up. People who are busy are more likely to spend time with you if you have put some effort into your attempt to see them. Busy people can read your note when they want rather than having to be dragged away from their jobs to receive your phone call. Often, people who receive your note will schedule an appointment for you through their secretary, and you will get in to see them without ever having spoken to them. (On the other hand, some job hunters are in fields where people are used to picking up the phone. "Cold calling" can work for them.)

- Identify the link between you and the person you wish to meet; state why you are interested in talking to that person.
- Give your summary and two short examples of achievements that would interest the reader.
- Indicate that you will call in a few days to see when you can meet.

A SAMPLE NOTE FOR INFORMATION-GATHERING

Dear Mr. Brown:

    Jill Doaks suggested I contact you because she thought you could give me the information I need.

    I'm interested in heading my career in a different direction. I have been with Acme Corporation for seven years and I could stay here forever, but the growth possibilities in the areas that interest me are extremely limited. I want to make a move during the next year, but I want it to be the right move. Jill thought you could give me some ideas.

    I'm interested in Human Resources Management. My seven years' experience includes the development of an Executive Compensation System that measures human resources' complex variables. For the past two years, I have been the main liaison with our unions and am now the head of the Labor Relations section. In this position, I managed the negotiation of six union contracts—and accomplished that feat in only ninety days.

    I'd like some solid information from you on the job possibilities for someone like me. I'd greatly appreciate a half hour of your time and insight. I'll call you in a few days to see when you can spare the time.

        Sincerely,

Enclose your résumé if it supports your case. Do not enclose it if your letter is enough or if your résumé hurts your case.

4. Call to set up the appointment (first, build up your courage). When you call, you will probably have to start at the beginning. Do not expect a person to remember anything in your letter. Don't even expect him to remember that you wrote. Say, for example, "I sent you a letter recently. Did you receive it?"

Remind him of the reason you wrote. Have your letter in front of you —to serve as your script—because you may again have to summarize your background and state some of your accomplishments.

If the person says the company has no openings at this time, that is OK with you—you were not necessarily looking for a job; you were looking for information or advice about the job possibilities for someone like yourself, or you wanted to know what is happening in the profession, company, or industry.

If the person says he is busy, say, "I'd like to accommodate your schedule. If you like, I could meet you in the early morning or late evening." If he's still too busy, say, "Is it OK if we set something up for a month from now? I would call you to confirm so you could reschedule our meeting if it's still not a good time for you. And I assure you I won't take up more than twenty minutes of your time." Do your best to get on his calendar—even if the date is a month away. (Remember that you are trying to form lifelong relationships. Don't force yourself on people, but do get in to see them.)

Don't let the manager interview you over the phone. You want to meet in person. You need face-to-face contact to build the relationship and to be remembered by the manager.

Rather than leave a message, keep calling back to maintain control. If no one returns your call, you will feel rejected. But be friendly with the secretary; apologize for calling so often. An example: "Hello, Joan. This is Florence McLaughlin again. I'm sorry to bother you, but is Mr. Johnson free now?"

"No, Ms. McLaughlin, he hasn't returned yet. May I have him call you?"

"Thanks, Joan, but that will be difficult. I'll be in and out a lot, so I'll have to call him back. When is a good time to call?"

Expect to call seven or eight times. Accept it as normal business. It is not personal.

> . . . we know that suffering produces perseverance; perseverance
> character; and character hope.
>   —ROMANS 5: 3–4

5. Prepare for the interview. Plan for a networking meeting as thoroughly as you would any other business meeting. Follow the agenda listed in step six. Remember that it is *your* meeting. You are the one running it. Beforehand:

- Set goals for yourself (information and contacts).
- Jot down the questions you want answered.
- Find out all you can about the person, and the person's responsibilities and areas of operations.
- Rehearse your two-minute pitch and accomplishments.

Develop good questions, and tailor your questions to get the information you need. Make sure the questions are appropriate for the person you are meeting with. You wouldn't, for example, say to a senior vice president of marketing, "So, tell me how marketing works." That question is too general. Instead, do your research—both in the library and by talking with more junior people. Then when you meet the senior vice president, ask questions that are more appropriate for someone of that level. You may want to ask about the rewards of that particular business, the frustrations, the type of people who succeed there, the group values, the long-range plans for the business. Prepare three to five open-ended questions about the business or organization that the person will be able to answer.

If you find you are asking each person the same questions, think harder about the information you need, or do more library research. The quality of your questions should change over time as you become more knowledgeable, more of an insider—and more desirable as a prospective employee. In addition, you should be giving information back. If you are truly an insider, you must have information to give.

6. Conduct the interview. If this is important to you, you will continually do better. Sometimes people network forever. They talk to people, but there is no flame inside of them. Then one day something happens: they get angry or just fed up with all of this "talking" to people. They interview better because they have grown more serious. Their time seems more important to them. They stop going through the motions and get the information they need. They interview harder. They feel as though their future is at stake. They don't want to "chat" with people. They are hungrier. They truly want to work in that industry or in that company. And the manager they are talking to can sense their seriousness and react accordingly.

FORMAT OF AN INFORMATION-GATHERING INTERVIEW

Prepare for each interview. The questions you want to ask and the way you want to pitch, or position, yourself, will vary from one meeting to another. Think it all through. Review the following format before *every* networking meeting. If you use it, you will have a good meeting.

- **Pleasantries**—this is a chance to size up the other person and allow the other person to size you up. It's a chance to settle down. Say two or three sentences of small talk, such as "Your offices are handsome," or "Your receptionist was professional. She took good care of me," or "You must be thrilled about your promotion."

- **Why am I here?** For example: "Thanks so much for agreeing to meet with me. Joe Brown thought you could give me the advice I need. I'm trying to talk to CEO's in the Chicago area because I want to relocate here." If this meeting is *in response to a targeted mailing*, say something like "I'm so glad you agreed to meet with me. I've been following your company's move in the international area, and thought it would be mutually beneficial for us to meet." Remind the person of how you got his or her name and why you are there, because she may have forgotten the contents of your letter or who referred you. Here are a few suggestions on "Why I'm here" (going from early on to later in the search process):

- I'm trying to decide what my career path should be. I have these qualifications and I'm not sure what they add up to. For example, I'm good at . . . What I think they add up to is . . . What do you think?

- I've moved here from upstate New York because I wanted to get into the publishing industry. I think it's important for me to meet people in the field so I can find out what it's like. Dr. Cowitt, my dentist, knew you worked in this industry and thought you would be a good person for me to talk to.

- For the past three or four months, I've researched the publishing industry and I think the operations area would be a good fit for me. I was especially interested in learning more about the operations area in your company, and I was thrilled when Helen Boney at the Publishing Association suggested I contact you.

- I have met with a number of people in the publishing industry, and I think some of these meetings may turn into job offers. I'd like your insight about the companies and which ones might be the best fit for me. I wrote to you because I will be in this industry soon, and I know you are one of the most respected publishers in it.

- I've worked in the publishing industry for ten years and have also learned sophisticated computer programming at night. I am looking for a new situation that would combine both of these areas of expertise because I find the growth opportunities are limited at my present firm. John Blazon thought you would be a good person for me to talk with since your company is so highly computerized.

- **Establish credibility with your two-minute pitch.** After you tell the person why you are there, they are likely to say something like

"Well, how can I help you?" Then you respond, for example, with, "I wanted to ask you a few things, but first let me give you an idea of who I am." There are a number of reasons for doing this:

1. The person will be in a better position to help you if he or she knows something about you.
2. It's impolite to ask a lot of questions without telling the person who you are.
3. You are trying to form a relationship with this person—to get to know each other a bit.

• **Ask questions** that are appropriate for this person. Really think through what you want to ask. Consider having your list of questions in front of you so you will look serious and keep on track. Remember: *you* are the interviewer. As the person is answering your questions, *tell them more about yourself if appropriate.* For example, you might say, "That's interesting. When I was at XYZ Company, we handled that problem in an unusual way. In fact, I headed up the project." By the time you leave the meeting, you should know something about each other.

• **Ask for referrals if appropriate.** For example, "I'm trying to get in to see people at the companies on this list. Do you happen to know anyone at these companies? May I use your name?"

This is an opportunity to extend your network. As you meet with people, show them your target list of companies, and ask questions:

"I've made a list of companies I'm interested in. What do you think of these companies? Which ones do you think I should contact, and which ones do you think I should stay away from?"

"Are there other companies you would suggest?"

"Who do you think I should contact at each of the good companies on this list?"

"Could you tell me something about the person you suggested at that company?"

"May I use your name?"

As you probe, they may respond that they do not know of any job openings. That's OK with you. You simply need to meet with more people in this industry, whether or not they have positions available: "I'm just trying to get as much information as possible."

Some job hunters get annoyed when they go away without contacts. They are thinking short-term and are not trying to build long-term relationships. Remember, you were not *entitled* to a meeting with the manager, or any information at all. The manager was being kind simply by meeting with you.

If you get no contacts, be very grateful for what you do get. Assume the manager is giving you whatever he can. It may be that the manager has no names to give. On the other hand, so many people network incorrectly (aggressively and abrasively) that many managers are reluctant to give out names until the job hunter has kept in touch for a number of months and proved his or her sincere interest. Many managers feel used by job hunters who simply want names and are not interested in *them*.

- **Gather more information about the referrals.** (Such as: "What is Sandra Bandler like?")
- **Formal time of gratitude.** Thank the person for his time.
- **Offer to stay in touch.** Remember that making a lot of contacts is not as effective as making contacts and then *recontacting* people later: "May I keep in touch with you [to let you know how I'm doing]?" You might call these people later for future contacts, information, etc.
- **Write a follow-up note, and be sure to follow up again later.** This is most important and a powerful tool. State how the interview helped you or how you used the information. Be sincere. If appropriate, offer to keep the manager informed of your progress. *Recontact your network every two to three months.* Even after you get a job, these people will be your contacts to help you in your new job—and maybe you can even help them! See Chapter 20: Following Up When There Is No Immediate Job.

Remember:

- You are *not* there simply to get names. It may often happen that you will get excellent information but no names of others to contact. That's fine.
- Be grateful for whatever help people give you, and assume they are doing their best.
- Remember, too, that this is *your* interview and you must try to get all you can out of it.
- This is not a job interview. In a job interview, you are being interviewed. In a networking meeting, you are *conducting* the interview.

OTHER INTERVIEW POINTERS

- The heart of the interview is relating your good points in the best way possible. Be concise and to the point. Don't be embarrassed about being good. Be able to recite your two-minute pitch and key accomplishments without hesitation.
- Keep control of the interview. Don't let the person you're meeting with talk too much or too little. If he goes on about something inappropriate, jump in when you can and relate it to something you want to say. Remember, this is *your* interview.

- Find out which of your achievements he's really turned on by. That's his hot button, so keep referring to the achievements he likes.
- Be self-critical as you go along with this process. Don't become so enamored with the process that you become inflexible. Don't become a professional information-gatherer or job hunter.
- Interview hard. *Probe.* Be prepared to answer hard questions in return.
- Take notes when you are getting what you want. This lets the manager know that the interview is going well, and encourages more of the same. The person you are talking to is just like everyone else who is being interviewed—everyone wants to do well.
- Show enthusiasm and interest. Lean forward in your chair when appropriate. Ask questions that sincerely interest you, and sincerely try to get the answers.
- Don't be soppy and agree with everything. It's better to disagree mildly and then come to some agreement than to agree with everything 100 percent.
- Remember your goals. Don't go away from any interview empty-handed. Get information or the names of other contacts.
- Don't overstay your welcome. Fifteen minutes or half an hour may be all a busy person can give you. Never take more than one and a half to two hours.
- If you are meeting over lunch, go someplace simple so you are not constantly interrupted by waiters.
- If you are looking for a job, don't conceal that fact.
- If the person you are interviewing suggests passing your résumé on to someone else, that is usually not helpful—unless you know who the person is and can follow up yourself. Say, "I hate to put you to that trouble. Would you mind if I called her myself and used your name?" If the manager does not agree to this, then you must accept his wishes.
- If the person you are meeting tells you of a job opening, say, "I'd like to know more about that job possibility, but I also had a few questions I'd like to ask you." Continue to get your questions answered. If you follow up only on the job lead, you will probably wind up with no job and no information.
- It is important to remember that these are only suggestions. You must adapt your own style, your own techniques. You'll find that the more you meet with people, the better you'll get at it. Start out with friends, or in low-risk situations. You do not want to meet with your most promising prospects until you are highly skilled at networking meetings. The more you practice, the better.

WHO IS A GOOD CONTACT?

A contact is any connection between you and the person with whom you are hoping to meet. Most often the contact is someone you've met in another information-gathering interview, but think a little, and you will find other, creative ways to establish links with people. (Also see the section on targeted mailings in Chapter 17.) Here are a few real-life examples:

Example one: A man's mother used to clean the office of the president of a good-sized corporation. One day the son wrote to the president, "My mother cleaned your office for twelve years." He was granted an interview with the president and shown a good deal of courtesy. This may seem far-fetched, but it happened.

Example two: Eileen wanted to leave a company where she had worked for nine years. She thought about the person who had taught her data processing twelve years earlier. Her teacher had left the company to form his own business. She had never kept track of him, but he had impressed her as worldly, and she thought he would be a good person to give her advice.

She wrote to him on personal stationery:

Dear Mr. Jones:

You taught me data processing in 1972. I remember it well since it was the start of my career, and I thought you would be a good person to give me the advice I need.

I'm interested in making a move during the next year or so, but I want it to be the right move.

I now have ten years of computer experience, specializing in financial and personnel systems. I have used third-generation languages and have designed complicated systems. For example:

• Led a three-person team in developing a human resources system that linked salary administration, performance reviews, and employee benefits packages.

• Developed a sophisticated accounting system that allowed all of the PC's in the company to access certain information on the mainframe. All departments in the company could see the same, updated information.

I'll call you in a few days to set up a mutually convenient time to get together.

Of course, the man did not know Eileen from Adam. She had been one of twenty-eight students in the class he taught at a large company, and was probably the most shy of the group. In fact, after she wrote to him, she became afraid and did not call for two weeks.

When she finally did call, she was told the business had been acquired by another firm and her former teacher had moved from Philadelphia to Chicago. She felt like a fool calling Chicago, but she finally got up the nerve.

When she identified herself to the secretary, she heard, "Eileen Lavin! We've been trying to reach you everywhere. Your note didn't contain a phone number!" The secretary said Eileen's former teacher was now a senior vice president in Chicago—and had sent the note to the head of the Philadelphia office.

When she called the Philadelphia office, the secretary said, "Eileen Lavin! We were hoping you would call. Your note didn't have your phone number."

The secretary arranged for Eileen to see the head of the Philadelphia office, who developed a job description for her. According to company policy, the job would have to be posted internally and the head of the Philadelphia office would have to interview qualified in-house candidates. After developing a job description to suit Eileen, however, the chances were good that he would not find someone internally with her same qualifications.

Eileen went to work at the company, and it was many months before she finally met the man who was her former teacher. Neither one of them recognized each other, but that was fine!

Shown on page 186 is another networking cover letter.

OTHER SOURCES OF CONTACTS:

Be sure to read Chapter 13 for lots of ideas about associations, alumni groups, and so on. In addition, you can consider:

- Contacting acquaintances—even more so than friends. Friends may be more reluctant to act as a contact for you. You are more of a reflection on them than you would be for an acquaintance. And if things don't work out, they could lose your friendship—but acquaintances don't have anything to lose.
- Network every chance you get—on the bus, at parties. Don't be like those job hunters who don't tell anyone they are looking for a job. You never know who knows someone who can help you. Everyone you meet knows lots of people.

KEN WALTERS

February 2, 19xx

Mr. Peter S. Dompster
Executive Vice President
Green Card International, Inc.
888 Sixth Avenue
New York, New York 10000

Dear Mr. Dompster:

Lucas Frybath suggested I get in touch with you.

I am a seasoned financial services marketer at PremiereBank with a strong packaged goods background, and extensive experience in product development and merchandising, branch management, electronic banking and innovative distribution planning.

- I created the PremierBank Investment Portfolio, the bank's first complete presentation of its retail savings and investment products, and developed successful ways to sell the PremierDip account in the retail setting.
- As an Area Director in the New York retail bank, I doubled branch balances in mid-Manhattan in only three years.
- Prior to PremierBank, I rebuilt the baby shampoo division for Johnson & Johnson, and managed all bar soap marketing at Lever Brothers.
- Most recently, I have been developing a set of PC-based funds transfer products for PremierBank's Financial Institutions Group.

A résumé is enclosed for additional background.

I am seeking to move to a new assignment that would take full advantage of my consumer financial services marketing experience, and am extending my search outside of PremierBank as well as inside. Lucas thought that it would be worthwhile for us to meet briefly. I'll call in a few days to set up an appointment, if appropriate.

I'm looking forward to meeting you.

       Sincerely

       Ken Walters

- Don't contact someone on the strength of *Dun and Bradstreet, Poor's,* or other directories. There is no true link between you and that person. Use your imagination to think of a better link.

OUT-OF-TOWN SEARCH

The principles are the same wherever you are. If you have targeted another city, sometimes it is difficult to get face-to-face meetings with some of the people you would like to talk to. But plan ahead. If you are making business trips to, or attending seminars or taking a vacation in, that city, think about whom you would like to make contact with there for your network. Telephone or write to him or her well in advance for an appointment. Keep your ears open about who might be coming through your area, and try to get time with him or her if you can.

SUMMARY

Networking is a powerful job hunting tool—if it is used properly, which it most often is not. It is also a life skill that you can and should use throughout your career. Become expert at it, and do not abuse people. Give them something back.

> Keep away from people who belittle your ambitions. Small people always do that, but the really great make you feel that you, too, can become great.
> —MARK TWAIN

> Business is a game, the greatest game in the world if you know how to play it.
> —THOMAS J. WATSON, JR.
>   former CEO of IBM

CHAPTER 17

HOW TO CONTACT COMPANIES DIRECTLY

I don't know anything about luck. I've never banked on it and I'm afraid of people who do. Luck to me is something else: hard work and realizing what is opportunity and what is not.
—LUCILLE BALL

BETH CONDUCTED FIVE direct-mail campaigns. She selected five clear targets and developed lists of names for each, ranging in size from fifty to two hundred names. She mailed a cover letter and résumé to her first list. When she started to get calls for interviews, she mailed to her second list. At approximately two-week intervals, Beth would send out another mailing. She received an excellent response (that is, calls for interviews) from three of her five mailings.

To develop her interviewing skills and investigate each target area, Beth first interviewed at firms she did not care about. She treated these interviews as networking meetings. Beth probed, for example, to find out what the manager thought of other companies on her list. If the comments were generally negative, she dropped those companies. If the comments were positive, she asked if the manager might know someone in that company whom she could contact. She got a lot of mileage out of her campaign because she combined direct mail with networking, and worked the system with great energy.

The entire process took only one and a half months. Beth had clear targets, followed the process, and prepared thoroughly for her meetings. She explored career possibilities she had been somewhat interested in, and refined her career direction. She turned down a number of job offers before she accepted a high-level position that allowed her to combine her strongest skill area with something that was new to her and satisfied her long-range motivated skills. Beth took a two-week vacation before she started that job. She deserved it.

Jack's campaign strategy was very different. Jack is intelligent, articulate, research-oriented—and also very shy. He targeted an industry that would result in a career change for him. He had read a lot on this industry, and wanted to find out the job possibilities within it.

Jack meticulously researched companies and selected twenty he was seriously interested in. They were huge corporations, and that made it relatively easy to get the names of people to contact. If he had simply mailed to that list, however, he might have gotten no response. As you will see later, twenty names is generally not enough for a direct-mail campaign. The effort would have been even more futile in Jack's case because he had, essentially, no hands-on experience in that field.

Jack did a targeted mailing—that is, he wrote to the twenty people, and *followed up with phone calls* to all of them. His well-written and convincing letter proved his sincere interest in and knowledge of the field. He sent it—without a résumé, because he was making a major career change—and told each of the twenty he would call him or her. He sent all the letters at once, and called every person. It was quite an effort. Jack got in to see just about every person on his list, and—as usually happens —some of them took a personal interest in his case. They gave him the names of others, and told him how to break into the field. Two of his contacts volunteered to sponsor him in their company's training program.

HOW IT WORKS

Approximately 20 percent of all jobs are found through direct-mail campaigns. This technique is even more effective when combined with networking—as both Beth and Jack did.

You will do better in your direct-mail campaign when you:

- have clearly identified your target market
- are familiar with the problems faced by companies in that market
- know what you have to offer to solve its problems

Know enough about your target market to compose an appropriate cover letter and to hold your own in an interview. If you don't know enough, learn more through library research or networking. If you feel that you may be caught off guard in an interview because of a lack of knowledge of your target market, do not use this technique until you have gained at least some knowledge.

These are not job interviews, but exploratory meetings that may lead to:

- more information (which is just fine)
- names of other people to contact
- a job interview

Conduct the meeting using the same format as a networking meeting's.

Don't tell the interviewer you blanketed the market. If a company wants to see you, quickly do a little research on it. Tell the manager you wrote to him as a result of your research, and name something specific about the company that interested you. Don't offend someone by saying you have written to everyone in the industry.

It doesn't matter if your contacts come from a direct contact or from networking. What matters is that you get active contacts with people who are in a position to hire you.

BENEFITS OF THIS TECHNIQUE

Direct mail blankets the market. In one fell swoop, you can find out what the chances are for someone like you in that market. You "market test" what you have to offer, and also get your name out quickly to prospective employers. This technique is fast and as complete as you want it to be, as opposed to networking, which is slower and hits your target in a spotty manner.

WHAT IS A TARGETED MAILING?

A targeted mailing is direct mail followed by a phone call. Use it when you would like to see every person on your small list. Research so you can write customized letters (you may want to call for annual reports, for example, or talk to people to get information about a company). Follow the process for networking, paying special attention to the follow-up call, which requires a great deal of persistence. Just like networking, you want to meet with people whether or not they have a job to offer.

AN EASY WAY TO CONTACT LOTS OF PEOPLE

Typically, job hunters do not contact many people. Either the job hunter is unemployed and has the time to contact lots of people but may be suffering from low self-esteem—or is employed and simply does not have the time to contact people during the day. The direct-mail campaign allows a person to contact lots of potential employers despite shyness or a lack of time.

Sometimes job hunters hit a slump and find networking overly stressful. Direct mail can help you get unstuck. You can hide away for a short while and grind out a mailing. You can sound more self-confident on paper than you actually feel, and can get your act together before you go out and talk to people. A direct-mail campaign can be a way out of a bind. But you must eventually talk to people. You cannot get a job through the mail. Don't use this technique to avoid people. You are writing so you can get in to see them.

THE NUMBERS YOU'LL NEED

In a small industry, your list will be smaller. In a larger industry, your list may be so large that you'll want to hit only a portion of it, as a test, and then hit another portion later.

The "response rate" is measured by the number of interviews you get divided by the number of pieces you mailed. Interviews count as responses; rejection letters do not. Interviews count because there is the possibility of continuing your job search in that direction. Rejection letters, no matter how flattering, have ended your search in that specific direction.

In direct mailing, a 4 percent response rate is considered very good. The basic rule of thumb is this:

- A mailing of two hundred good names results in
- seven or eight interviews, which result in
- one job offer.

If your list is smaller, you may still do OK if you are well suited to that target and if there is a need for your services. If, however, your list has only ten names, you must network in, or use a targeted mailing with a follow-up phone call.

Another factor that affects your response rate is the industry you are writing to. Certain industries are very people-oriented and are more likely to talk to you. Targeting industries that have a great demand for your service should result in a lot of responses.

Assuming that the job you are seeking is reasonable (that is, you have the appropriate qualifications and there are positions of that type available in the geographic area you are targeting), persistent inquiries will eventually turn up some openings.

SHOULD YOU ENCLOSE YOUR RÉSUMÉ?

If your résumé helps your case, enclose it. Beth enclosed her résumé; Jack did not. Direct-mail experts have proved that the more enclosures, the greater the response rate. You never know what may "grab" the reader, and the reader is likely to glance at each enclosure. Your résumé, if it supports your case and is enticing, is another piece to capture the reader's attention. I have been called for interviews because of what was on page three of my résumé.

If, however, your résumé hurts your case, change it—or leave it out altogether. A résumé may hurt your case when you are attempting a dramatic career change, like Jack was. (Read Chapter 2 on career changers to get more ideas on how you can support your case.)

COVER LETTERS

The format you follow for your cover letter can be essentially the same whether you enclose your résumé or not. Your cover letter focuses your pitch more precisely than your résumé does and makes the reader see your résumé in that light. You can pitch to a very precise segment of the market by making only minor changes in the letter. The format for your cover letter is:

Paragraph 1—The grabber. Start with the point of greatest interest to your target market. This is the equivalent of a headline in an ad.

If your background is enough of a grabber for the target market you are writing to, use it. For example, if you want a job in sales and have an excellent track record in that area, then open with a terrific sales accomplishment. Or if your expertise is in turnaround management, your cover letter might start like this:

> As Vice President of a $250 million company, I directed the turnaround of an organization that was in serious financial difficulty. As a result, this year was more profitable than the previous 10 profitable years combined. . . .

On the other hand, you can open your letter with a statement that shows you understand the problems faced by the industry you are selling your services to. A successful letter to advertising agencies started like this:

> Many ad agencies are coping with these difficult times by hiring the best creative and sales people available. While this may maintain a competitive edge, many agencies find their bottom line is slipping. The usual response is to send in the accountants.

These agencies, and perhaps your own, need more than accounting help. As Vice President of Operations . . .

Here's a variation on the same theme—but aimed at companies that are probably doing well financially:

I know this is a time of rapid growth and high activity for outplacement firms. I believe this is also a time when outplacement firms must be as effective as possible to maintain their competitive edge. If you are looking for new counselors, either on an ad hoc or a permanent basis, consider a person like me.

If you work for a well-known company in an area that would be of interest to your target market, you could start your letter like this:

I am presently with X Company in a position where I . . .

Perhaps your background itself would be your key selling point:

I started out in computers in 1976 and have been involved with them ever since. I am presently at . . .

If you are targeting a small number of companies, mention your specific interest in each company:

I have been interested in [your company] for a number of years because of . . .

Paragraph 2—A summary of your background aimed at a target—perhaps taken from the summary statement on your résumé.

Paragraph 3—Your key accomplishments that would be of interest to this target market. These can be written in a bulleted or paragraph format. Make them lively and interesting.

Paragraph 4 (optional)—Additional information. This could include references to your education or personality, or other relevant information, such as:

I am high in energy and integrity—persuasive, thorough, and self-confident —a highly motivated self-starter accustomed to working independently within the framework of a company's policies and goals. I thrive on long hours of work, and enjoy an atmosphere where I am measured by my results, where compensation is directly related to my ability to produce, and where the job is what I make it.

Final paragraph—The close. Such as:

I would prefer working in an environment where my leadership and problem-solving abilities are needed, and would be pleased to meet with you to discuss the contribution I could make to your organization.

Or a statement like this one—which excludes those who may be interested in hiring someone lower level:

> Hiring me would be an investment in the mid-$70,000 range, but the return will be impressive. I would be pleased to meet with you to discuss the contribution I could make to the performance of your organization.

TARGETED MAILINGS—JUST LIKE NETWORKING

Paragraph 1—The opening paragraph for a targeted mailing would follow the format for a networking letter: state the reason you are writing and *establish the contact* you have with the reader.

> Congratulations on your new position! I know you are extremely busy (I've heard about it from others). After you are settled in, I would be interested in meeting with you. I think it would be mutually beneficial for us to meet, although I have no fixed idea of what could come of it.

After you have found out something about the person or the company you are writing to, pretend you are sitting with that person right now. What would you say to him? Here's what one job hunter wrote to an executive:

> I agree. Your position *is* truly enviable.
> With the merger of AT&T and United Telecom completed, AT&T is now positioned to become an even greater force in shaping telecommunications for the future, both domestically and internationally. However, with all the challenges come the inevitable need for control, resolution of legal and regulatory issues, competitive threats, pricing issues, and reexamination of both the positioning and global packaging of AT&T. Clear, focused strategic and business plans become essential for success. I believe I can help you in these areas.

Here's another letter that reflects a great deal of thought:

> As the banks look back on their risky involvement with groups like Campeau, it is clear that a better understanding of the retail business would have saved them from considerable losses. As a result, I'm sure many banks and lending institutions have gone to the opposite extreme. Another solution, however, would be to have an unbiased expert merchant involved in evaluating their retail plans.

Your opening should reflect whatever you know about the company or the person:

> Whenever people talk about companies with excellent internal outplacement firms, Chase's name always comes up. In fact, the people who run the Amalgamated Center, where I am now assigned, speak often of the quality of your services. I am interested in becoming a consultant in this field, and I hope to meet with you.

Paragraph 2—Give a *summary about yourself.*

Paragraph 3—Note a few *key accomplishments that would be of interest to this target.*

Paragraph 4—Ask for *half an hour* of their time, and say you will *call them in a few days,* such as:

> I am sure a brief meeting will be fruitful for us both. I will call your new secretary in a week or so to see when I can get on your calendar.

or

> I hope you will allow me half an hour of your time and insight to explore this area. I will call you in a few days to set up a mutually agreeable time.

If you plan to *follow up with a phone call,* say so. But if you say so, do it —or you may get no response while they wait for your call.

VARIATIONS AND ADDITIONAL PARAGRAPHS:

For an *out-of-town search* (perhaps placed next to the last paragraph):

> As a result of many years' travel to Seattle, I would prefer to live and work in that area. In fact, I am in Seattle frequently on business and can arrange to meet with you at your office.

As we have seen, other variations include *the use of underlining key points,* which can increase your response rate and helps the busy reader scan your note. Underlining makes certain key points pop out at the reader points anywhere in your text. Underline parts of sentences in no more than five places. Read the underlined parts to make sure they sound sensible when read together, have a flow, and make your point.

Ignoring all of this can sometimes be very effective. Do what works in your target area. Nat, who was interested in Japanese banks, wrote to forty banks with a four-line cover letter that said something like: "Enclosed please find my résumé. I have had twenty years of banking experience, am mature, . . ."

Nat knew his market. He thought the Japanese would be put off by the typically aggressive American approach. He got an excellent response rate—and the kind of job he wanted.

Remember, it is sometimes better to follow your instincts rather than listen to the experts. You're smart. You know your market better than we do. Make up your own mind.

THE FOLLOW-UP CALL (AFTER A TARGETED MAILING)

When you call, you will probably have to *start again from the beginning*. Do not expect the reader to remember anything in your letter. Don't even expect her to remember that you wrote. For example, when you phone:

- say, "I sent you a letter recently. Did you receive it?"
- Remind her of the reason you wrote. You may have to again summarize your background, and state some of your accomplishments.
- If she says she has no job openings at this time, that is OK with you —you were not necessarily looking for a job *with the company;* you were looking for information or advice about the job possibilities for someone like you, or perhaps you wanted to know what is happening in the profession, company, or industry.

Leave messages that you called, but do not ask to be called back. When no one calls, you will feel rejected. However, be friendly with the secretary, and apologize for calling so often. If she would like to have her boss call you back, tell her thanks, but you will be in and out and her boss will be unable to reach you: you will have to call again. *Expect to call seven or eight times.* Do not become discouraged, but accept it as normal business.

THE MEETING

When you go in for your meeting, *handle it as you would a networking interview* (unless the manager turns it into a job interview):

- Exchange pleasantries.
- State the reason you are there and why you wanted to see this particular person.
- Give your two-minute pitch.
- Tell the manager how he or she can help you. Get the information you want, as well as a few names of other people you should be talking to.

Be grateful for whatever assistance this person gives you. People are helping you the best they can. If a person does not give you the names of people to contact, perhaps he cannot because he feels insecure in his own job. Appreciate whatever he *does* give you.

FORM A RELATIONSHIP

Take notes during your meeting. Your follow-up letters will be more appropriate, and then you will feel free to contact this person later. Keep in touch with people on a regular basis. Those who know you well will be more likely to help you.

A targeted mailing is a very powerful technique for hitting *every* company in a small target area. A direct-mail campaign hits every company in a large target. Both can dramatically move your job hunt along. Try them!

FOLLOW UP

Follow up with a customized note specifically acknowledging the help you received, just as you would after a networking interview. (See Chapter 20: Following Up When There Is No Immediate Job.)

FINAL THOUGHTS

You will strike sparks with certain people you meet. They will develop a sincere interest in you and will surprise you with their help. I have had people invite me to luncheons to introduce me to important people, or call me when they heard news that would interest me. I have even made new friends this way.

Of course, I have done my part, too, by keeping in touch to let them know how my campaign was going. If you are sincere about your search, you will find that the people you meet will also be sincere and will help. It can be a very warming experience.

> Without effort we cannot attain any of our goals in life, no matter what the advertisements may claim to the contrary. Anyone who fears effort, anyone who backs off from frustration and possibly even pain will never get anywhere. . . .
> —ERICH FROMM
>   *For the Love of Life*

> Unless you call out, who will open the door?
> —AFRICAN PROVERB

Following are sample letters from successful direct-mail and targeted-mail campaigns. Rather than simply copy them, think of *one* person on your list to whom you are writing, and think of the compelling things you should say to make that person want to meet with you. That way, your letters will sound more sincere and have more life.

SAMPLE DIRECT-MAIL LETTER

Sent to seventy people. Resulted in *five* calls for jobs—with no follow-up phone calls.

Dear:

As a fellow member of the Organization Development Network, I am writing to explore with you potential opportunities. Currently with Gotham as an internal Corporate Human Resources consultant, I am seeking an opportunity in organization and management development. Perhaps it would facilitate this process if I share key highlights of my backgound:

- Management Development specialist with over **6 years experience** in developing and making presentations.
- At **Gotham,** I am responsible for designing and implementing projects to enhance the professionalism of over **2,000 managers worldwide.**
- Hold a **degree in Organizational and Counseling Psychology.**

What do you think? Do you know of possibilities for someone with my skills and experience? I realize you are busy and I don't want to be intrusive by phoning; however, if there is an interest or if you would just like to discuss some ideas, please contact me at 216-555-1212. Attached is my résumé. I look forward to your input. Thank you.

Sincerely,

SAMPLE DIRECT-MAIL/TARGETED-MAIL LETTER

If your target list contains hundreds of companies, divide them into separate markets. Tailor your letters to each target market, such as the "inorganic chemicals industry" in this example. Add the last line for those you plan to call directly, perhaps twenty out of every one hundred mailed.

MOHAMMAD GHAFFARI

April 20, 19xx

Name
President or CEO
Company
Address
City, State, Zip

Dear Mr. [Name]:

In many companies [or, in the inorganic chemicals industry], the use of **technology has not kept pace with the expansion of markets** and the need for more sophisticated information to service those sales opportunities. The need for logical, manageable information and its dissemination is paramount in today's world. I can help you with solutions to these issues.

I am a **Senior Information Systems Executive** with experience in **managing the information needs for companies ranging from** $250 million to over $1 billion in annual sales. As a key member of the management team, I can direct the implementation of technology to achieve the profit objectives of your organization.

Here are some specific examples of my accomplishments:

- Developed a composite information data base. Resulted in **higher market share** and greater penetration into existing markets.
- Saved $1 million annually on a $5 million data processing budget.
- Consolidated the systems of $1 billion in acquisitions.

I am a strong hands-on strategic planner and leader and I would welcome the opportunity to discuss how my skills and experience could contribute to your company's objectives. I will call you in a few days to set up a mutually convenient time for us to meet.

Sincerely,

Moe Ghaffari

Enclosure

A FORMULA YOU CAN FOLLOW FOR COVER LETTERS

- Paragraph 1:
  For targeted mail and networking:
     State the reason you are writing, and establish the contact you have with the reader.
  For search firms:
     State your target (industry or company size, position, geographic area) and perhaps the salary range you are seeking.
  For direct mail:
     Start with your strongest point—a "grabber."

- Paragraph 2:
  Give a summary about yourself.

- Paragraph 3:
  Note a few key accomplishments that would be of interest to this target.

- Paragraph 4 (Close):
  For targeted mail and networking:
     Ask for half an hour of the reader's time, and say you will call her in a few days.

TARGETED MAILING

November 10, 19xx

Mr. Vincent Frank
President
Creative Concepts
155 Fifth Avenue
New York, New York 10000

Dear Mr. Frank:

Would you like to meet an effective sales professional with a successful track record in your industry? After running my own business for the last couple of years, I am considering a change. Because of the caliber of your company, I think you would be an excellent person to talk with.

I've been in the corporate communications business for twelve years as president of my own company and as a sales executive with a leading producer of industrial shows and meetings.

As head of sales for Thurmond and Osgood, Inc., I:

- Increased their business by more than $3 million.
- Initiated proposal bids for an additional $2 million of potential sales.
- Put their name on the map with such companies as Johnson & Johnson, Toshiba, Lever Brothers, CBS Records, and ABC-TV.

I would appreciate half an hour of your time and insight to explore opportunities in this changing industry.

I'll give you a call within a week.

Sincerely,

TARGETED MAILING: OUT-OF-TOWN SEARCH

RUSSELL WORTH

November 10, 19xx

Mr. Joseph Thorn
SVP & Controller
Bankers Trust
433 Market Street
San Francisco, CA 94000

Dear Mr. Thorn:

I am writing to you as I am seeking a senior financial and/or operations position in the San Francisco Bay area. Although I enjoy working for Chase Manhattan Bank, I'm afraid my 12 years in San Francisco has spoiled me forever, certainly relative to living in New York.

I am a senior financial manager with a strong background (Bank of America, Wells Fargo, Chase) in financial control and analysis, budgeting, forecasting and data processing operations. I have strong management and administrative skills, have managed large groups of people and have successfully turned around problem operations. I have an extensive knowledge of personal computers as well as data-base and spreadsheet applications.

I would very much appreciate the opportunity to meet with you for half an hour to introduce myself, discuss the current environment at Bankers Trust, and identify any areas of the bank which may, in the future, have a need for someone with my background and experience. I would also appreciate your ideas on other financial institutions in San Francisco which may offer future career opportunities.

I will be in the Bay area in early December (I still maintain my home in San Rafael) and will call you in advance to schedule a mutually convenient time. I appreciate your consideration and look forward to the possibility of meeting you.

Sincerely,

DIRECT-MAIL CAMPAIGN

Nick sent this letter to two hundred banks. It resulted in eight interviews and two job offers.

NICHOLAS AVANTI

Street Address
City, State, Zip
(212) 555-2231 (day)

May 10, 19xx

Name
President
Bank Name
Address
City, State, Zip

Dear [Name]:

Many companies' banking relationships are being disrupted because of new controls and regulations and the impact of mergers and acquisitions. In addition, frequent changes in account officers and terms of service are causing a loss of understanding between bank and customer.

Smooth-running banking relationships can make all the difference in the effective conduct of business. How can you, as President of XXX Bank, stay abreast of what is happening and even benefit from current developments?

I can help you with these issues. I offer twenty years' experience in banking, most recently as Vice President with Mellon Bank's International Department. Furthermore, few have my connections in and knowledge of the industry.

Here are two specific areas where my experience could benefit you:

Banking Relationships: I know my way around the industry and know what a bank should be able to do for its customers. My experience would enable you to maximize the services available from your bank and enhance the degree of comfort the banks feel toward you, their customer.

Assessment of Credit Risk: Much of my career has been spent in the area of credit assessment, and my broad experience could help you avoid many of the pitfalls inherent in doing business.

I have the maturity and sophistication to be able to deal with a wide variety of personalities and problems, and the persistence to see things through to a satisfactory conclusion.

I would welcome the opportunity to discuss with you how my skills and background could contribute to your company's goals.

Yours sincerely,

Nicholas Avanti

DIRECT-MAIL CAMPAIGN

Sent to sixty presidents of small/medium-sized advertising agencies or the appropriate people in large agencies. Resulted in five exploratory interviews, which then led to additional interviews and three job offers.

M. CATHERINE WENDLETON

Street Address Lancaster, PA.
(xxx) 555-2231

May 10, 1983

Dear [Name]:

Many agencies are coping with these difficult times by hiring the best creative and sales people available. While this may maintain a competitive edge, many agencies find that their bottom line is slipping. The usual response is to send in the accountants.

These agencies, and perhaps some of your own subsidiaries, need more than accounting help. As Vice President of Operations for a $10 million advertising agency, I directed the turnaround of a company that was in serious financial difficulty. As a result, 1982 was the most profitable year in company history, and 1983 promises to be better yet.

This experience has taught me what can cause an agency to get into trouble. I know the danger signs, and I can teach a company how to run itself with true efficiency and economy—not just with heavy-handed frugality. I have a record of success in making an agency run more smoothly and profitably:

- Troubleshoot in all areas of agency operations (except Creative output).
- Improved employee productivity by 30%. Reduced the number of unprofitable accounts by 83%.
- Set up a management information system that gets to the core of the problems and encourages managers to act. Cleaned up a flawed computer system.
- Dramatically reduced the number of crisis situations in Creative and the number of overbudget situations.
- Instituted a comprehensive salary and performance review system. Developed hiring procedures to reduce turnover.
- As Chairman of the Executive Committee, instituted tight budgetary controls, improved responsibility accounting, and account margin and cost controls.

I have an M.B.A. as well as 12 years of progressive management responsibility in finance and strategic planning, data processsing, personnel, and advertising and marketing.

As a result of many years' travel to New York, I would prefer to live and work in the New York area. In fact, I'm in New York frequently.

Hiring me would be an investment in the $[xx,xxx] range, but the return will be impressive. I would be pleased to meet with you to discuss the contribution I could make to the performance of your organization.

Yours truly,

DIRECT-MAIL CAMPAIGN

This same letter could be used to contact search firms. Just change the next to the last sentence to read: "If you have a search that requires these skills, I would like very much to get together."

KEN WALTERS

February 2, 19x

Name
Title
Company
Address
City, State, Zip

Dear Mr. [Name]:

I am a seasoned financial services marketer with **ten years at PremierBank** and heavy package goods experience at Lever Brothers, Johnson & Johnson and Proctor & Gamble.

My experience is in **developing and marketing financial products and services,** including electronic banking products, investment packages and basic banking services, to both consumer and corporate markets. I also have a strong track record in **building effective sales teams and turning around troubled businesses.** I am currently exploring opportunities to build a financial services business or to inject new life into an existing one.

A résumé is enclosed for additional background. If you would like to discuss the possibilities, I would like very much to get together.

I look forward to hearing from you.

Sincerely,

Ken Walters

HOW TO WORK WITH
SEARCH FIRMS

Once-in-a-lifetime opportunities come along all the time—just
about every week or so.
—GARRISON KEILLOR
A Prairie Home Companion

IF YOU UNDERSTAND how search firms work, your expectations will be more reasonable, and you will better understand how to
approach them.

Contrary to what some people think, a recruiter in a search firm does
not place hundreds of managerial and professional people. A recruiter is
generally happy to place one or two people a month.

The work recruiters do is in some respects similar to the work done
by realtors. They find positions that need to be filled (the equivalent of
houses for sale), and they find people to fill those positions (house hunters).
They try to find a match just as realtors match up house hunters with the
houses on their lists. Yet in both fields, possibilities are often presented
as "once in a lifetime" opportunities.

There are excellent search firms, just as there are excellent realtors.
But recruiting is basically sales-oriented. Therefore, the more marketable
you are, the more likely a search firm will be interested in handling you.
If you are too difficult to categorize or are asking an unreasonable price or
have other drawbacks, you will be ignored.

Make it easy for search firms to market you. Here are a few suggestions:

- Summarize your marketable characteristics in your cover letter.
  They need to categorize you anyway, so make it easy for them to sell
  you.

- Clearly state your target market (geographic area, industry and position) and your salary range. For example: "I'm interested in a financial position in the direct marketing industry in the New York or Chicago areas. I'm looking for a salary in the $65,000 to $70,000 range."
- Next, state your key selling points—your summary and accomplishments. Tell them what to say to sell you. It will make their jobs easier and increase your chances of being handled by the search firm.

Here is what may happen if you have made it easy for them. They make a few phone calls. "Joe," they say, "I've got someone you may be interested in." And then they may read from your cover letter. "He's got fifteen years of financial experience in the direct-marketing industry, most recently with X Company. He's an energetic, ambitious guy—a real self-starter. I think you may want to take a look at him. . . . Oh, I know you don't have any openings, but you should look at him—just to keep him in mind."

A WORD OF WARNING ABOUT SEARCH FIRMS

If you are belittled or badgered by a search firm, do not take it personally, but do move on. The possible damage to your ego isn't worth it. Some search firms give the industry a bad name. A recruiter may, for example, tear down your ego so that you will accept a position that is very low in salary. The recruiter will call you back in six months to a year—to "see how you're doing." When you say you're not doing so well, he will offer to "help" you again.

Search firms work for the companies that hired them, not for you. Some want the best fee and don't care about a good placement for you. Some want to place you quickly at the lowest salary level possible and move on.

Recruiters will not touch you if you are not marketable. If they want to deal with you, that should give you confidence about your marketability. Once they find you are marketable, they often keep track of you and contact you again.

If you refuse a job offer, a search firm is *not* likely to drop you. Getting an offer proves you are marketable. If you've gotten one offer, most will conclude you can get another. So don't be afraid to turn down an offer, even though the search firm will say that you'll probably have to wait a year or two for another one. A recruiter is just doing his job when he says that. Contact a number of search firms, but use other job hunt methods, too.

WHICH COMPANIES USE SEARCH FIRMS?

Search firms are used by smaller companies to replace the personnel department and to screen candidates. In addition, smaller companies are forced to use search firms because applicants don't contact them as often as they do larger companies.

Search firms are also used to fill jobs where there is a labor shortage. This could be for a specialty that is much in demand at the moment, an executive-level position, or a field that is so unusual that the search firm may have to look outside the company's normal geographic area.

To find the names of search firms, use the *Directory of Executive Recruiters*. Despite its title, it lists firms for most job levels and job categories, and also by geographic area. It is carried by many libraries, or you can get your own copy from Kennedy Publications, Templeton Road, Fitzwilliam, NH 03447.

RETAINER VS. CONTINGENCY SEARCH FIRMS

Search firms are hired by companies to fill positions. In an up economy or an up profession, jobs are being created, and search firms are often needed to fill those jobs. In a down economy or profession, search firms are not needed. Companies pay search firms about a third of the new person's salary. Retainer firms receive an exclusive assignment to fill a position, and get paid whether or not they find the person for it. Contingency firms are paid only if they fill the position, and a number of contingency firms could be working on filling the same position. The one that fills it gets the fee.

Do not send your résumé to search firms unless you know their reputation. Disreputable agencies could blanket the market with your résumé, and cheapen your value. Make sure the search firm tells you before it sends your résumé to anyone. The biggest worry for you is that the firm could become your competition: if a search firm has sent your résumé to lots of places, it will have gotten to companies before you have had a chance to get in on your own. If a company has a policy of not paying a fee to search firms, it will not consider you for a position because you were "introduced" by a search firm. If it *is* willing to pay a fee, but two search firms have sent in your résumé, the company will not hire you because it does not want to get into an argument about which search firm to pay. Simply have a search firm tell you ahead of time which companies it wants to contact on your behalf. You can find reputable search firms by asking your networking contacts for the names of the firms they use.

HOW CAN I GET THE SEARCH FIRM TO INCREASE THE SALARY BEING OFFERED?

You can't. A search firm is hired to fill a certain position at a certain salary. You thought a search firm could get you a job, didn't you? You forgot that search firms can only get you an interview; you have to do the rest yourself. Decide if you want the interview, turn it into an offer by *following up with the company, not with the search firm,* and negotiate the compensation yourself.

SAMPLE SEARCH FIRM LETTER

Search firms need to know your target: the kind of job you want and where. They also need to know your salary requirements. This letter follows our formula format from page 200.

Dear:

In the course of your search assignments, you may have a requirement for a technically knowledgeable IBM AS400-System 38 professional.

I have been both a "planner" and a "doer" of the phases of the System Development Life Cycle at companies such as General Motors and Proctor & Gamble, where I have spent most of my career. My accomplishments span the gamut, including the following:

- Evaluation of Application and System Software and Hardware;
- Installation/set up of a new computer site;
- Conversion of RPG and COBOL programs;
- Requirements for and design of applications;
- Development and programming;
- Quality assurance and testing;
- Optimization of performance for Applications and Systems.

At this juncture, after many years of commuting to Manhattan, I'm interested in seeking permanent employment in New Jersey, where I live.

The enclosed résumé briefly outlines my experience over the past 15 years. My base is now in the $70,000 range, plus the usual fringes.

If it appears that my qualifications meet the needs of one of your clients, I would be happy to further discuss my background in a meeting with you.

Yours truly,

HOW TO ANSWER ADS

Of all sad words
Of tongue and pen
The saddest are these
"It Might Have Been."

Let's add this thought
unto this verse:
"It Might Have Been
A Good Deal Worse."
—ANONYMOUS

SOME PEOPLE GET excited after they have answered an ad in the paper. They know this is the job for them.

Do not be surprised if you answer thirty or fifty ads and get no interviews. Your résumé is with perhaps thousands of other responses. What's more, your résumé is not being screened by the hiring manager.

Chances are, your cover letter and résumé will be screened by someone like a twenty-year-old I met. She reviewed résumés on behalf of blue-chip companies, screening thousands of professionals and managers in the $40,000 to $100,000 range. She decided who would get interviewed.

This young woman was good at her job, and often took a personal interest in the people whose résumés she saw—but she was only twenty years old. Writing a cover letter to "intrigue" or strike a responsive chord in her wouldn't have worked.

While intrigue, subtlety, and personality may work in direct-mail campaigns and networking, stick to the basics in answering ads. If the ad asks for specific qualifications and experience, highlight those areas from your background. Respond point by point to each item mentioned. Show how you have everything they want. Keep your cover letter crystal clear. Remember, the reader of your letter may be twenty years old. If you don't fit exactly, you will probably be screened out.

If an average ad in *The Wall Street Journal* or *The New York Times* gets a thousand responses, you have 999 competitors. Answer ads (I

SAMPLE LETTER FOR ANSWERING AN AD
WHERE YOU QUALIFY

RICHARD F. BUCKNELL

March 23, 19xx

Glenna Ambach
Employment Manager
National Data Labs
22 Parns Avenue
East Hamstart, MO 59684

Dear Ms. Ambach:

I believe I am a good fit for the Assistant Controller position that was advertised in the *Hamstart Times* on March 20, 19xx.

Having been continually challenged and rapidly promoted at Gotham, I have a proven track record in controllership fucntions. As you may be aware, Gotham has a rigorous budgeting, financial analysis and cost accounting process, similar to National Data Labs', and this has contributed to the success of the organization.

Here is a breakdown of my experience vs. your requirements:

Your Requirements	My Experience
• 12+ years' experience in private accounting/management	• 14+ years' experience in financial management
• A BBA, MBA a plus.	• BBA in Finance MBA in Financial Management
• Financial Analysis/Cost Accounting Skills	• Strong Financial Analysis skills —Controllership functions

I consider myself a sophisticated management professional with a significant number of business accomplishments, coupled with an excellent ability to communicate both orally and in writing.

I would welcome an interview with you to review my experience in financial management.

Sincerely,

Richard F. Bucknell

believe in doing everything to help your job hunt), but be clear and to the point.

If you qualify for the job, make that clear by following the format of the letter on the following page. If you do *not* qualify, use the paragraph format used in networking cover letters. If you don't get in by responding to the ad, *network* into the company or contact someone there directly (not the person mentioned in the ad).

FOLLOWING UP WHEN THERE IS NO IMMEDIATE JOB

Contrary to the cliché, genuinely nice guys most often finish first, or very near it.
—MALCOLM FORBES

DURING EACH MEETING, you have taken up the time of someone who sincerely tried to help you. Writing a note is the only polite thing to do. Since the person has gone to some effort for you, go to some effort in return. A phone call to thank a person can be an intrusion, and shows no effort on your part. Make some effort.

In addition to being polite, there are good business reasons for writing notes and otherwise keeping in touch with people who have helped you. For one thing, hardly anyone does it, so you will stand out. Second, it gives you a chance to sell yourself again and to overcome any misunderstandings that may have occurred. Third, this is a promotional campaign, and any good promoter knows that a message reinforced soon after a first message results in added recall.

If you meet someone through a networking interview, for example, she will almost certainly forget about you the minute you leave. She will go back to her business. Sorry, but you were an interruption.

If you write to people almost immediately after your meeting, this will dramatically increase the chance that they will remember you. If you had waited two weeks before writing, they may remember meeting someone, but not remember you specifically. If you waited longer than two weeks, they probably won't remember meeting anyone—let alone that it was you.

Promptly follow the interview with a note. It is important to remind those to whom you write who you are, when they talked to you, and some highlight of the meeting. Contact them again within a month or two. It is just like an advertising campaign. Advertisers will often place their ads every four weeks in the same publication, but rarely less often than that because of the drop in how many people remember the ad.

WHAT MICHAEL DID

This is a classic—and it worked on me. I wanted to hire one junior accountant for a very important project, and had the search narrowed down to two people. I asked my boss for his input. We made up a list of what we were looking for and we each rated the candidates on twenty criteria. The final scores came in very close, but I hired Judy instead of Michael.

In response to my rejection, Michael wrote me a note telling me how much he still wanted to work for our company, and how he hoped I would keep him in mind if something else should come up. He turned the rejection into a positive contact. Notes are so unusual, and this one was so personable, that I showed it to my boss.

A few months later, Michael wrote again saying that he had taken a position with another firm. He was still very much interested in us, and he hoped to work for us someday. He promised to keep in touch, which he did. Each time he wrote, I showed the note to my boss. Each time, we were sorry we couldn't hire him.

After about seven months, I needed another helping hand. Whom do you think I called? Do you think I interviewed other people? Do you think I had to sell Michael to my boss? Michael came to work for us, and we never regretted it. Persistence pays off.

WHAT TO SAY IN YOUR FOLLOW-UP NOTE

This kind of follow-up may sometimes be more informal than a follow-up to a job interview. Depending on the content of your note, you may type or write it. Generally use standard business-size stationery, but sometimes Monarch or other note-size stationery, ivory or white will do. A *job* interview follow-up should almost always be typed on standard business-size ivory or white stationery.

After an information-gathering interview, play back some of the advice you received, any you intend to follow, and so on. Simply be sincere. What did you appreciate about the time the person spent with you? Did you get good advice that you intend to follow? Say so. Were you inspired? Encouraged? Awakened? Say so.

If you think there were sparks between you and the person you met with, be sure to say that you will keep in touch. Then do it. Follow-up letters don't have to be long, but they do have to be personal. Make sure the letters you write could not be sent to someone else on your list.

SAMPLE FOLLOW-UP TO A NETWORKING MEETING

KEN WALTERS

To: Gerry Ghaffari:

Thanks again for contacting Brendan for me, and for providing all those excellent contact names.

There's such a wealth of good ideas in that list that it will take me a while to follow up on all of them, but I'm getting hard at it and will let you know what develops.

Again, thanks for your extraordinary effort. (By the way, should you ever want to "review your career options," I would be delighted to share a few names, or more than a few, with you.)

Stay tuned!

Ken

JANE WESTFALL

163 York Avenue - 12B
New York, New York, 10000
(212) 555-2231 (day)
(212) 555-1674 (message)

June 25, 19xx

Ms. Sandra Bandler
Director of Outplacement
Chase Manhattan Bank
8 Pine Street
New York, NY 10001

Dear Ms. Smith

Thanks so much for seeing me. Your center is very impressive and seems very well run. But of course, that's what I had heard before I met you.

As you suggested, I sent for information on ASTD, and was pleasantly surprised to see your name in there! It sounds like a great organization, and I can't wait until they start to have meetings again in the fall.

I will definitely follow up with Gloria, and appreciate your giving me her name. I've called her a few times, but she and I are very busy.

After I left your place, I wished I had asked you more about your own career. It was only at the very end that you brought up the interesting way you got your job. I had wrongly assumed that you came up through the ranks at Chase. Perhaps some other time I can hear the rest of the story.

I will keep you posted regarding my activities, and perhaps I'll even run into you at ASTD meetings.

Thanks again for your time and insight. Till we meet again.

Cordially,

Jane Westfall

To keep in touch, simply let interviewers/network contacts know how you are doing. Tell them whom you are seeing and what your plans are. Some people, seeing your sincerity, will keep sending you leads or other information.

It's never too late to follow up. For example: "I met you a year ago and am still impressed by. . . . Since then I have . . . and would be interested in getting together with you again to discuss these new developments." Make new contacts. Recontact old ones by writing a "status report" every two months of how well you are doing in your search. *Keeping up with old networking contacts is as important as making new ones.*

Some job hunters use this as an opportunity to write a proposal. During the meeting, you may have learned something about the company's problems. Writing a proposal to solve them may create a job for yourself. Patricia had a networking meeting with a small company where she learned that it wanted to expand the business from $5 million to $50 million. She came up with lots of ideas about how that could be done—with her help, of course—and called to set up a meeting to review her ideas. She went over the proposal with them, and they created a position for her.

However, you are not trying to turn every networking meeting into a job possibility. You *are* trying to form lifelong relationships with people. Experts say that most successful employees form steady, long-term relationships with lots of people and keep in touch regularly throughout their careers. These people will keep you up to date in a changing economy, tell you about changes or openings in your field, and generally be your long-term ally. And you will do the same for them.

Has a man gained anything who has received a hundred favors and rendered none? He is great who confers the most benefits.
—RALPH WALDO EMERSON
"Essay on Compensation"

HOW TO HANDLE REJECTION LETTERS

In nature, there are neither rewards nor punishments—there are consequences.
—ROBERT GREEN INGERSOLL

COMPANIES GENERALLY SEND the same rejection letter to everyone. These letters often compliment the applicant on his or her credentials and offer regret that there are no appropriate openings at that time. It is important to realize that **a rejection letter is truly a rejection only when it follows an interview.**

REJECTION LETTERS IN RESPONSE TO A DIRECT-MAIL CAMPAIGN

If you received a respectable response rate from your campaign, try another campaign of the remaining companies in a few months. Direct marketers say you should then expect approximately half the response you got with your first mailing. As an alternative, network into the companies that interest you, contact someone else in the same firm, or use a targeted-mailing approach.

If your response rate from your mailing was poor, you picked the wrong market for what you have to offer, or the package you sent was lacking. Chances are, you were not as knowledgeable about this market as you thought. Research or network to learn more, or network to find out what was wrong with your package.

REJECTION LETTER IN RESPONSE TO AN AD

This is par for the course. The company probably received a thousand résumés. Or perhaps the ad was not for a legitimate opening.

If a company name was listed, network in, do a targeted mailing to someone who could be the hiring manager, or contact a search firm that handles the type of position mentioned. Your résumé was probably rejected by someone other than the hiring manager, so it's worth further effort if you're interested in the position. Some companies have a policy of immediately sending out rejection letters to everyone. Then they call those people they're interested in—even though the applicants have already been "rejected." For companies that always send rejection letters, this approach saves time.

REJECTION LETTER IN RESPONSE TO A NETWORKING CONTACT YOU TRIED TO MAKE

The person did not understand that what you wanted was information. If many people respond to you this way, reassess your approach to networking.

REJECTION LETTER FOLLOWING A JOB INTERVIEW

This is a true rejection letter. It used to be that it took seven job interviews to get one offer. That figure may now be higher. If you are still interested in the company, don't give up. (Read what Michael did in Chapter 20: Following Up When There Is No Immediate Job.)

LESSONS TO LEARN

When you get a rejection note in response to an interview, think about it. How interested are you in that firm? Did you hit it off with the interviewer? If you think there was some mutual interest, see if there might be other jobs with the company later—perhaps in another department. Or perhaps the person hired instead of you might not work out. Keep in touch. People rarely do, but we all like to hire people who truly want to work for us.

CASE STUDY: STAN
Turning a Rejection into an Offer

Stan was told an offer was being made to another candidate. He was crushed, but he immediately dashed off a letter to the hiring manager and hand-delivered it. A brief letter, it said, in part:

> I was disappointed to hear that you have offered the position to someone else. I truly believe I am right for the position, and wish you would keep me in mind anyway. You never know—something could happen to the new person, and you may need a replacement. Please consider me no matter when this may occur, because I believe I belong at your institution.

The next day, Stan received a call with an offer. Some people may think the offer to the other candidate fell through. However, I believe Stan's letter influenced the hiring manager. When he saw Stan's letter, he thought to himself, We're offering the position to the wrong person! and he allowed the negotiation with the other candidate to lapse.

CHAPTER 22

CONTROLLING YOUR CAMPAIGN AND DEVELOPING MOMENTUM

There is a tide in the affairs of men,
Which, taken at the flood, leads on to fortune;
On such a sea we are now afloat;
And we must take the current when it serves,
Or lose our ventures.
     —SHAKESPEARE
     Julius Caesar

CONTROLLING YOUR CAMPAIGN

YOUR OVERALL CAMPAIGN can be managed with just a few important worksheets. Use the Interview Record (in Chapter 26) for *every* meeting—both networking and job. Consider using a separate calendar to record your search activities—so it will be clear to you how much (or how little) you are doing. Use the Contact List (from Chapter 16) to keep track of whom you have contacted in each of your targets. Finally, and most important, list the six to ten things you have in the works on the Measuring the Effectiveness of Your Job Hunt worksheet in this chapter.

ARE YOU CONDUCTING A GOOD CAMPAIGN? MEASURING THE *QUALITY* OF YOUR CAMPAIGN

When you are networking, do people say, "Boy, I wish I had an opening. I'd sure like to have someone like you here"?

Getting a job offer is not the way to test the quality of your campaign. A real test is when people say they'd want you—but not now. Then you are interviewing well with the right people. All you need now are luck and timing to help you contact (recontact) the right people when they also have a need.

If people are not saying they want you, find out why. Are you inappropriate for this target? Are you aiming at the wrong targets? Or perhaps you seem like an outsider.

During the beginning of your search, you are gathering information to find out how things work. You look like an outsider, and outsiders are rarely given a break. Why should someone hire an outsider? There are lots of competent people who have the experience and can prove they will do a good job.

If you think you are in the right target, talking to people at the right level, and are not early on in your search, you need feedback. Ask people, "If you had an opening, would you consider hiring someone like me?"

Become an insider—a competent person who can prove that she has somehow already done what the interviewer needs. Prove that you can do the job, and that the interviewer is not taking a chance by hiring you.

MEASURING THE *QUANTITY* OF YOUR CAMPAIGN

You need to find a lot of people who would hire you if they could. You know by now that you should always have six to ten contacts in the works at all times. This is the only true measure of the effectiveness of your campaign to get interviews in your target area. If you have fewer than this, get more. You will be more attractive to hiring managers, will interview better, and will lower the chances of losing momentum if your best lead falls apart.

Use the worksheet Measuring the Effectiveness of Your Job Hunt. It contains your current list of active contacts. At the beginning of your search, these will simply be networking contacts with whom you want to keep in touch. At that stage, your goal is to come up with six to ten contacts you want to recontact later, perhaps every two months. In the middle of your search, the quality of your list will change. The names will be of the right people at the right level in the right companies. Finally, the six to ten names will represent prospective *job* possibilities that you are trying to move along.

If you have six to ten job possibilities in the works, a good number of them will fall away through no fault of your own (job freezes, or the hiring manager changing his/her mind about the kind of person they want). Then you'll need to get more possibilities in the works. With this critical mass of ongoing possible positions, you stand a chance of getting a number of offers and landing the kind of job you want.

DEVELOPING MOMENTUM IN YOUR SEARCH

A campaign builds to a pitch. The parts begin to help one another. You focus less on making a particular technique work and more on the situation you happen to be in. This chapter gives you a feel for a real campaign.

In your promotional campaign to get interviews, you see people who are in a position to hire you or recommend you. Keep in touch with them so they will . . .

- think of you when a job opens up, or
- invite you to create a job for yourself, or
- upgrade an opening to better suit you, or
- give you information to help you in your search

When you are in the heat of a real campaign, a critical mass of activity builds, so you start:

- hearing the same names
- seeing the same people
- contributing as much as you are getting
- writing proposals
- getting back to people quickly
- feeling a sense of urgency about this industry
- writing follow-up letters, making follow-up phone calls

MEASURING THE EFFECTIVENESS OF YOUR JOB HUNT
(Your current list of active contacts)

Measure the effectiveness of your job hunt by *listing the number of people you are currently in contact with on an ongoing basis,* either by phone or mail, who are in a position to hire you or recommend that you be hired. The rule of thumb is this: if you are seriously job hunting, **you should have six to ten active contacts going at one time.** Keep adding names to your list, because certain people will become inappropriate. Cross their names off. You should probably have some contact once every month or two with the people who remain on your list.

For target # _____:

Geographic area: _____
Industry or company size: _____
Position/function: _____

Name of Contact	Company	Position	Date of Last Contact	Targeted Date of Next Contact
1.				
2.				
3.				
4.				
5.				
6.				
7.				
8.				
9.				
10.				
11.				
12.				
13.				
14.				
15.				

HOW YOU KNOW YOU ARE IN A CAMPAIGN:

- You feel as though you know a critical mass of people in that industry.
- When you "interview," you contribute as much as you take away. Your information about the industry puts you on a par with the interviewer—and you share that information.
- You are a contributor—an insider. You know what's going on.
- You feel some urgency and are more serious about this industry. You are no longer simply "looking around"—playing it cool. You are more intense. You don't want anything to stand in your way, because you know that this is what you want.
- You become more aware of any little thing that can help you get in. Your judgment becomes more finely tuned. Things seem to fall into place.
- You are working harder at this than you ever could have imagined. You read everything. You develop proposals almost overnight and hand-deliver them.
- Your campaign is taking on a life of its own. At organizational meetings, you seem to know everybody. They know you are one of them and are simply waiting for the right break. When someone mentions a name, you have already met that person and are keeping in touch with him or her.
- The basic job hunting "techniques" no longer apply. You are in a different realm, and you feel it. This is a real campaign.

> . . . the secret is to have the courage to live. If you have that, everything will sooner or later change.
> —JAMES SALTER, *Light Years*

Eventually, and often after the survival of a long and profound crisis, often after the painful shedding of one skin and the gradual growth of another, comes the realization that the world is essentially neutral. The world doesn't care, and is responsible neither for one's spiritual failures nor for one's successes. This discovery can come as a profound relief, because it is no longer necessary to spend so much energy shoring up the self, and because the world emerges as a broader, more interesting, sweeter place through which to move. The fog lifts, as it were.
—FRANK CONROY, *New York Times Book Review*, January 1, 1989

PART FOUR

GETTING WHAT YOU WANT

HOW TO INTERVIEW AND NEGOTIATE

All my life people have said I wasn't going to make it.
—TED TURNER
CEO, Turner Enterprises

HOW TO HANDLE THE INTERVIEW

Just know your lines and don't bump into the furniture.
—SPENCER TRACY

AN INTERVIEW IS not simply a conversation; it's show time, folks. You will be competing against people who are well rehearsed and who know their lines.

DEVELOP YOUR LINES

In an interview, an inability to express yourself clearly is worse than a lack of experience. Refine your sales pitch by listing on a three-by-five card:

- the main reason the employer would want to hire you
- your "pitch," or summary statement: what you have to offer in the way of experience, credentials, and personality
- two key accomplishments to support your interest in this position
- an answer to what you think might be the employer's main objection to you, if any
- a statement of why you want to work for this company

Keep this card in your pocket and review it just before going in for the interview, so you will know your lines. Then you can concentrate on the interviewer and the problem areas he or she may be facing. You can ask:

- What are the major problems you seem to be facing right now?
- What are your most important goals?
- What is standing in the way of your reaching those goals?

LOOK AND ACT THE PART

Remember, this is show biz. Even if you don't feel self-confident, act as if you do. If you come in looking defeated, like a loser, why would anyone want to hire you? Managers don't want to hire people with problems. Act as if you are successful and feel good about yourself, and you will increase your chances of actually feeling that way. Enthusiasm counts. Every manager is receptive to someone who is sincerely interested in the company and the position.

Looking and acting the part increases your chances for success. Some job hunters who have worked for one employer for a long time can get very relaxed about their appearance and have no idea what they look like compared with other job hunters. Look as good as you can and act as though you are doing just fine.

DURING THE INTERVIEW—PLAY THE PART
OF A CONSULTANT

> The world is moving so fast these days that the man who says it
> can't be done is generally interrupted by someone doing it.
> —Harry Emerson Fosdick

Pretend for a minute that you own a small consulting company. When you first meet a prospective client, you want to probe to better understand the problems this person is facing. If the client has no problems, or if you cannot solve them, there is no place for you.

You are also there to sell your company. Therefore, as the client talks about company problems, you reveal your own company's experience and credentials by asking questions or by telling how you have handled similar situations. You want to see how your company fits in with this company.

If the conversation goes astray, lead it back to the main topic—the work you would do for them and your abilities. That way you can make your points in context. If you want the job, it is your responsibility to reassure the manager that everything will work out. The manager does not want to be embarrassed later by discovering he'd made a hiring mistake. It is almost as if you are patting the manager on the arm and saying, "There, there. Everything will be fine. You can count on me."

Display self-confidence in your ability to handle the position. If you are not confident, why should the hiring manager take a chance on you? If you want the job, take a stand and say that you believe it will work. If you are asked how you would handle a situation, reassure the manager that even though you do not know specifically what you would do (because, after all, you are not on the job yet), you can figure it out because:

- It won't be a problem. I'm good at these things.
- I'm very resourceful. Here's what I did as company controller. . . .
- I've been in that situation before. I can handle your situation even though I don't know the specifics.

Let the manager air his or her doubts about you. If you are told what these reservations are, you can reassure the manager right then, or you can mull it over later and reassure the manager in writing.

Do not appear to be "shopping around." Be sincerely interested in this particular company—at least during the interview.

Follow up on your meetings. Address the important issues, stress your interest and enthusiasm, and state your major selling points—especially since you now know what is of interest to the interviewer.

DO YOUR HOMEWORK

Before the interview, research the company and the industry. If you're asked why you are interested in them, you will have your answer. Do library research. Call the company's public relations department and ask for literature or an annual report. Ask others about the company. Show up early and read company literature in the reception area, talk to the receptionist, and observe the people. Get a feel for the place.

THE REHEARSAL

It may sound like a contradiction, but you achieve spontaneity on the set through preparation of the dialogue at home. As you prepare, find ways of making your responses seem newly minted, not preprogrammed.
—MICHAEL CAINE
Acting in Film

Even experienced job hunters need practice. Each interview smooths out your presentation and responses. As you get better, your self-confidence grows.

By now, you've had networking or information-gathering interviews. You will have practiced talking about yourself and will have information about your area of interest and the possibilities for someone like you.

When I was unemployed, I had lots of interviews, but I was not doing well in them. I was under so much stress that I kept talking about what I wanted to do rather than what I *could* do for the company. I knew better, but I could not think straight. An old friend who used to belong to The Five O'Clock Club helped me develop my "lines" for my three-by-five card. Then we practiced. After that, my interviews went well.

GET A JOB OFFER

> To take what there is and use it, without waiting forever in vain for the preconceived—to dig deep into the actual and get something out of that—this doubtless is the right way to live.
> —HENRY JAMES

Sincerely intend to turn each interview into a solid job offer. Do your best to make the position and the pay into something acceptable. Make the most of each interview. Negotiate changes in the job itself. Suggest additional things you can do for the company—jobs often can be upgraded a level or two. Or perhaps the manager could refer you to another area of the company. You should make every effort to turn an interview into a reasonable job offer.

- This is an opportunity to practice your negotiation skills and increase the number of interviews you turn into offers. You can always turn the job down later.
- Getting a job offer helps your self-esteem. You can then say you received a number of offers, but they didn't seem right for you. This puts you in a stronger negotiating position.
- Even if you turn down an offer, stay friendly with the hiring manager. This may lead to another offer later that is more appropriate.
- When you get an offer you are not sure about, say that you have a few other things you must attend to, but will get back to them in a week. Then contact other companies that were of real interest to you. Tell them you have received an offer but were hoping to work something out with them. They may tell you to take the other offer —or they may consider you more seriously because the other offer makes you more valuable. Sometimes getting another offer is the only thing that will make a company act.

- You may be surprised: perhaps what you originally found objectionable can be changed to your liking. If you end the process too early, you lose the possibility of changing the situation to suit you. Having a job created especially for you is the best outcome.

> Blessed is he who has found his work; let him ask no other blessedness.
> —THOMAS CARLYLE

COMING IN AS A CONSULTANT

Some job hunters are willing to work for a company as a consultant and hope the company will later put them on the payroll. This rarely happens. If you are doing a great job for little money, the company has no incentive to change that arrangement. If you want to be "on salary," consult only if you are sure you have the self-discipline to continue job hunting after you start consulting.

You can parlay a consulting assignment into a full-time job at a decent salary if you do outstanding work on the assignment, and get a decent offer somewhere else. Then tell your manager that you enjoy what you are doing and would like to be a salaried employee—but have received another job offer. You would prefer working for his company, but this temporary arrangement is not what you want.

AIMING FOR THE SECOND JOB OUT

Sometimes the job you really want is too big a step for you right now. Instead of trying to get it in one move, go for it in two moves. Make your next job one that will qualify you for the job you really want.

WHAT DO YOU REALLY WANT?

> I am proud of the fact that I never invented weapons to kill.
> —THOMAS A. EDISON

> If I had known, I should have become a watchmaker.
> —ALBERT EINSTEIN, on his role in making the atomic bomb possible.

To get ahead, many people compromise what they want. A lot of compromising can result in material success but also feelings of self-betrayal and not knowing who you really are.

It can be difficult to hold on to your values and live the kind of life that is right for you. You may feel there is no hope for change. If you are really honest, you may discover that you have tried very little to make changes. Ask yourself honestly what you have done to improve your situation.

Deciding where you want to work is a complex problem. Many unhappy professionals, managers, and executives admit they made a mistake in deciding to work for their present companies. They think they should have done more research and more thinking before they took the job.

The stress of job hunting can impair your judgment. You may make a decision without enough information because you simply want to "get a job." Ego can also be involved: you want to get an offer quickly so you can tell others and yourself that you are worth something. Or you may deceive yourself into thinking you have enough information. Even if you are normally a good decision maker, you can shortcut the decision-making process when it comes to your own career.

You will make better decisions when you are not deciding under pressure. Start now to see what your options are. Then you will have already thought them through in case you have to make a move quickly later.

Objectively evaluate the information you come up with, and develop contingency plans. Decide whether to leave your present position, and evaluate new opportunities. List the pros and cons of each possibility for you and those close to you.

You may decide, for example, that a certain position is higher level, higher paying, and more prestigious, but you will have less time for your family, and the job will make demands on your income because you will have to take on a more expensive life-style. You may even decide that you don't like the kind of work, the conditions, or the people, or that your lack of leisure time will push you farther away from the way you want to live.

Depending on your values, the job may be worth it or it may not. If you list the pros and cons, you are more likely to adhere to your decision and have fewer regrets. You are more likely to weigh the trade-offs, and perhaps think of other alternatives. You will decide what is important to you. You will have fewer negative surprises later, and will be warned of areas where you may need more information. You will make better decisions and have more realistic expectations about the future.

WHAT IF YOUR INTERVIEWS ARE NOT TURNING INTO JOB OFFERS?

> If one man says to thee, "Thou art a donkey," pay no heed. If two speak thus, purchase a saddle.
> —THE TALMUD

Listen. You may find that your target market is declining, or that you don't have the required background, or whatever. One of my clients kept saying that managers insulted her. If you have the same experiences again and again, find out what you are doing wrong.

Perhaps you are unconsciously turning people down. A job hunter may make unreasonable demands because, deep inside, he or she knows there are things dramatically wrong with a situation, and asks for more money or a better title to make up for the unacceptable working conditions. Then the company rejects the applicant. The job hunter thinks he or she was turned down for the job. In reality, *he* turned down the job. He did not let an offer happen because he knew the job was not right, and he made it fall through. There is nothing wrong with this—so long as he knows he could have had a job offer if he had wanted one.

Job hunters are under tremendous pressure to answer to a lot of people who want to know "how your job hunt is going." If you say you are still looking and have not gotten any offers, you may feel bad. That's why you may want to get a few offers—even though you are not interested in those particular jobs. On the other hand, if your job hunt seems to be going very quickly, you may not want to waste your time on practice offers.

Make sure you are addressing the company's problems—not your own. A major mistake that I have made myself is focusing on what I want rather than on what the company or the manager needs.

Perhaps you are not talking to the right people. Are you interviewing with people two levels higher than you are—those in a position to hire you? If you are spending a lot of time talking to people at your own level, you can learn about the field, but this is unlikely to result in job offers.

If you don't know why, ask them. If appropriate, you may want to call a few of the people you interviewed with to find out why you did not get the job. If you are really stuck and feel you are not interviewing well, this can be very valuable feedback for you. You may even be able to turn a negative situation around.

DO YOUR BEST AND THEN LET IT GO

> . . . you ought to say, "If it is the Lord's will . . ."
> —JAMES 4:15

You are trying to find a match between yourself and a company. You are not going to click with everyone anymore than everyone is going to click with you. Don't expect every interview to turn into a job offer. The more interviews you have, the better you will do at each one.

And don't punish yourself later. Do your best, and then do your best again.

Hang in there. Get a lot of interviews. Know your lines. and don't bump into the furniture. You will find the right job. As M. H. Anderson said: "If at first you don't succeed, you are running about average."

> A man should always consider how much he has more than he wants, and how much more unhappy he might be than he really is.
> —JOSEPH ADDISON

> Whensoever a man desires anything inordinately, he is presently disquieted within himself.
> —THOMAS À KEMPIS

QUESTIONS IN A JOB INTERVIEW

A sudden, bold, and unexpected question doth many times surprise a man and lay him open.
  —Francis Bacon
    "Of Cunning"

QUESTIONS YOU MIGHT ASK

The meeting of two personalities is like the contact of two chemical substances; if there is any reaction, both are transformed.
  —Carl Jung
    Modern Man in Search of a Soul

IN AN INTERVIEW, you are there not only to answer the interviewer's questions, but also to make sure you get the information you need. Ask questions that are appropriate: what do you really want to know? Here are a few to get you thinking in the right direction:

- What are the key responsibilities of the job?
- What is the most important part of the job?
- What is the first problem that would need the attention of the person you hire?
- What other problems need attention now? Over the next six months?
- How has this job been performed in the past?
- Are there other things you would like someone to do that are not a formal part of the job?
- What would you like to be able to say about the new hire one year from now?
- What is your background?
- How would you describe your management style?
- How is the department organized?

DIFFICULT INTERVIEW QUESTIONS
AND POSSIBLE ANSWERS

> Shy persons often act like they were captured and are being
> interrogated.
> —GARRISON KEILLOR

Business is a game, and interviewing is part of the game. You are asked a question to see how well you handle it—to see how well you play the game. This is not like a discussion with a friend. Don't take questions literally.

For example, if the interviewer asks you why you didn't go to college, should you tell the truth? such as:

- I came from a town where no one went to college, or
- my mother died and I had to help out, or
- I didn't have the money.

These answers are negative and also take you both away from what should be the main discussion: the company's needs and how you can help.

The interviewer is not interested in you and your mother. There is a job to fill. Talking about certain subjects weakens your position—regardless of who brought them up. Keep the interview positive, and do not discuss subjects that are offtrack.

A businesslike answer moves the interview along. Many times hiring managers say to me, "Why did Joe [the applicant] have to tell me that? I was ready to hire him, but now I can't. When my boss confronts me about Joe's lack of college, I don't have a good answer."

Some job hunters insist on being "honest." They think, I'll just tell them the way it is, and if they don't hire me, then so be it. These job hunters are putting their responsibility on the interviewer. We've all had problems. The interviewer doesn't have to hear about them.

Let's try the question again—from a responsible, businesslike point of view.

> LETTICE: Let me play the interviewer for once: you be the victim.
> —PETER SCHAFFER
> *Lettice & Lovage*

WHY DIDN'T YOU GO TO COLLEGE?

I like to be out there doing things. I thought about college a few times (or: I took a few courses), but I wanted to get more done. And that's what my bosses have always said: I'm someone who gets things done. They've all been happy with me.

Briefly and politely handle those questions that might take you off course. Do not go into long discussions, but smoothly move the conversation back to the company's needs or your abilities—the things on your three-by-five card that you had planned to cover. Give your answer, and then say, for example, "but I really wanted to tell you about a special project I worked on." It is your responsibility to get the conversation back on track.

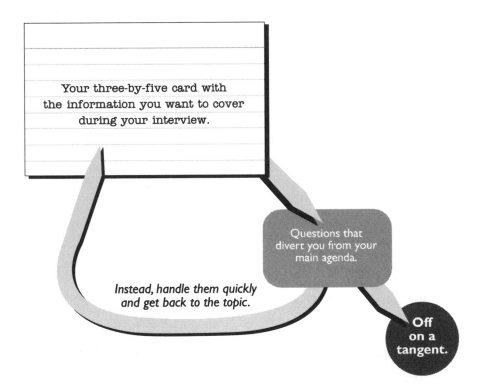

Your three-by-five card with the information you want to cover during your interview.

Questions that divert you from your main agenda.

Instead, handle them quickly and get back to the topic.

Off on a tangent.

Let's try a few other questions, but remember to find your own answers, depending on your situation.

WHAT WOULD YOU LIKE TO BE DOING FIVE YEARS FROM NOW?

Actually, I'd like to do the best job I can possibly do in the position we're talking about right now. I know that if I do a great job, good things will happen to me later. They always have.

TELL ME ABOUT YOURSELF

See Chapter 15: Your Two-Minute Pitch.

TELL ME ABOUT THE WORST BOSS YOU'VE EVER HAD.

No matter what your bosses have been like: I've been really lucky. I've been blessed with good bosses. They've all been different, but I've learned from each of them.

WHY ARE YOU LOOKING?

My company is going through a reorganization. I had the option of taking another job internally, but I decided to look elsewhere.

Or

XYZ Company has been great for me, but the career possibilities in the areas that interest me are extremely limited.

Or

Perhaps you've heard that the _____ industry has been going through a major restructuring. I was caught, along with three thousand others.

Or

Your own answer for this one.

WHAT ARE YOUR GREATEST WEAKNESSES?

After taking time to mull it over:

> Actually, I can't think of any work-related weaknesses. My bosses have always thought I was great. I'm the kind not only to do my own job, but to also notice what else needed to be done in other areas and pitch in to help.

Or, name a weakness and show how you have resolved it, such as:

> Sometimes I get impatient with people because I want the job to get done, but I make sure I find out what's going on and help them with whatever may be stopping them.

WHAT IS YOUR CURRENT SALARY?

See Chapter 27.

> There are no hopeless situations; there are only men who have grown hopeless about them.
> —CLARE BOOTHE LUCE
> *Europe in the Spring*

HOW LONG HAVE YOU BEEN UNEMPLOYED?

If you've been unemployed a while, and you answer, "twenty-six months," how likely are you to be hired? I have run job hunt groups of people who have been unemployed two years or more. The first thing we work on is an answer to this question. From a moral point of view, I must help these people develop a good story so they can get back to work. It would be cruel for me to insist they tell the truth. Who will hire an applicant that says, "When I was fired, I got depressed for six months and couldn't move, and then my mother got sick and I had to help. By then, I had been unemployed eleven months, and no one would hire me. I'm hoping you will give me a chance."

It makes sense that no one will give this person a chance. By "telling the truth," this job hunter is saying, "I've had all these problems, but I'm better now. Will you risk your business for me?" It's not fair to burden the interviewer. All the interviewer wants to do is fill a job—not save lives.

Develop a good answer you can live with. Think of what you have actually been doing. Have you been working on your computer? Helping at your church or synagogue? Helping friends with their businesses? Most people can think of something they've been doing—even something little —that they can build a story around.

If you really haven't been doing anything at all, then go do something. You are unlikely to interview well if you haven't been out there at all. Get your adrenaline going. Walk dogs, pick strawberries, usher at church. Get active.

Better yet: learn a new skill. Try computers. Volunteer your skills, or get paid something nominal. Then think up a good story:

1. I've actually been looking only a month or two. After I left XYZ Company, I spent some time working on a special project for a small company.

Or

2. I've been looking only a few weeks now. After working for more than twenty years, this was my first time off, and I took advantage of the time to (fix up my house, take care of a sick family member, learn tax accounting, etc.). I was glad to have the opportunity to (help out, learn something new, etc.). But now I'm ready to get back to work and put in another twenty years.

Or

3. Take the work you've done:

I've been doing public relations work for a small firm. I thought it would be fun to try after so many years with a big corporation, but now I know I like corporate life and I want to get back.

If your answers aren't working and are causing you not to get hired, change them.

CHAPTER 25

CONSIDER YOUR COMPETITION

Bullock shrugged. He'd been thinking about Bill that afternoon, trying to decide how to fit him into Deadwood Brickworks, Inc. It wasn't a question he could be useful. Anybody could be useful when you decided where they fit. That was what business was.
—PETE DEXTER
Deadwood

SO FAR IN the interview process, we have considered you and the hiring manager. By acting like a consultant, you can negotiate a job that's right for both you and him. But there are other players and other complexities in this drama. First, you have competitors. They may be other people the interviewer is seeing, or your competition can be an ideal candidate in the interviewer's mind. In addition, there are all the other people you meet during the hiring process. They are influencers and, in fact, may influence the hiring decision more than the hiring manager does. These are people the hiring manager trusts and on whose opinions he relies. Finally, there are complexities such as outside influencers, the timing of the hiring decision, and salary considerations.

This chapter contains case studies of how some people considered and dealt with their competition. In the next chapter, we'll give you the guidelines they followed, that helped them decide what they could do to win the job. Remember, the job hunt starts after the interview. What can you do to turn the interview into an offer? You may think you have done a lot of work so far in your job hunt, but you still have a long way to go. This is the part of the process that requires the most analysis and strategic thinking. But since most of America is mindlessly watching TV right now, you have a chance to win if you spend some time thinking. Think *objectively* about the needs of the organization and of everyone you met, and think about what you can do to influence *each* person.

If you're in a seller's market, however, you may not need to follow up: you'll be brought back for more meetings before you have a chance to breathe. *If you're in a buyer's market*, you will probably have to do some thoughtful follow-up to get the job.

Because effective follow-up is a lot of work, your first decision should be, Do I want to get an offer for this job? Do I want to "go for it"? If you are ambivalent, and are in a competitive market, you will probably *not* get the job. Someone else will do what he or she needs to do to get it.

Follow-ups will not guarantee you a specific job, but extensive follow-ups on a number of possibilities increase the number and quality of your offers. If you focus too much on one specific situation and how you can *make* them hire you, that won't work. You need both breadth and depth in your job hunt: you have both when you are in contact on a regular basis with six to ten people who are in a position to hire you or recommend that you be hired. You must have six to ten of these contacts in the works, *each* of which you are trying to move along.

Ideally, you will get to a point where you are moving them along together, slowing certain ones down and speeding others up, so you wind up with three concurrent job offers. Then you can select the one that is best for you. This will usually be the job that positions you best for the long run—the one that fits best into your Forty-Year Plan. It will rarely be sensible to make a decision based on money alone.

Therefore, if one situation is taking all of your energy, stop right now for ten minutes and think of how you can quickly contact other people in your target area (through networking, direct contact, search firms, or ads). It will take the pressure off, and prevent you from trying to close too soon on this one possibility.

> Mediocrity obtains more with application than superiority without it.
> —BALTASAR GRACIÁN
> *Oraculo Manual*

CASE STUDY: THE ARTIST
Status Checks Rarely Work

> Without competitors there would be no need for strategy.
> —KENICHI OHMAE
> *The Mind of the Strategist*

Most people think follow-up means calling for the status of the search. This is not the case:

At Citibank, a project I managed needed an artist. I interviewed twenty and selected the work of three to present to my boss and my boss's boss.

I came up with two piles: One of seventeen rejects, and another of the three I would present. A few people called to "follow-up." Here's one:

ARTIST: I'm calling to find out the procedure and the status. Do you mind?

ME: Not at all. I interviewed twenty people. I'll select three and present them to my boss and my boss's boss.

ARTIST: Thanks a lot. Do you mind if I call back later?

ME: No. I don't mind.

The artist called every couple of weeks for three months, asked the same thing, and stayed in the reject pile. To move out, he could have said things like:

- Is there more information I can give you? Or
- I've been giving a lot of thought to your project and have some new ideas. I'd like to show them to you. Or
- Where do I stand? How does my work compare with the work others presented?

If all you're doing is finding out where you are in the process, that's rarely enough. *The ball is always in your court.* It is your responsibility to figure out what the next step should be. Job hunters view the whole process as if it were a tennis game where—*thwack*—the ball is in the hiring manager's court. Wrong.

Me to job hunter: "How's it going?"

Job hunter to Kate: *(Thwack!)* "They're going to call me."

When they call, it's to say, "You are not included." If you wait, not many of your interviews will turn into offers.

CASE STUDY: RACHEL
Trust Me

> A man is not finished when he's defeated; he's finished when he quits.
> —RICHARD MILHOUS NIXON

Rachel had been unemployed for nine months. This was her first Five O'Clock Club meeting. She was disgusted. I had an interview, she said. I know what will happen: I'll be a finalist and they'll hire the other person.

Rachel was nice, enthusiastic, and smart; she was always a finalist. Yet the more experienced person was always hired.

Here's the story. Rachel, a lobbyist, was interviewing at a law firm.

The firm liked her background, but it needed some public relations help and perhaps an internal newsletter. Rachel could do those things, and wrote a typical thank-you note playing up her strengths, playing down her weaknesses, and ignoring the firm's objections. She highlighted the lobbying, and said that PR and a newsletter would not be a problem. She could do it. She was asking the firm to "trust her."

LOTS OF JOB HUNTERS TAKE THE "TRUST ME" APPROACH

THE GROUP: Do you want this job? Are you willing to go through a brick wall to get it?

RACHEL: Yes. I am. I really want this job.

ME: Let's think about overcoming their objections. If you can write a PR plan after you get hired, why not do it now? Why ask them to trust you?

Two people in the group had old PR plans, which they lent her. Remember: the proposals or plans or ideas you write will probably be wrong. That's OK. You're showing the company you can think the problem through and actually come up with solutions.

Rachel's lack of experience with newsletters was also an objection. We suggested Rachel call law firms in other cities and get their newsletters.

After doing research, Rachel sent a very different note. In this one she said she had been giving it more thought, and was very excited about working for the firm. She had put together a PR plan, *which she would like to review with them,* and had gotten copies of newsletters from other law firms, which gave her ideas of what she could do in a newsletter for them. Of course, she got the job.

UNCOVERING THEIR OBJECTIONS

He who knows only his own side of the case, knows little of that.
—JOHN STUART MILL, *On Liberty*

Rachel got the job because she overcame the objections of the hiring committee. Start thinking about how you can overcome objections. This will change the way you interview, and you will become more attuned to picking up valid objections rather than quashing them. Then you can even solicit negatives. For example, you can ask:

- Who else is being considered?
- What do they have to offer?
- How do I stand in comparison with them?
- What kind of person would be considered an ideal candidate?
- What would you like to say about a new hire one year from now?

Get good at interviewing so you can solicit valid objections to hiring you.

ACT LIKE A CONSULTANT

Since most jobs are created for people, find out what the manager needs. Hiring managers often decide to structure the job differently depending on who they hire. Why not influence the hiring manager to structure the job for you?

Probe—and don't expect anything to happen in the first meeting. If you were a consultant trying to sell a $30,000 or $130,000 project (your salary), you wouldn't expect someone to immediately say, "Fine. Start working." Yet job hunters often expect to get an offer during the first meeting.

Forget about job hunting. This is regular business. You're selling an expensive package. Do what a consultant or a salesperson does: Ask about the company's problems and its situation; think how you could get back to the interviewer later. Get enough information so you can follow up and give the interviewer enough information so he'll want to see you again. Move the process along: Suggest you meet with more people there. Do research. Have someone influence the interviewer on your behalf. Then get back to him again. That's what a consultant does. Remember to move the process along, and kill off your competition.

CASE STUDY: KEN
Identifying the Issues/Timing

Ken was the first person interviewed for a senior vice president of marketing position. When Ken asked, the interviewer said he would see five or six more people. As you will see shortly, being first is the weakest position. Kill your competition quickly, or find ways to maintain the interviewer's interest and meet with him again.

Ken identified the company's most important issue—it was not wondering what Ken would do as the head of marketing, but something more basic: it was debating the *role* marketing should play in the new organization.

Determining the real issues is critical in deciding your follow-up plan. And since the timing was against him, Ken acted fast. He wrote a handsome four-page proposal about the role marketing should play, and he sent it overnight.

When Ken was called for a second round of interviews, he found there were no other candidates. Ken had killed off his competition. Ken not only identified the issues, he was in sync with the company's timing. It was planning to decide quickly, so he acted quickly, too.

CASE STUDY: LEON
How Did He Get The Job?

> He said, however, that the real secret of his fortune was that none of his mules worked as hard and with so much determination as he did himself.
> —GABRIEL GARCÍA MÁRQUEZ
> *Love in the Time of Cholera*

Leon came to The Five O'Clock Club after fifteen months of interviews. After three meetings, he got two job offers—simply because he followed the group's advice and wrote proposals. When he told the group his good news, someone asked him how he got the two jobs, and he said that one offer was from a search firm, and one was from networking. Leon had been pursuing jobs through networking and search firms for fifteen months, but it wasn't until he decided to follow up on these that he was offered a job.

CASE STUDY: JOHN
Consider Your Likely Competitors and Go For It

> The successful person has the habit of doing things failures don't like to do. They don't like doing them either necessarily. But their disliking is subordinated to the strength of their purpose.
> —E. M. GRAY
> *The Common Denominator of Success*

Most job hunters think *anxiously* about the "competition out there." Instead, be *objective* about your likely competitors.

John thought he was job hunting for a year. He answered ads, met with search firms, and even went on interviews, but he wasn't job hunting: *in a tight market, the job hunt starts* after *the interview.*

At our first meeting, John recounted his activity. One ad he'd answered was for a job at the Kennedy Foundation, and he'd met three people there two weeks earlier. He was waiting for their call. Before John went on, I stopped him.

"John," I said, "do you want that job?"

"Well," he replied, "I'll see what happens next. If they call me, I'll consider it."

"The way things stand, John, you are *not* going to get that job. If they call, they'll say they found a better match. Are you willing to go through a brick wall to get that job? If you are, I can help you—and it's a *lot* of work. But if you essentially want to sit on the bench answering ads, there's not much a coach can do."

John said he was willing to go after the job. A job hunter's commitment is absolutely necessary or he will not be willing to do or even notice what needs to be done to win the job.

WHO ARE JOHN'S LIKELY COMPETITORS?

The Kennedy Foundation wanted a controller. John had been a controller in a major corporation for twenty years. What kind of controller would the Kennedy Foundation most likely want?

Develop a prototype of your likely competitors. We have to guess about our competition, but then we'll have a target and can develop a plan. Remember, your competition might not be real people, but an ideal in the mind of the hiring manager. Kill off that competitor, too, or the hiring manager will continue looking for them.

John thought his likely competitors were people who had been controllers in not-for-profit organizations. I suggested that he spend a day at The Foundation Center (a library), and research the controllership function at other foundations. I told him to make sure he could handle the work and knew the jargon.

John came back with good news: "I know how to do that kind of accounting. It's actually what I've done all along."

HOW DOES JOHN *NOW* STAND IN RELATION TO HIS LIKELY COMPETITORS?

> Don't forget that it (your product or service) is not differentiated until the customer understands the difference.
> —TOM PETERS
> *Thriving on Chaos*

John now has twenty years of corporate controllership experience and a day in the library. His likely competitors have real hands-on experience.

At this stage, John is *not* even with them. He has to do more if he wants the job.

John and I searched his background for areas that might interest the Kennedy Foundation—experience his likely competitors would not have, such as securities accounting.

Look at all the work and thought John has put in so far—without a request from the hiring manager. The ball is *always* in your court. But here the game is not tennis, but golf. The person who is farthest from the goal must keep hitting until he gets ahead.

John had met with three people at the Kennedy Foundation. Among the three was a financial person, and someone from personnel. His first draft of the letter to the financial person was negative: "Despite the fact that I have no not-for-profit experience, I believe my credentials . . ."

Wrong. Come up with something that *beats out* your competition. You must be in a position to say, in so many words, "Unlike others who have spent a lot of time doing this work, I bring something extra to the party."

Also remember that you are interviewing with individuals—not organizations. You are *not* interviewing with the Kennedy Foundation or IBM. Each person you meet has her own opinions about the issues that are important to her, the things she likes about you, and the reasons she might not want you there. Address these points with *each* person.

THE OTHER DECISION MAKERS/INFLUENCERS

> The people you want to reach . . . should be viewed as distinct
> target audiences that require different approaches and strategies.
> —JEFFREY P. DAVIDSON, marketing consultant
> *Management World,* September/October 1987

Many job hunters assume the hiring manager is the only person who matters. Big mistake. Others are not only influencers; in some cases, they may actually be the decision makers.

I'm a good example. I make terrible hiring decisions: everyone seems fine to me. So I have others interview the candidates. Their opinions weigh more than mine. Any applicant who ignores them is ignoring the decision makers—or at least the serious influencers.

Take seriously every person you meet. Don't be rude to the receptionist. She may say to the boss, "If you hire him, I'm quitting." That receptionist is definitely an influencer.

IDENTIFYING THE ISSUES

> You must call each thing by its proper name or that which must get done will not.
> —A. Harvey Block

When John met with the personnel person at the Kennedy Foundation, she asked him questions such as, "So, what do you do on weekends?" and, "Where do your kids go to school?" Assuming these were not idle questions, what issue was she getting at?

We decided the issue was *fit*. When John wrote to her, he said he was excited about the position and had spent a day doing research—and he addressed the issue of fit.

Three months, eleven grueling interviews, and seven in-depth reference checks later, John's credentials were presented to the board of directors for approval. To make sure his important arguments were brought before the board, John prepared one more follow-up letter (see page 251). By the way, John had three more interviews after the board meeting. He got the job—and he's still there.

Many job hunters ask John how he got the job. They are asking the wrong question. They mean, "How did you get the interview?" John is forced to reply, "I got it through an ad." I hope you can see that John got the *job* through his analysis and follow-up. He got the *interview* through an ad.

WHAT HAPPENS AS TIMES PASSES

> He had made a fortune in business and owed it to being able to see the truth in any situation.
> —Ethan Canin
> *Emperor of the Air*

Most jobs are *created* for people: most interviewers don't clearly know what they will want the new person to do. Yet job hunters expect the hiring manager to tell them exactly what the job will be like, and get annoyed when the manager can't tell them.

Generally the job description depends on who will be in the job. Therefore, help the hiring manager figure out what the new person should do. If you don't help him, another job hunter will. This is called "negotiating the job." You are trying to remove all of the company's objections to hiring you, as well as all of *your* objections to working for them. Try to make it work for both of you. But time is your enemy. Imagine what happens in the hiring process as time passes:

Mr. Jim Johnston
The Kennedy Foundation
1234 13th Street, NW
Washington, D.C. 12345

Dear Jim:

Now that you are at the final stage of your search, I wanted to take the opportunity to summarize my feelings about the position and address what I see as some of the major issues affecting your decision.

Long-term commitment

My almost twenty-year career at Gotham unequivocally attests to my loyalty and commitment to my employer and my job. It is only because this opportunity is so exceptional that, for the very first time, I am seriously considering leaving Gotham. You can be assured that this sense of loyalty will remain with me at the Foundation.

Profit-making background

I feel strongly that my experience in the for-profit sector represents value added to the Foundation. I base this upon the following:

- My experience in securities accounting, clearance and custody, where virtually 100% of your assets and revenues reside, is critical to your organization.
- My review of the Marwick Report on its review of the Comptroller's Office very interestingly included recommendations identical to the initial conclusions I drew from some of the specifics we discussed Thursday.
- The cultural changes you are introducing represent concepts ingrained in me. My experience in the for-profit sector would nicely complement, support and help expedite your initiatives to become more businesslike in your operations.
- My independent research on foundation accounting, primarily at the Foundation Center, illustrated the striking similarity in the Statements on Financial Accounting Standards and the Statements on Financial Accounting Concepts between the two sectors.
- My in-depth study of the Foundation's Annual Report assured me that the differences in accounting and financial reporting between the two sectors are insignificant. My conversation with Bob Dana, Senior Manager at Ernst & Young, confirmed my conclusion.

I have a very positive feel for the Foundation, its philanthropic work, its infrastructure and its personnel practices, both in general and as it would affect me directly.

Jim, I believe that I and the Foundation are ideally suited for each other. My broad managerial and technical expertise is needed for the immediate tasks at hand but will also be of value in your other areas of responsibility. My experience in operating in a decentralized environment has honed my decision-making skills and my ability to interface with others at all levels.

I am looking forward to your favorable decision.

Very truly yours,

John H. Charmon

You have an interview. When I, your counselor, ask how it went, you tell me how great it was: the two of you hit it off, and you are sure you will be called back. You see this interview as something frozen in time, and you wait for the magical phone call.

But after you left, the manager met with someone else, who brought up new issues. Now his criteria for what he wants has changed somewhat, and consequently, his impression of you has also changed. He was honest when he said he liked you, but things look different to him now. Perhaps you have what he needs to meet his new criteria, or perhaps you could convince him that his new direction is wrong, but you don't know what is now on his mind.

You call to find out "how things are going." He says he is still interviewing and will call you later when he has decided. Actually, then it will probably be too late for you. His thinking is constantly evolving as he meets with people. You were already out of the running. Your call did nothing to influence his thinking: you did not address his new concerns. You asked for a status report of where he was in the hiring process, and that's what you got. You did nothing to get back into the loop of people he might consider, or find out the new issues that are now on his mind.

> Oh I could show my prowess,
> be a lion not a mou-esse,
> if I only had the nerve.
> > —The Cowardly Lion in the movie *The Wizard of Oz*
> > (from the book by L. Frank Baum) by E. Y. Harburg and
> > Harold Arlen

The manager meets more people, and further defines the position. Interviewing helps him decide what he wants. You are getting farther and farther away from his new requirements.

You are not aware of this. You remember the great meeting you two had. You remind me that he said he really liked you. You insist on freezing that moment in time. You don't want to do anything to rock the boat or appear desperate. You hope it works out. "The ball is in his court," you say. "I gave it my best. There's nothing I can do but wait." So you decide to give it more time . . . time to go wrong.

> Annie: . . . you want to give it time—
> Henry: Yes—
> Annie: . . . time to go wrong, change, spoil. Then you'll know it
> wasn't the real thing.
> > —Tom Stoppard
> > *The Real Thing*

You have to imagine what is going on as time passes. Perhaps the hiring manager is simply very busy and is not working on this at all. Or perhaps things are moving along without you. Statistics prove that the person who is interviewed last has the best chance of being hired. That's because the last person benefits from all the thinking the manager has done and is able to discuss all of the issues that are of interest to the manager.

WHAT YOU CAN DO DURING THE INTERVIEW

If you come into an interview with the goal of getting a job, you are putting too much pressure on yourself to come to closure. When you walk away without an offer, you feel discouraged. When you walk away without even knowing what the job is, you feel confused and lost.

> Boone smiled and nodded. The muscles in his jaw hurt. "What I meant was did you ever shoot anybody but your own self. Not that that don't count. . . ."
> —PETE DEXTER
> *Deadwood*

Instead of criticizing managers who do not know what they want, understand them: "I can understand that there are a number of ways you can structure this position. Let's talk about your problems and your needs. Perhaps I can help."

Your goal in the interview is not to get an offer, but to build a relationship with the manager. This means you are on the manager's side —assessing the situation, and figuring out how to move the process along so you can continue to help define the job.

PAY ATTENTION TO YOUR COMPETITION

Most job hunters think only about themselves and the hiring manager. They don't think about the others being considered for the position. But you are different. While you are moving it along, you think about your competition.

> Therefore be as wise as serpents and as harmless as doves.
> —MATTHEW: 10:16

You are acutely aware at all times that you have competition. Your goal is to get rid of them. As you move the process along, you can see the competition dropping away because you are doing a better job of addressing the hiring manager's needs, coming up with solutions to his problems, researching and showing more interest and more competence than your competitors.

You are in a problem-solving mode: "My goal isn't to get a job immediately, but to build a relationship. How can I build a relationship with this person—so that someday when he or she gets his act together and decides what he wants, he'll want me?" You have hung in there. You have killed off your competition. You have helped define the job in a way that suits both you and the hiring manager, and you are the one he wants. You have the option of saying, "Do I want this job or don't I?"

Big shots are only little shots who keep shooting.
    —CHRISTOPHER MORLEY

CHAPTER 26

PLANNING YOUR FOLLOW-UP

It may be that the race is not always to the swift, nor the battle to the strong—but that's the way to bet.
  —DAMON RUNYON

YOU HAVE READ a few examples of job hunters turning job interviews into offers. They had to think hard about what to do next. They objectively and methodically analyzed *all* the interviews they had and developed strategies for addressing every issue for *each* person they met with. They thought about who their likely competitors were, and what the hiring managers probably preferred. Who are your likely competitors? How do you stack up against them? Prove you're better than they are, or you won't get the job.

The heights by great men reached and kept
Were not attained by sudden flight,
But they, while their companions slept,
Were toiling upward in the night.
  —HENRY WADSWORTH LONGFELLOW

WHY BOTHER WITH FOLLOW-UP?

- To influence both the decision makers and the influencers
- To move things along
- To show interest and competence
- To knock out your competition
- To reassure the hiring manager

- To turn a losing situation into a winning one
- To make it difficult for them to reject you
- To set the right tone/buy yourself time after you are hired

In a tight market, follow-up helps. But still *strive to have six to ten contacts in the works at all times*. The job you are interviewing for may vanish: the manager may decide not to hire at all, or hire a finance instead of a marketing person. There may be a hiring freeze, or a major reorganization. Follow-up techniques will generally not help in these situations. If you are in a competitive market, put extra effort into those job possibilities that are still alive.

> Nothing is more dangerous than an idea when it is the only one you have.
> —EMILE CHARTIER

And if you have lots of other contacts in the works, you will be less likely to allow yourself to be abused by hiring managers trying to take advantage of "desperate" job hunters. You can assess ridiculous requests and be more willing to walk away.

The following Interview Record is a checklist of items to consider in assessing your interviews and planning your follow-up. Try to remember everything that happened at each of your meetings. Many job hunters take notes during the interviews so they will do a better follow-up. After all, wouldn't a consultant take notes during a meeting? How else can you remember all the important issues that come up? At the very least, take notes immediately after the meeting. Some job hunters keep track of every person they met with by using the Interview Record. Make plenty of copies of the form for your job search. Keep them in a folder or a three-ring binder, in alphabetical order within target area.

ASSESS THE INTERVIEW(S)

> The strain and discouragement of frankly facing the complex tangle of motives at work in most human situations tempt everyone into the errors of oversimplification.
> —Henry S. Dennison
> *Organization and Management*

> Anyone who listens well takes notes.
> —DANTE

INTERVIEW RECORD

Name: _____

Position: _____

Company: _____

Address: _____

_____

_____

Phone: Bus: _____

Home: _____

Referred by:

Link to referral:

People spoken to (May require separate sheets.):

Issues (advice, problems, plans, etc.):

Key points to remember:

Referrals (Write additional names on back.):

Name: _____

Position: _____

Company: _____

Address: _____

_____

_____

Phone: Bus: _____

Home: _____

Date of initial contact: _____

Method used: _____
              (If letter, copy and attach
                   to this sheet.)

Planned date of follow-up call to

set up appointment: _____
  (Also record date on job-hunting calendar.)

Actual dates of calls to set up

appointment: _____

_____

_____

_____

Appointment: _____

Follow-up note mailed: _____
                    (Copy attached.)

Follow-up 2: _____

Follow-up 3: _____

Follow-up 4: _____

Follow-up 5: _____

Follow-up 6: _____
                (Copies attached)

Other comments:
Such as:
• tone of the meeting • positives about you
• objections to you   • key issues to address
• logical next steps   • influencers
• your feelings about the job

Effective follow-up depends on knowing what happened in the interview. In fact, you will begin to interview very differently now. You now know you are there to gather enough information so you can follow up, and to give enough information back so the interviewer will be willing to meet with you again. As your counselor, I'd want the following:

BACKGROUND INFORMATION

- How did it go? What did they say? What did you say?
- How many people did you see?
- How much time did you spend with each?
- What role does each of them play?
- Who is important?
- Who is the decision maker?
- Who is the hiring manager?
- Who most influences the decision?
- Who else did you meet (secretaries, receptionists, future peers or subordinates, bosses from other areas)? How influential might they be? (Do not dismiss them too readily. They may be more influential than you think. A trusted secretary, for example, has a lot of influence. She had better want you there.)
- How quickly do they want to decide? A year? A month? Next week?
- What do you have to offer that your competition doesn't?
- What problems did the interviewer have? Do you have any solutions to those problems?
- How badly do you want this job?

FOLLOW UP INFORMATION FOR *EACH* PERSON

He said, however, that the real secret of his fortune was that none of his mules worked as hard and with so much determination as he did himself.
—GABRIEL GARCÍA MÁRQUEZ
Love in the Time of Cholera

For *each* person with whom you interviewed, analyze and craft a follow-up note that addresses:
- **the tone of the conversation.** This is the tone you should use in your follow-up. Was it friendly? Formal? Familylike?
- **the positives about you,** why this person would want you there. If you interviewed with peers, why would they want you on the team? In

the interview, it is *your* job to make sure each person you meet can see
the benefit of having you as an employee.

- **the objections to hiring you**—for *each* person you met,
whether or not these objections were expressed. For example, you may
know that the company typically hires someone with a background that is
different from yours, or you may not have certain experience it is looking
for, or your past salary may be too high, or it may see you as overqualified.
A future peer may see you as a threat (let that peer know you are not) or
thinks you will not fit in. You may be seen as too old or too young or too
something else. If you think the company is worried about having you on
board for some reason, address that reason. For example, if someone sees
you as too old, think of the benefits that come with age. Then you might
say, "I hope you are interested in hiring someone with maturity and a
broad base of experience."

> Even in a highly controlled meeting, there is a lot . . . going on.
> The real process of making decisions, of gathering support, of
> developing opinions, happens before the meeting—or after.
> —Terrence E. Deal and Allan A. Kennedy, *Corporate Cultures*

Many job hunters want to ignore or gloss over the objections; instead,
pay attention to why *each* person may not want you there. Joel DeLuca,
Ph.D., author of *Political Savvy*, noted that if you are observant, you
should come out of a meeting with a good sense of how hard a sell this is
going to be, as well as some idea of the political lay of the land.

> If [a man] is brusque in his manner, others will not cooperate. If he
> is agitated in his words, they will awaken no echo in others. If he
> asks for something without having first established a [proper]
> relationship, it will not be given to him.
> —*I Ching*

- **the key issues.** Was the interviewer concerned about interde-
partmental relationships? Work overload? The political situation with a
key vendor? How you will support people in other areas? How you can
make their job easier? What makes you different from your competition?
Identify those issues that are key to the interviewer(s).
- **your feelings about the job.** If this is the one place you really
want to work, say so. If you would enjoy working with your prospective
manager and peers, say so. In addition to competence, people want someone they'd like to work with and someone who wants to work with them.
Write your follow-up note with enthusiasm. Let your personality come
through.

- **the next steps.** Regardless of who should take the next steps, what exactly are they? What will move the process along?

> The average sale is made after the prospect has said "no" six times.
> —JEFFREY P. DAVIDSON, marketing consultant
> *The Washington Post*, May 20, 1985

For example, the next step could be:

- another meeting to discuss something in greater detail.
- meeting(s) with other people.
- another meeting after the other candidates have been interviewed.
- an in-depth review of documents.
- discussing a few of your ideas with them.
- drafting a proposal of how you would handle a certain area.

> Let him who wants to move and convince others be first moved and convinced himself.
> —THOMAS CARLYLE

State the "next steps" in your follow-up note. For example, "I'd like to get together with you to discuss my ideas on . . ." or, "If I don't hear from George in a week or so, I'll give you a call."

If you were the first person interviewed, try to be interviewed again: "As you interview others, you may more clearly define what you want. I would appreciate the opportunity to address the new issues that may arise."

INFLUENCE THE INFLUENCERS

> A great number of objections indicate a tough road but still can be used to develop strategy. Every objection or reservation shows a concern that needs to be taken into account or an agenda item of the manager who is objecting.
> —JOEL DeLUCA, PH.D.
> *Political Savvy*

Most job hunters pay attention to the hiring manager and ignore everyone else. However, most hiring managers want the input of others. You may be rejected if a future peer or subordinate says that you seem difficult to work with, or the receptionist complains that you were rude to her. Remember that everyone is an influencer. *Follow up with everyone you met formally*. Cultivate as many advocates as you can. Have people inside rooting for you. It's better if your future peers, for example, say that you would be great to have on the team. Influence the influencers with a letter or phone call.

Tell outside influencers the position you are interested in and why, and how they can help you. Joe, a well-known top-level executive, felt one of his interviews went very well, but he was afraid the interviewer would tap into the corporate pipeline and hear untrue negative rumors about him. Joe has two choices: he can hope the interviewer doesn't hear the rumors, or he can fight for the job he deserves.

Joe has to try to control the pipeline—the key influencers in this situation. First, Joe called some influential people who thought well of him and who the hiring manager would respect. He stated why he wanted this job, and asked them to put in a good word for him. Second, Joe thought of the people the hiring manager was most likely to run into or call for information. Joe called them first and did his best to influence them to support him.

This is hard work, but do you want to control your fate? How badly do you want the job? When you are playing for big stakes, you have to work to do better than your competition.

BE IN SYNC WITH THEIR TIMING

Even if you're on the right track, you'll get run over if you just sit there.
—WILL ROGERS

Move the process along to the next step, but at the *interviewer's* pace, not yours. The timing depends on the personality of the interviewer and his sense of urgency. If the situation is urgent, write your letter overnight and hand-deliver it in the morning. If the manager is laid-back, an urgent delivery is inappropriate. These are not thank-you notes: your primary goal is not to thank the interviewer, but to influence him or her. If your letter will not be an influence, don't send it.

Use your judgment. If things are going along at a good clip, and you are being brought in every other day, you may want to let it ride if you think you have no competition.

Also be aware that if things are *not* moving along quickly, it may have nothing to do with you. It may well be that the interviewer is not doing *any*thing about filling the position—he may be busy with other business. You'll notice this the next time you are hiring someone. You can't work on the hire every minute, because you have your regular job to do. You thought you would have the new person in place within a month, but you keep getting called away to meetings, your secretary caught the flu, and your boss had an emergency project for you to work on.

If you have no idea what is going on, it would help if you've formed a good relationship with the hiring manager's secretary. Then you could call and say, "Hi, Jane. This is Joe. I was wondering if you could help me with something. I haven't heard from Ellis [her boss] for two weeks and I had expected to hear something by now. I was going to drop him a note, but I didn't want to bother him if he's really busy with other things. I was wondering if he's still interviewing other people or if he's been tied up with other things, or what." Who knows what she'll say? But if she says he had a death in the family and has been out of town, that gives you some idea of what is happening. He is not sitting around talking about you all day long. He is doing other things, and the hiring process often moves more slowly than you think.

> Understanding is a wellspring of life to him that hath it.
> —Proverbs 16:22

HOW CAN YOU TELL IF A FOLLOW-UP LETTER IS A GOOD ONE?

> There is no such thing as "soft sell" or "hard sell." There is only "smart sell" and "stupid sell."
> —CHARLES BOWER, President, BBD&O
> *Editor & Publisher*, December 7, 1957

A good letter is *tailored* to the situation. It would be impossible to send it to someone other than the addressee. *It sells you, separates you from your competition, addresses all issues and objections, and states a next step.* Finally, its tone *replicates* the tone of the interview (or creates a good tone if the interview wasn't so good). For example, John's various follow-up notes to those he met at the Kennedy Foundation addressed each of the managers' issues.

Your letters to some people will be very detailed and meticulous. These may take you half a day to write. For others, you will write a simple letter saying that you thought they would be great to work with, and addressing the issues they brought up.

Most job hunters err, however, when they assume someone who is lower level has no influence. Be careful about who you dismiss. During the interview, try to pick up on the relationships between people. In brief, remember to influence the influencers. Write notes to prospective peers you have met. They have some say in the hiring decision—maybe a lot of say. If they don't want you, you might not get hired. For each person you met, think of why he or she would want you there. What's in it for him? What do you bring to the party? Make sure you are not a threat. Overcome his objections. Address any issues raised. Use the tone set in the interview.

Following is a letter from a job hunter, Philip, to a *prospective peer*, Jonathan. Philip considers Jonathan an important influencer, and noted the following from his meeting with Jonathan:

- Philip sensed that Jonathan was worried about losing his standing as the second-in-command to George, the hiring manager, when the new person came in.
- He was also concerned that the new person might not be a team player or a hard worker, or be willing to help out with his special projects, which involved computer simulations.
- He was concerned about losing the camaraderie in the department, and hoped the new person would have a good sense of humor to offset the stress of working under deadline.
- Jonathan was obviously trying to conduct a very professional interview, and asked Philip a number of times what he thought of the questions.
- Jonathan was relieved when Philip said he would enjoy developing materials for the department, although it was not central to the job. This is a project none of the other competitors would be able to handle.
- Jonathan wondered about the department's reputation outside the company.

The conversation had been light and friendly. Philip considered Jonathan to be the key influencer, and thought George, the hiring manager, would be making the decision with Jonathan. Philip wrote to each of his prospective peers and also to George. This is what he wrote to Jonathan:

PHILIP JOHNSON

Dear Jonathan:

I was glad finally to have a chance to meet you. George had spoken of you so proudly, I knew you had earned everything you've gotten at Bluekill and have worked very hard. I, too, am a hard worker, and I know we would complement each other.

I liked your professional approach to the interview, and found your questions and direction quite interesting. I hope I "did OK." I believe I could work out a schedule to accommodate your many projects—and one thing you can count on is that I'm good at developing computer simulations. In my last position, I was considered the best, and would enjoy doing the same for you. I work very hard at it, and it pays off.

My impression is that George depends on you a lot, and perhaps I could help out also. I think I could develop materials that could be used both inside and with customers, and I will be glad to hear your ideas on the matter. I've developed a great deal of material in the past that I will be happy to show you.

All things considered, I think I would make a good addition to the group, and I believe you and I would enjoy working together. As I said to you when we met, I've worked in a few companies, and I do my best to make every place I work as enjoyable as it can be. Your sense of humor surely helps, and I'm sure mine will also.

Cordially,

Philip Johnson

Time passed. Philip met again with George and with other peers. But he was concerned about whether Jonathan would still be in favor of him in light of the number of additional applicants Jonathan had met by then. Philip decided to contact Jonathan again, this time more informally. In reviewing his notes, he fixed on what Jonathan had said about the reputation of the department. Philip then arranged a networking meeting with an important person in the industry so he would have something to contact Jonathan about. The information would also help him make up his mind in case he received a job offer. Then he wrote, on informal stationery:

Dear Jonathan,

In our meeting, you wondered about the reputation of your department. I'm sure you will be happy to hear, as I was, that your department is thought of as the best in the industry. I met with Cheryl Jenkins yesterday and she raved about each person in your group—including you. You should be proud of her commendation, and I admit that I was proud as well because I sincerely hope I wind up working with you.

I mentioned to you that I would be happy to show you the computer simulation materials I have developed in the past. I have finally put them together, and will call you to see if you still want to look at them. It shouldn't take more than fifteen minutes of your time.

Hope all is well.

Best regards,
Philip

Sometimes an important influencer is the best way to influence the hiring manager. Philip got the job, but he got much more: he started the job with a very good relationship with each of the people he would be working with. When you analyze what is important to each person, you not only increase your chances of getting the job, you increase your chances of having the new job go smoothly.

> Sometimes I go off on a tangent, but I follow my intuition and if it doesn't work, it doesn't matter. There's no such thing as failure; you just learn from it and go on.
> —DAVID HOCKNEY
> (from the audiocassette: *David Hockney: A Retrospective* Metropolitan Museum of Art, 7/88)

> If God does not give you that which you like, he will give you that which you need.
> —THOMAS WATSON
> *All Things for Good*

> Whoever loves discipline loves knowledge, but he who hates correction is stupid.
> —Proverbs 12:1

CHAPTER 27

FOUR-STEP SALARY NEGOTIATION STRATEGY

I've got all the money I'll ever need if I die by four o'clock.
—HENNY YOUNGMAN

NOW YOU KNOW you not only have to impress the hiring manager, but also the other influencers so they will want to have you on board. In addition you have to think about your likely competitors, and how you can convince everyone you meet that you are the best choice. During the interview, a job hunter may also think about salary.

When job hunters ask about salary negotiation, they usually want to know how to answer the questions What are you making now? and What are you looking for? We'll cover these issues in detail a little later, but it is more important to first look at salary negotiation from a strategic point of view. From the very first meeting, you can set the stage for compensation discussions later.

Most job hunters think about salary—unconsciously and anxiously —during their first interview. They think, I'm making $50,000 now (or $150,000), but I know this person won't pay more than $35,000 (or $135,000). Most job hunters try to get rid of the anxiety. They don't want to waste their time if this person isn't going to pay them fairly. So when the hiring manager mentions money, the job hunter is relieved to talk about it.

HIRING MANAGER: How much are you making now?
JOB HUNTER: I'm making $50,000.
HIRING MANGER: That's a little rich for us. We were thinking about $35,000.
JOB HUNTER: I couldn't possibly take a job for $35,000.

End of discussion. Another wasted interview. But there is a better way. Intend to turn every job interview into an appropriate offer. Overcome the company's objections to hiring you, and overcome your *own* objections to working there. If the salary or something else bothers you about the job, think about how you can change it. We'll see how later.

Think more consciously and more strategically. *Intend* to negotiate. Most job hunters don't negotiate at all.

- They don't negotiate the job. They passively listen to what the job is, and try to fit themselves into it.
- They certainly don't negotiate the salary. They listen to the offer, and then decide whether they want to take it.

We'll see how you can be more proactive rather than passive. The following guidelines will allow you to take more control and more responsibility for what happens to you. Following these steps will not guarantee you the salary you want, but you will certainly do much better than if you do not follow them. Remember the four steps you will learn here—and pay attention to where you are in those steps.

STEP 1. NEGOTIATE THE JOB.

> If your ship doesn't come in, swim out to it.
> —JONATHAN WINTERS

By now, you have already negotiated the job. You have created a job that suits both you and the hiring manager. Make sure it is at an appropriate level for you. If the job is too low level, don't ask about the salary—upgrade the job. Add responsibilities until the job is worth your while. Make sure the manager agrees that this new job is what he or she wants. Don't negotiate the salary yet.

STEP 2. OUTSHINE AND OUTLAST YOUR COMPETITION.

> The heart and soul of competing is knowing how to appeal to your customers.
> —DON PETERSEN, former CEO, Ford Motor Co.

By now, you have already killed off your competition. You have kept in the running by offering to do more than your competitors. You have paid attention to the progress made in your meetings, and you have moved the process along. For some jobs, it can take five interviews before the subject of salary is discussed. All the while, your competitors have been dropping out. Postpone the discussion of salary until they are all gone.

STEP 3. GET THE OFFER

> With the help of my God, I shall leap over the wall.
> —Book of Common Prayer

Once a manager has decided that you are the right person, you are in a better position to negotiate a package that is appropriate for you. Until you actually get the offer, postpone the discussion of salary.

STEP 4. NEGOTIATE YOUR COMPENSATION PACKAGE.

> You can get more with a kind word and a gun than you can get with a kind word alone.
> —JOHNNY CARSON

> No modest man ever did or will make a fortune.
> —LADY MARY WORTHY MONTAGU

Most job hunters hear the offer and then either accept or reject it. This is not negotiating. If you have never negotiated a package for yourself, you need to practice. Why not try to get some offers that don't even interest you, just so you can practice negotiating the salary?

IT WORKS AT ALL LEVELS

Once I did a salary negotiation seminar for low-level corporate people. One person had been a paper burster for twenty-five years: he tore the sheets of paper as they came off the computer. But because he had been at the company for twenty-five years, his salary was at the top of the range of paper bursters. He had the same kind of salary problem a lot of us have.

The four steps worked for him, too. He told hiring managers, "Not only can I burst paper, but I can fix the machines. This will save you on machine downtime and machine repair costs. And I can train people, which will also save you money."

He was	**1. Negotiating the job**
And:	**2. Killing off his competition**
And after he:	**3. Gets the offer**
He'll have no trouble:	**4. Negotiating the salary**

Know where you are in the four steps. If you have not yet done steps one, two and three, try to postpone step four.

CASE STUDY: KATE, 1980
All four steps in action

I was earning around $60,000 in 1980. A search firm called me about a job that paid $40,000. Remember, search firms are a means for getting *interviews*—not for getting jobs. Don't negotiate salary with the search firm. Simply decide whether you want the *interview*.

I asked the recruiter what the job was. "It's with an advertising agency," she said. "They're looking for a woman to supervise the secretarial staff."

I had an MBA, was making $60,000, and specialized in turning around troubled firms. A recruiter cannot negotiate job content but *can* give information. When she described the situation, it seemed to me that the company was in trouble and was using the wrong solutions to solve their problems. I told her I would like to meet with the president. She said, "You *would*?"

I like situations where I know who my competition is: people who want to supervise secretaries for $40,000. I asked the president:

- How is your company organized?
- What are your biggest accounts?
- What is the profit margin on each?
- Do you have a cost accounting system?
- May I see your computer system?
- Did you know that certain reports would give you better profit control?

His eyes lit up. I was headed in the right direction—and was killing off my competition while I created a job more appropriate for myself. I kept talking to him about his business and what we could do to turn it around. I was trying to move it along, move it along, move it along—and kill off my competition.

After the offer, we got into the formal discussion of salary. At this point, I wanted

- the title "VP of Operations"
- to chair the executive committee so we could turn the company around
- easy access to the CPA firm. They would be my partners in this.

The actual salary was not a problem. But you can see that it would have been had I discussed it too early, when the president was thinking about a much lower level job. After we defined a new job and he definitely wanted me, we were in a better position to discuss a salary that was right for the new position.

"Salary negotiation" involves more than salary. Negotiate what you need to do the job well, and anything having to do with your compensation.

CASE STUDY: GEORGIA
Using all four steps

It was the day before Thanksgiving. Georgia had interviewed to head a small profit center at a hospital. She would be involved with eleven radiologists who gave cancer tests in a mobile unit, and two administrators. She also had competition.

Georgia had met with six doctors. One particularly unpleasant one asked for a proposal on how she would handle the job. This was Wednesday; he wanted it back the Monday after Thanksgiving. Boy!

Georgia and I worked at my dining room table over Thanksgiving. "You can be sure no one else is putting in this much effort," I told her.

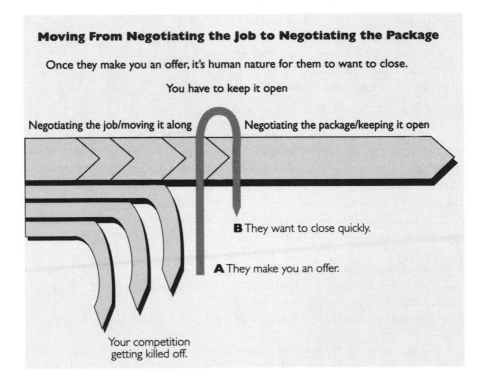

Moving From Negotiating the Job to Negotiating the Package

Once they make you an offer, it's human nature for them to want to close.

You have to keep it open

Negotiating the job/moving it along | Negotiating the package/keeping it open

B They want to close quickly.

A They make you an offer.

Your competition getting killed off.

Georgia hand-delivered not one proposal, but *six*, and on time. She did not want her fate in the hands of one nasty doctor. Her cover notes were different, but essentially said, "Dr. So-and-So asked for this proposal. I felt duty-bound to give you a copy as well, since the things we discussed are reflected here."

Within an hour of the delivery, Georgia got a call from her future boss (not the nasty doctor). He was elated: "We want to offer you the job. If you don't take it, we're stuck. We don't want any of the other people who interviewed, and we'll be forced to start our search over." This was music to my ears. He told her that she *no longer had competitors*.

Now we were in a different phase of the search. It's human nature that a person making the offer simply wants to come to closure. However, you need time to discuss things.

I said to Georgia, "You've spent plenty of time defining the job. You need an equal amount of time to define the compensation."

She said to the doctors, almost verbatim, "We've spent plenty of time defining . . ."

They immediately backed off: "We'll spend whatever time it takes."

They didn't want to lose Georgia. She had paid her dues, and now she was in a strong position to negotiate. They made her a written offer, and then we worked up a counteroffer.

- She wanted a certain base pay.
- She would need entertainment expenses to sell this program.
- The bonus was a problem.

CALCULATING THE BONUS

We wanted a bonus based on the volume the $250,000 trucks could handle. We decided that each truck would probably need one day of maintenance a month, and that each radiologist would be able to do x number of tests.

With the bonus based on truck volume, we figured what Georgia's maximum salary would be. To allow for year two, we asked the hospital to buy another truck if the volume reached a certain amount.

When Georgia delivered the counteroffer, the doctors couldn't believe it; they now had a truck operating at almost no volume, and Georgia was talking about buying another truck!

Georgia got the compensation she wanted, and something else. . . .

GEORGIA GOT TO KEEP HER JOB

Georgia bought six months of safety in the job: she could do no wrong. The very first day, Georgia realized she'd had a misunderstanding during the interview process and needed to change something about the way the job was done. It was no problem. A job hunter who is thorough in the search process has laid the foundation for keeping her job. Unlike other new hires, the jury is *not* out on her. Georgia had proved herself. The doctors knew that no one knew more about this business than she did. She even knew more than *they* did!

That's why you want to follow up with *everyone* during your search. You may be working with them later. And if any of them has an objection to hiring you, try to settle it during the search, rather than handling it after you are hired. Build strong relationships during the interview process.

Know where you are in the process. Take the steps in sequence. You will not get the offer until after you have negotiated the job and also killed off your competition.

If a job pays $20,000 less than you want, that's fine for now. Postpone the salary discussion. Remember that you are there not for this specific job, but for a position that has not yet been completely defined—and in which you have some say.

A skilled negotiator has a different approach—and much more power—than someone who does not know these techniques. A skilled negotiator chases companies, not jobs. A certain position may not be right, but the job hunter wants to make a good impression anyway because there may be other places in the organization that are right for her.

WHAT ARE YOU MAKING NOW? WHAT ARE YOU LOOKING FOR?

Now we'll look at the questions you've been waiting for. But we'll look at them strategically—so you can *plan* an appropriate answer depending on your situation. First, you need to develop some background information before you can plan your strategy for answering the questions. The strategy will also give you hints for postponing the discussion of salary until you have an offer.

Background Information: Figure out what you really make. Start with your base salary, but also include your bonus and any perqs, such as a company car, a savings plan, deferred compensation, company lunches, company contribution to insurance plans, and so on. That's what you really make—but that may not be what you will tell the prospective employer.

Background Information: Figure out what you are worth in the market. Talk to search firms, ask people at association meetings, look at ads in the paper, and—most of all—network. At networking meetings, ask, "What kind of salary could someone like me expect at your company?" A few networking meetings will give you a good idea of the market rates for someone like you.

Background Information: Compare what you are making (total compensation) with what the market is paying. You need to know if you are presently at market rates, below market, or above market. *This is the key* to how you will answer a hiring manager or search firm that asks you, "What are you making?" or, "What are you looking for?"

HOW TO ANSWER: IF YOU ARE WITHIN THE MARKET RANGE

Most companies want to know what you are making and, if you are within the market range, they will pay you 10 to 15 percent above what you are currently making. Therefore, if you are making $40,000 and you know the market is paying $43,000 to $45,000, then you could say, "Right now I'm at $40,000, but I'm looking to move a little away from that." The only time you can safely state your current compensation is when you are at market rates.

HOW TO ANSWER: IF YOU ARE ABOVE MARKET RATES

A counselor asked me to have a meeting with his client Sam, who was having problems finding a job because of his high salary. I did an interview role play with Sam. At one point I said, "So, Sam, what are you making now?" Sam replied, "Two hundred thousand dollars-plus-plus-plus." I said, "I know you're a very competent person, but we simply cannot afford someone at your high level." Sam's salary was not hurting him, but his way of talking about it was. Even if your salary isn't $200,000-plus-plus-plus, you can easily put off the hiring manager if she thinks your salary will be a problem. You have to give her a chance to find out about you, and you have to think about how you can create a job that is appropriate for your salary. You must tell her, "Salary will not be a problem"—*especially if you know it is a problem.* You have to think to yourself that it won't be a problem when she gets to know you better and understands what you will do for her. Otherwise, you will not get anywhere.

If you are making more than the market rate, do your best to create a job that warrants the salary you want and defer the discussion of salary until you have the offer. When you're asked, "What are you making now?" use a response from the list below to reassure the hiring manager that you are both on the same team and can work this out. These responses are listed in sequence from easiest to most difficult. Try the easy response first. If the hiring manager persists, you may have to move on to one of the other responses. You are simply trying to postpone the discussion of salary until she knows you better and you have an offer.

The manager asks, "What are you making now?" You respond:

- "Salary won't be a problem. But I'm not exactly sure what the job is, so maybe we can talk more about that. I'm very flexible, and I'm sure that when we come to some agreement on the job, we can work out the salary."
- "Salary won't be a problem. I know that you do not want to bring someone in at a salary that makes you resentful, and I'm sure you do not want me to be resentful either. I know that we'll come to a happy agreement."
- "I'm making very good money right now, and I deserve it. But I'd hate to tell you what it is because I'm afraid it will put you off. I know that salary will not be a problem. I'm a fair person and I'm sure you are, too. I know we'll come to an agreement."
- "I'm being paid very well, and I'm worth it. But I'm very interested in your company and I'm willing to make an investment in this if you are. As far as I'm concerned, salary won't be a problem."

Marie successfully postponed the discussion of salary for two years. When she came to The Five O'Clock Club, she had been unemployed for a long while. It took six months before she was on the verge of a job offer at a major fashion house, the company of her dreams. On the day she was to receive the offer, the company went into play—that is, another company was trying to take this one over, so all hiring was put on hold. Marie was more desperate than ever. Within a month or two, she received an offer from a major entertainment company, went to work there, and continued to keep in touch with the fashion house. Over the next year and a half, she had meetings with the president and most of the senior executives at the fashion house. Each one asked her about her salary, and to each one she replied with one of the statements listed above. She eventually got a tremendous offer—after having postponed the discussion of salary for two years. By the way, Marie's boss at the entertainment company told her that he hired her because she was so persistent in her follow-up. He thought she acted a little desperate, which she was after having been unemployed for so long, but he gave her the job because it seemed to mean so much to her. And, of course, she later got the job at the fashion house because she followed up with them for *two years*! If this desperate job hunter could postpone the discussion of salary, so can you. But you need to practice with someone. It does not come naturally.

HOW TO ANSWER: IF YOU ARE MAKING BELOW MARKET RATES

Again, you have a few options. For example, if a manager asks what you are making, you could answer instead with what you are looking for:

> MANAGER: "What are you making right now?"
> YOU: "I understand the market is paying in the $65,000 to $75,000 range."
> MANAGER: "That's outrageous. We can't pay that."
> YOU: "What range are you thinking of for this position?"

Note: You haven't revealed either what you are making or what you want —but you've still tested the hiring manager's expectations. The person who states a number first is at a negotiation disadvantage.

Or you could say, "My current salary is $32,000. I know the marketplace today is closer to $45,000. I have been willing to trade off the salary in order to build my skills [or whatever]. But now I am in a position where I don't need to trade off money, and I'm ready to take a position at market rates."

IF YOU ARE PUSHED TO NAME YOUR SALARY

Don't simply state your salary—develop a line of patter to soften it. Simply stating a number can be very confrontational, as with the $200,000-plus-plus-plus job hunter. If you have exhausted all the responses, and the hiring manager throws you up against the wall and shouts, "I want to know what you are making!" you can still soften your answer by saying, for example:

- "I'm earning very good money right now—in the $90,000 to $120,000 range, depending on bonus. And I'm certainly worth it. But I'm very interested in your company, and I know we can work something out."

- "My salary is very low—only $20,000, and I know that's dramatically below market rates. But I was willing to do that as an investment in my future. Now, however, I expect to make market rates."

You should name your salary only as a last resort. Managers want to know your last salary as a way of determining your worth to them, but it is certainly not the most reasonable way to decide what you are worth. For example, you would want to be paid more if the job requires seventy hours a week and lots of travel, versus one that requires only thirty-five hours a week. How do you know how much you want unless you know what the job entails? You are being sensible to talk about the job first and the salary later.

Some managers cannot deal that way, so you have to be prepared in case you are forced to discuss salary prematurely. And even if you do name your salary, there are different ways you can couch it. For example:

- "My current salary is $32,500."
- "I make in the high sixties."
- "My base is around $25,000 and my bonus [commissions] is usually around $15,000, which brings my total package to $40,000."
- "I make in the range of $100,000 to $200,000, depending on my bonus." (This, of course, tells them very little.)

Remember to soften your mention of your salary with a line of patter, or your response will sound too confrontational and too much like a demand: "I make . . . but salary won't be a problem because . . ."

You are trying to postpone the discussion of salary until after you have an offer, but in real life that is not always possible. Postpone it if you can. If you can't, be sure you know how you want to answer the questions. What are you making now? and, What are you looking for?

NO ABSOLUTE ONE WAY

> I was taught that the way of progress is neither swift nor easy.
> —MARIE CURIE

Salary negotiation is the most nerve-wracking part of the job hunting process. At the beginning of your job hunt you are at loose ends—not knowing where you are going, and feeling like you will never get there. But salary negotiation is the part people fear the most. It is a surprise monster at the end of your search.

You are in a great negotiating position if you can walk away from the deal. Therefore, make sure you have six to ten contacts in the works. If this deal is the only thing you have going, see how quickly you can get something else going.

WHAT IS NEGOTIABLE?

Everything's negotiable. That doesn't mean you'll *get* it, but it is negotiable. First, think of what is important to you. Make a personal list of what you must have versus what you want. Decide where you can be flexible, but also know the issues that are deal breakers for you.

Think of your musts versus your wants. If you get everything you "must" have, then perhaps you won't even mention items on your "want" list. Go in knowing your bottom-line requirements, what you would be willing to trade off, and what benefits/perqs could compensate you if you hit a salary snag. Have your own goals in the negotiation clearly in mind.

Salary is not the only form of compensation that might be negotiated. Other items might include:

- the timing of the first review
- closing costs on a new home or a relocation package
- use of a company car
- association or club memberships
- reimbursements for education
- bonus

Which is the most meaningful or valuable to you?

NEGOTIATING ITEMS THAT ARE NONNEGOTIABLE

Peter received a written offer from a major corporation. He liked it all except the job title: he'd been offered the title of vice president, but he wanted senior vice president. The company policy was that no one could be hired from outside with a title higher than vice president.

I said to Peter, "Are you willing to walk away from the job if you don't get the title you want?" I needed to know that so I could help Peter plan his strategy. Peter said he would walk away from it. Then I needed to know why. Peter said he had had the title of vice president fifteen years ago, and it was too much of a blow to his ego to go back to that title. Furthermore, he felt he would not be able to do a good job if he had the lower-level title, because everyone would know what his title was and they would not respond to his requests. He felt he would fail in the job if he had the title of vice president.

The rule here may surprise you. If you are at an impasse where the hiring manager wants to give you one thing and you want another, you have only one recourse: *Talk about the job!* If Peter had directly addressed the title issue, they probably would not have come to an agreement. He would have been quoted company policy. In fact, when job hunters are negotiating, hiring managers sometimes get the impression that the job hunter does not care about the job, but only about the salary and the benefits. Therefore, be different. Talk about the job to reassure him that the job is what is most important to you. Below is a shortened, paraphrased version of the letter Peter sent to the hiring manager. Please note the italicized part, which is an important strategy for you to use:

> I was thrilled to receive your offer to head up the Rickety Division, and am eager to get in there and work with you to move it in a new direction. I know we will hit all of the targets you and I spoke about.
>
> I was pleased with the compensation package you offered, and am also glad about the car situation. However, *I find it difficult to accept the offer* with the title of vice president. I had that title fifteen years ago, so I feel I'd be going backward in my career. But I am also concerned that the lower title will affect my credibility and effectiveness.
>
> I am sure we can come to some agreement. I am very eager to dig in and am looking forward to hearing from you.

Peter did not reject the offer: he said he really wanted to work there, but would find it difficult to accept. It took three weeks for the company to get back to him and give Peter the title he wanted. But that was not necessarily the only result that would have been positive. For example, the company could have said, "Come in and get started, Peter. We can give you the title after three months." Or it could have said, "Peter, I'm sorry, our hands are tied on this one. But I assure you that you will not experience the problems you are dreading. Our employees will know you are division head, and that will matter to them more than the vice president title. Lewis Segal came in as vice president only two years ago, and look at him now."

Peter kept the process open until he heard the final offer. That allowed him to hear the best offer, or to change his mind and take the job with the lower title and the reassurances from the company that it would be OK.

That's what you want to do also. Hear the entire offer before you decide. *Do not accept or reject any job until it is offered to you.* Before their first interview with a company, some job hunters say, "I really want this job," or, "I don't want this job." They don't even know what the job is and they have already made up their minds. This is the wrong attitude. Go into each interview intending to make it into the best job for you and for the company. This means you will probably have to negotiate—both the job and the compensation.

WHEN THERE IS AN IMPASSE

Let's review the rule to follow when you come to an impasse—when what they offer is different from what you want:

Talk first about the job. Then explain why you want something.

Let's say, for example, you want a company car. Don't say, "I want a car." Instead, say, for example, "I appreciate your offer, and cannot wait to get started. I know we will really turn that place around. I am looking forward to starting on the twenty-third, and am pleased with the package you have offered. However, I was wondering what we might do about a car. I was thinking that I would have to do a lot of traveling between these three cities, and wonder what we might do about that. I have no car at present, and I think that renting a car might be a big expense. Is there any possibility that we could lease a car? It would be much cheaper."

WIN-WIN

You want a win-win situation—one you can both live with. After you have received a job offer, the situation is no longer adversarial. You and the company are both on the same side of the table trying to make this deal work.

Actually, it is up to you to control this part of the process. You have the most at stake. The fact is, once a hiring manager has made an offer, he or she usually wants to close quickly. Her job is done. Now your job begins.

Therefore, you must make sure you bring up everything you want in a way that is collaborative. Set a tone that reassures the hiring manager that you are thrilled to have the job, cannot wait to get started, but just have a few details to work out. You can say, for example, "I really appreciate your spending this time. Some of these things may not mean much to you, but they mean a lot to me."

LOOK AT THE ENTIRE PACKAGE

Look at the entire compensation package. Do your homework so you know the typical compensation for a similar position in the industry, and make allowances—especially in the area of benefits—as you move from one industry to another. The benefits may differ, but they should be on a par.

Find out which items are automatic benefits and which are negotiable; every company's plan is different.

Be reasonable. In the past, it has almost been a given that job seekers would move only for a salary increase of 20 percent or more. In these economic times, lateral moves are much more common. Know your market worth.

SEARCH FIRMS

Search firms must know the *range* of salary you are making or the amount you are looking for. They do not need an exact amount.

ADS

In answering ads, you will rarely give your salary requirements. The trend at the moment is for many ads to read, "Please state salary requirements." Most job hunters do not, and the hiring company does *not* exclude them. Stating your salary or requirements not only puts you at a negotiating disadvantage, it also allows you to be eliminated from consideration because you are too high or too low.

On the other hand, some ads state, "You will absolutely not be considered unless you state your salary requirements." Then, you should state them.

> History records the successes of men with objectives and a sense of direction. Oblivion is the position of small men overwhelmed by obstacles.
> —WILLIAM H. DANFORTH

In summary, think about where you are in the four steps. It will help you concentrate on what you should be doing. If you still have competitors, for example, it is too early to negotiate salary. And practice. This takes a lot of skill but is worth it when you wind up getting paid what you are worth.

> Armies of worried men in suits stormed off the Lexington Avenue subway line and marched down the crooked pavements. For rich people, they didn't look very happy.
> —MICHAEL LEWIS, *Liars Poker*

PART FIVE

KEEPING IT GOING

AFTER YOU'VE GOTTEN THE JOB YOU WANT

The pace of events is moving so fast that unless we can find some way to keep our sights on tomorrow, we cannot expect to be in touch with today.
—DEAN RUSK

CHAPTER 28

STARTING OUT ON THE RIGHT FOOT IN YOUR NEW JOB

Now, *here*, you see, it takes all the running you can do to keep in the same place. If you want to get somewhere else, you must run at least twice as fast as that!
 —LEWIS CARROLL
 Alice in Wonderland

STARTING OUT CAN be tricky. It is a time of trial. You are often being watched to see if you will work out. Here are some things you need to do to start out on the right foot and keep moving in the right direction.

BEFORE YOU START

• **Say thank you.** Contact all the people who helped you get the new position. On page 283 is a sample letter to go out to those you met in your search.

Consider doing something more for those who have been especially helpful in your search, such as sending them flowers or a gift. It's the only polite thing to do, but it is also pragmatic. Often people don't make this effort because they feel they'll be in the new job a long time. Today, when the average American changes jobs every four years, the odds say you're going to change jobs again soon. You need to keep up those contacts. Think about ways to keep in touch with them—if you read something that someone on your list would appreciate, clip it and send it.

RONA BERKELEY

400 First Avenue
Dayton, Ohio 22090

Addressee name
Address
City, State, Zip

Dear XXXXX:

The happy news is that I have accepted a position at Ohio State Trust as Controller for their Ohio branches. I'll be responsible for financial reporting and analysis, loans administration, budgeting and planning. I think it's a great match and will make good use of both my management skills and banking experience, and the environment is congenial and professional.

I really appreciated your interest in my job search. I very much enjoyed speaking with people like you about your career and I appreciated your advice and encouragement. The fact that you so willingly gave of your time meant a great deal to me, and certainly was beneficial.

If I can reciprocate in some way, please feel free to get in touch with me. I will also probably be in contact with you in the months ahead. My new office is a 75 Rockfast Corner, Dayton 22091. You can reach me at 200-555-1212.

Sincerely,

RIGHT AWAY

- **Don't fix things or do anything daring for the first three months.** That is the biggest mistake people make. Take time to learn the system, the people, and the culture.

You cannot possibly understand, in those first months, the implications of certain decisions you may make. You may be criticizing a project that was done by someone important. Or you could be changing something that will affect someone on the staff in ways in which you aren't aware.

- **Make yourself productive immediately.** This does not contradict the point just made. Do things that are safe. For example, install a new system where there has been none. This is "safe" because you aren't getting rid of some other system. What isn't safe? Firing half your staff the first week!

- **Introduce yourself to everybody.** Be visible—walk around and meet people as soon as possible, including those who work for you. Too many managers meet only the "important" people, while ignoring those who will actually do the work.

- **Don't make friends too fast.** Someone who befriends you right away could be on the way out. That doesn't mean you shouldn't be friendly, however. Go to lunch with several people rather than becoming known as someone who associates only with so-and-so. Get to know everybody, and then decide with whom to get closer.

- **Take over compensation of your subordinates immediately.** Look at review and raise dates, and make sure no one is overlooked. You can't afford to wait three months to get settled while one of your people is stewing about an overdue salary review.

- **Get your budget—quickly.** If it isn't good, build a better one. If you spend some time at the beginning trying to understand the budget, the things you hear over the next few weeks will mean more to you.

IN THE FIRST THREE MONTHS

- **Learn the corporate culture.** People new to jobs often lose those jobs because of personality conflicts rather than a lack of competence.

Keep your head low until you learn how the company operates. Some companies have certain writing styles. Some expect you to speak a certain way. Certain companies have a special way of holding parties. Do people work with their doors open or their doors shut? All of these rules are part of the culture, and they are unwritten. To learn them, you have to pay attention.

> So I watched my step. There were a million little rules to obey; I knew none of them. Salesmen, traders, and managers swarmed over the floor, and at first I could not tell them apart. Sure, I knew the basic differences. Salesmen talked to investors, traders made bets, and managers smoked cigars. But other than that I was lost.
> —MICHAEL LEWIS
> *Liars Poker*

I had a client, for example, who lost his job because his management style rubbed everyone the wrong way. He was a "touchy feely" manager who, when he wants his employees to do things, schmoozes with them, saying things such as, "You know, I was kind of thinking about this and. . . ." But the corporate culture was such that the employees liked and expected to be asked straight out. His style made them feel patronized and manipulated. And his own staff did him in.

Pay your dues before doing things at variance with the corporate culture. After you build up some credits, you have more leeway. Let your personality emerge when you understand the company and after you have made some contribution.

- **Learn the organizational structure**—the real structure, not the one that is drawn on the charts. Ask your secretary to tell you who relates how with whom, who knows what, who thought of this project, who is important. You could be surprised.

- **As far as subordinates are concerned, find out other people's opinions and then form your own.** Consider that you may have a different perception because you have different values.

- **Find out what is important in your job.** For example, when I counsel people for a corporation, counseling is not the only important thing in my job. The people who come to me are sent by personnel, and I must manage my relationship with the personnel people. It doesn't matter how good a counselor I am if I don't maintain a good relationship with personnel.

- **Pay attention to your peers.** Your peers can prove as valuable to you as your boss and subordinates. Do not try to impress them with your brilliance. That would be the kiss of death because you'd have a very large reputation to live up to. Instead, encourage them to talk to you. They know more than you do. They also know your boss. Look at them to teach you and, in some cases, protect you.

I know one executive who found out that her last three predecessors were fired. She knew from talking to people that her boss was the type whose ego was bruised when someone had ideas. He had a talent of getting rid of this kind of person.

To protect herself, she built relationships with her peers, the heads of offices around the country. After a year and a half, her boss's brother took her to breakfast and told her that, unlike her predecessors, she could not be fired: it would have been such an unpopular decision that it would have backfired on her boss.

- **Don't set up competition.** Everyone brings something to the party and should be respected for his or her talent, even those who are at lower levels than you are. Find ways to show your respect by asking for their input on projects that require their expertise.

- **Set precedents you want to keep.** If you start out working twelve-hour days, people come to expect it of you—even if no one else is doing it. When you stop, people wonder what's wrong.
- **Set modest goals for your own personal achievement, and high goals for your department.** Make your people look good and you will look good, too.

> The secret of success in life is for a man to be ready for his opportunity when it comes.
> —Benjamin Disraeli

THREE MONTHS AND BEYOND . . .

- You'll be busy in your new job, and may not keep up your outside contacts. In today's economy, that's a big mistake. **Continue to develop contacts outside the company.** If you need information for your job, sometimes the worst people to ask are your boss and the people around you. A network is also a tremendous resource to fall back on when your boss is busy—and you will seem resourceful, smart, and connected.
- **Keep a "hero file" for yourself,** a hanging file in which you place written descriptions of all your successes. If you have to job hunt in a hurry, you'll be able to recall what you've done.

You will also use it if you stay. If you want anything, whether it be a raise or a promotion, or the responsibility for a particular project, you can use the file to build a case for yourself.

- **Keep managing your career.** Don't think, I'll just take this job and do what they tell me, because you might get off on some tangent. Remember where you were heading and make sure your career keeps going that way.

Be proactive in moving toward your goal. Take on lots of assignments. If a project comes up that fits into your long-term plan, do it. If one doesn't fit into your plan, you can do it or you can say, "Oh, I'd love to do that, but I'm really busy." You'll be making those kinds of choices all the time.

> I find the great thing in this world is not so much where we stand, as in what direction we are moving: to reach the port of heaven, we must sail sometimes with the wind and sometimes against it—but we must sail, and not drift, not lie at anchor.
> —Oliver Wendell Holmes

A man's work is in danger of deteriorating when he thinks he has found the one best formula for doing it. If he thinks that, he is likely to feel that all he needs is merely to go on repeating himself . . . so long as a person is searching for better ways of doing his work, he is fairly safe.
   —EUGENE O'NEILL

CHAPTER 29

HOW TO KEEP YOUR LIFE COURSE IN MIND

I learned three things in Zurich during the war. I wrote them down.
Firstly, you're either a revolutionary or you're not, and if you're not
you might as well be an artist as anything else. Secondly, if you
can't be an artist, you might as well be a revolutionary. . . .
I forget the third.
    —Tom Stoppard
    Travesties

SOMETIMES WE FORGET our important thoughts, or we
remember them and they sound strange, or we become afraid of them.
Afraid of success. Afraid of failure. Like writing this book. Some days I
became nauseated at the thought of working on it. On other days, I simply
"forgot" I was writing it, or I became afraid that it all sounded stupid,
harsh, boring, trite. Often, I couldn't remember why I was doing it; then
I was afraid I would never finish.

Writing a book is a lot like job hunting. Some days you forget why
you're doing it—you just know that you must. Or you become sick at the
thought of it. You can sometimes become afraid that you sound stupid, or
are doing the wrong things, or will embarrass yourself, or you'll never
finish.

But somehow—one day at a time—it gets done. A job hunter makes
a phone call, writes a proposal, researches a company. Every day you
make a new decision to do your best no matter how you feel about it. You
sit down and do what you must do. That is discipline: to continue to job
hunt—or to continue to write—regardless of how you feel. And then you
get into it and it flows.

Then you have to remember where you were trying to head yourself.
Job hunting—or writing a book—was supposed to take you somewhere.

When one lives without a clear value structure, it is both difficult to
direct life in the long run and difficult to experience a sense of

meaningfulness that comes from following a prescribed course. It is possible to sail a boat, for example, without charts or a compass. However, the absence of a chart prevents the possibility of a journey. One is limited to "day" sailing, so that new destinations and new challenges are out of reach. Eventually the same seascape and circumstances will produce a tedium not unlike the absence of meaning associated with a present-centered existence.
—HERBERT RAPPAPORT, PH.D.
Marking Time

Everyone is running to and fro, pressed by the stomach ache of business.
—FRÉDÉRIC-AUGUSTE BARTHOLDI,
French sculptor of Statue of Liberty
Letter to his mother, June 12, 1871

It is easy to get caught up in your day-to-day activities. Your life can get off course; you become distracted. You may even discover you have veered from your true path for a number of years. That's OK. Bring yourself back and walk toward your goal. Stay with your own direction—the one that is in your heart. Deep down, you know when things are right and when things are not. Keep walking toward your goal.

Don't be bound by your past. It is important to remember that you are not whatever your jobs have been. We don't exist on a sheet of paper—a résumé. Don't identify too strongly with it. Stay fluid behind those words on the page. They are not you, but simply a sales tool.

The power is in what you are doing now and in your pull toward the future. The power is in the act of living each day to the fullest. It is the direction we are each heading in that is important. Look to the future. We constantly gain new insights, new visions.

Taking the long view can give you satisfaction. A stone mason working on the Cathedral of St. John the Divine was asked how he could keep on cutting those stones year after year. He said he was not cutting stones—he was building a cathedral.

Of journeying, the benefits are many; the freshness it brings to the heart, the seeing and hearing of marvelous things . . . the meeting of unknown friends . . .
—SADI

Interviewing can soften you. It can broaden your horizons and make you realize there is a big world out there with lots of interesting things to do. In talking to people, you can see that it is not all so pat—so clearly spelled out—what a person should "be." There are endless variations, and when you realize how much variety there is, you also realize that, in the end, it is largely up to you to choose what you will be. We each have a place. Find your place. Live your part.

> I have a dream that my four little children will one day live in a
> nation where they will not be judged by the color of their skin but
> by the content of their character. I have a dream . . .
> —MARTIN LUTHER KING, JR.
> Speech to 200,000 civil rights demonstrators,
> Washington, D.C., August 28, 1963

Martin Luther King, Jr., was driven by his dream. *Your* main drives, threads, inclinations, also have power. You will come back to them again and again in your life because you are driven to do these things. They will come out. Why not harness that energy and direct it consciously rather than letting it rule you? In the right situations, your drives are a benefit and can add to your success. But in the wrong situations, they will still appear over and over, and they can harm you.

Better to find out clearly what they are, and go where they are valued. Then you will have a happy marriage between you and your environment. Then you will no longer be swimming against the tide, but will let the tide take you to new heights and a new sense of satisfaction.

They say, "Go with the flow." Go with your own flow. Go in the direction you were meant to take. Find out what it is that motivates you, and go with it.

> Everyone has a talent. What is rare is the courage to follow the
> talent to the dark place where it leads.
> —ERICA JONG

> . . . tendencies and aspirations are more important . . . it is more
> important what people want to be than what people actually are.
> —JOHN LUKACS
> *A History of the Cold War*

When you find out what you are inside, it will give you great energy and a happy obsession to realize it. When this happens, people say that their jobs are fun, and not work at all. There is nothing else they would rather be doing.

There is a freedom in fulfilling your function in the world—to know you are in the right place, doing what is right for you. You are fulfilled when you know what you are, know what you are supposed to be doing on this earth, and are doing it. When what you should be doing hits you, and you make it a conscious part of yourself, you won't get easily sidetracked. You will know what's right for you, and you will care.

Accept yourself as you are and be grateful. Then go for it. Be who God made you and do it all the way. Don't hold yourself back, but turn to face the world. Take your dreams and goals seriously, and your life will be simpler and have direction.

If you don't know what your dreams and goals are, then think about yourself. Live your life and observe yourself. Do the Seven Stories exercise and observe the real you—the you that does certain things no matter what. Ask a friend to help you find your threads.

> Choose a job you love, and you will never have to work a day in your life.
> —CONFUCIUS

> Many of us live as though the momentum in our lives is generated by others. There is often a sense of anguish when the realization emerges that we have to generate our own momentum by the images we have of ourselves and the future.
> —HERBERT RAPPAPORT, PH.D., *Marking Time*

You have plenty of time. How many more years do you have left? Let's say you'll be very active until the age of seventy or more. How many years is that? Perhaps I have thirty more active years—maybe forty. A lot can happen in thirty or forty years. Is it too late for me? Is it too late for you? Probably not.

Don't rush toward your dreams, but savor every step and enjoy the present. Reaching your goal is not the point. In fact, it does not matter whether you ever reach your goal. The point is the way we live each day.

Don't hurry through life on the way to your goal. Live your life, enjoy, and make the most of each day. Your goal is simply a guide—not a do-or-die phenomenon. If you can have a goal and enjoy the process of getting there, you have truly lived. It's the process that's important.

> Why, sometimes I believed as many as six impossible things before breakfast.
> —LEWIS CARROLL
> *Alice in Wonderland*

It's your life. Play a little. Take chances. You will succeed if you aren't too rigid about succeeding. Test things out. See what works. Don't try to hold on too tightly.

Our dreams recur. Perhaps yours are so deep and so quashed that you don't know what they are. Let them come out, then test them later to see how true they are for you. Dreams are serious things, and you might as well live them. Because, when you are old, you will find great satisfaction in having lived your dreams—in having lived your life. If you don't try to live your dreams, you may later be filled with regret.

> One of the common themes among depressed adults who I see in my practice is the deep sense of regret for not "stretching oneself" at different stages of life.
> —HERBERT RAPPAPORT, PH.D.
> *Marking Time*

> There is only one success—to be able to spend your life in your own way.
> —CHRISTOPHER MORLEY

Advance steadily in the direction of your goal and don't worry about how long it will take you to get there. If you advance steadily, you will get there as soon as you can, anyway. Just do what you can. I've seen people advance steadily for many, many years. They somehow wound up doing amazing things that would have seemed impossible and frightening if they had concentrated on them earlier. By taking life one step at a time, and not getting anxious about the future, they steadily advanced, taking small steps, but lots of them. The steps that followed seemed smaller still, and not frightening, and they became the persons they were meant to be. They followed their own, not completely defined dreams. As they lived each step, the next step became more clear.

Goals evolve as we test and see what feels right for us. We try a step, and sometimes step back rather than take our lives in a direction that we thought would be right but was not. And then, after a number of years, we look back, amazed at our own progress and surprised that this could happen to us—sure of our direction, still taking the steps one at a time, and testing our direction as we go.

And so our lives unfold. The excitement is in the present—the hope is in the future, and we know we are truly part of the universe as much as each star and each tree. We belong here—doing our part, full of life and living what was once a dream, and unafraid of failure.

> Ah, but a man's reach should exceed his grasp, Or what's a heaven for?
> —ROBERT BROWNING
> "Andrea del Sarto"

There are some elemental truths about yourself that define the real you. You may have buried them over time, but now stay tuned in and see if you can uncover them. Sometimes these deep dreams of yours may shock your family and friends, and may even shock you. Better that you should know what they are.

I once had a client who had very low self-esteem, and had been doing "safe" work at a major corporation. He would sit hunched, with his head turned up toward where I was sitting, and he would meekly talk about the interviews he was going on. He didn't have a clue about what he should do with his life. There was so much confusion between what he thought he should do and what he had done in the past, it was very difficult for him to find some direction to head toward.

Then one day, as we were discussing all the usual things, this timid, hunched-over person said in a bland tone, "You can't imagine how thrilled I'd be if I could be the leader, running the entire thing and being completely in control."

It seemed impossible that these strong words were coming out of this person's mouth. Looking at him made it seem even more unlikely, yet there was some deep, elemental truth about what he wanted for himself. I wrote down what he said because it was one of those truths that can be so easily lost—so easily dismissed with a "let's be realistic, honey."

I believe that if this person keeps his dream in mind, he will someday be an incredibly dynamic person, "in charge of the whole thing"—whatever that may be. He will learn to hold himself better, to sound more dynamic, and to look the part. And when this dynamic winner emerges, it will be the real him. I believe that the timid, play-it-safe person is not the real him, but some twisted person that emerged when the real him was submerged.

And, if this person remembers his dream, he will surely advance toward it. Ten years from now, he will look back and find it hard to believe that he is the same person. The living comes not in finally reaching his dream—the living comes in becoming the kind of person he truly is deep inside. The living comes in his day-to-day life as he simply lives it.

Those words were the most important he ever said during the many hours I spent with him. It will take him years to be the real him—that's been buried for so long. But what a happy way to spend ten years. I can't think of a better way to live them—concentrating each day on the task before him, but remembering the person he was meant to be. Finding his own place in the universe and being proud of it.

> I spent a large part of my life being a loser, which I think adds an interesting dimension to my personality.
> —MICHAEL CAINE
> *Acting in Film*

EPILOGUE

... the country demands bold, persistent experimentation. It is common sense to take a method and try it. If it fails, admit it frankly and try another. But above all, try something.
—FRANKLIN DELANO ROOSEVELT
Speech, Atlanta, 1932

THERE IS NO one way to job hunt; one neat solution to job hunting cannot answer it all. There are many ways.

The results of what you do in a job hunt are neither good nor bad; they are simply results to be observed and thought about. They are indicators of the correctness of the direction you are pursuing; they are not indictments. They are not personal; they are the world's feedback to what we are doing. These results can keep us on track, and if we look at them objectively, then they should not throw us offtrack.

Information is not good or bad, it is simply information. Things are changing so fast that we each need all the relevant information we can get. We may tend to block out information we find threatening—but that is precisely the information we need to get. Knowing the truth of what is happening around us may help us decide how to take care of ourselves. The information is not out to harm us—it is simply there.

To view your life as blessed does not require you to deny your pain. It simply demands a more complicated vision, one in which a condition or event is not either good or bad but is, rather, both good and bad, not sequentially but simultaneously.
—NANCY MAIRS (who has multiple sclerosis)
Carnal Acts

To be what we are, and to become what we are capable of
becoming is the only end of life.
—ROBERT LOUIS STEVENSON

There is a place for you, and you must look for it. Do not be stopped when
others seem as though they are moving ahead. You, too, have a lot to offer
if you would only think about yourself and not them. You are on your own
track. Put your energy into discovering what is special about you, and
then hold on to it.

You will be knocked down enough during your job hunting. Don't
knock yourself; push back. Push past the people who offer you discour-
agement. Find those nurturing souls who recognize your worth and encourage you.

. . . there are days when the result is so bad that no fewer than five
revisions are required. In contrast, when I'm greatly inspired, only
four revisions are needed.
—JOHN KENNETH GALBRAITH

Don't tell me the facts about yourself; tell me who you really are. When
you are writing to someone, ask yourself, What am I really trying to say to
this person? What would I say if this person were right here? You are
writing to a real person, and when your personality comes through and
you say what you mean to say, then your note is unique.

Read your work out loud. It will give you a sense of the timing, the
flow. You will find out if it is readable. You will notice where it stumbles.
Have someone else read it, too. Most people need an editor.

Take a few risks, but do it with some restraint. don't be self-
indulgent, but do let your personality seep through. You are not simply a
"banker with twenty years major banking experience." You are "mature,
with worldwide contacts, and a sense of stability."

Pare down your writing. Get rid of the lines that have no energy.
Think about getting rid of your first paragraph completely. Perhaps you
wrote it just to warm up.

Write to make an impact, to influence the reader.

It is impossible to enjoy idling thoroughly unless one has plenty of
work to do.
—JEROME K. JEROME

Continue to job hunt, but be easy on yourself. I worked on this book
whenever I could, but some days I didn't feel like thinking, so I researched
quotes, or made a chart, or organized my material. All of these things
later made my writing easier—so I was always making progress.

The same can be applied to your job hunt. Some days you may research an industry or a number of companies, or you may write a proposal or a follow-up note. But you have to spend most of your time interviewing—just as I had to spend most of my time writing.

Job hunting takes practice, just as writing takes practice. I am not a professional writer, and you are not a professional job hunter. Neither of us, you or I, is perfect. But we are each trying to understand the process. This understanding will make us each less anxious, and more patient, about what we are doing.

Develop tricks to nudge yourself along. Find someone to report your progress to. If you cannot join a job hunt group, then meet with a friend. Talking gives you perspective and gives you the energy to keep on going.

Set goals for yourself. For example, aim at all times to be in contact, either in person or in writing, with six people who are in a position to hire you or recommend that you be hired. Keep in touch with these six people. Strive to add more people to your list, because others will drop off. Plan to continue to network even after you find a job. Make networking a part of your life.

Keep pushing even when you get afraid—especially when you get afraid. On the other hand, if you have been pushing nonstop for a while, take a break completely, relax, and then push again.

Get together with a friend and talk about your dreams. In talking about them, they seem possible. And in hearing yourself say them out loud, you can test how you really feel about them. Then you can discover the central dream—the one that will drive you.

> Where I was born and how I have lived is unimportant. It is what I
> have done with where I have been that should be of interest.
> —Georgia O'Keeffe

> Far better it is to dare mighty things, to win glorious triumphs, even
> though checkered by failure, than to take rank with those poor
> spirits who neither enjoy much nor suffer much, because they live
> in the gray twilight that knows not victory nor defeat.
> —Theodore Roosevelt

You will find endless resources inside yourself. Get inside yourself and find out what the dream is, and then do it. Stir yourself up. Go for it.

The fact is, if you don't try, no one will care anyway. The only reason to do it is for yourself—so you can take your rightful place in the universe. The only reason to do it is because we each have our place, and it seems a shame to be born and then to die without doing our part.

> We are all controlled by the world in which we live. . . . The
> question is this: are we to be controlled by accidents, by tyrants, or
> by ourselves?
>   —B. F. SKINNER

The world is big. There are many options; some job hunters try to
investigate them all. Instead begin with yourself. Understand that part.
Then look at some options and test them against what you are. You can
hold on to that as a sure thing. You can depend on what you are for
stability.

> I am larger, better than I thought, I did not know I held so much
> goodness.
>   —WALT WHITMAN

A former client called me today. When I first met him, he had been out of
work for a year. Now he was calling to say that he had been made vice
president of his company. He has found his niche and has never been
happier. Everyone notices it. And he keeps on networking—keeps on
enjoying the process.

The world keeps changing. It won't stop. We must change, too. We
are the dreamers of dreams.

> We are the music-makers, And we are the dreamers of dreams . . .
> Yet we are the movers and shakers of the world for ever, it seems.
>   —ARTHUR O'SHAUGHNESSY
>   "MUSIC AND MOONLIGHT"

INDEX

Page numbers in *italics* denote notable people and works mentioned or quoted.

ABOUT THE AUTHOR

KATE WENDLETON is a nationally recognized authority on career development. She has been a career coach since 1978 when she founded The Five
O'Clock Club®, a job search–strategy group that can help job hunters of
all levels. The Five O'Clock Club of mid-Manhattan attracts thirty to fifty
professionals, managers, and executives a week, served by eight career
consultants. Other chapters have been or are being formed across the
country. In addition, Workforce America: The Five O'Clock Club of Harlem, is a not-for-profit organization serving adult job hunters in Harlem
who are not yet in the professional or managerial ranks.

Kate founded, and for seven years directed, The Career Center at
The New School for Social Research in New York. She counsels executives both in private practice and for major corporations. A former CFO
of two small companies, she has twenty years of business-management
experience in both manufacturing and service businesses.

Kate attended Chestnut Hill College in Philadelphia and received
her MBA from Drexel University. She is a popular speaker with groups
that include The Wharton Business School Club, the Yale Club, The
Columbia Business School Club, and New York University's School of
Continuing Education.

While living in Philadelphia, Kate did long-term volunteer work for
The Philadelphia Museum of Art, The Walnut Street Theatre Art Gallery,
The United Way, and the YMCA.

Kate currently lives in Manhattan.

The original Five O'Clock Club was formed in Philadelphia in 1891. It was made
up of the leaders of the day who shared their experiences and fellowship "in a
setting of sobriety and good humor."